A Reading Skills Book

mosaic one

A Reading Skills Book

mosaic one

Third Edition

Brenda Wegmann

Miki Prijic Knezevic

The McGraw-Hill Companies, Inc.

New York St. Louis San Francisco Auckland Bogotá Caracas Lisbon
London Madrid Mexico City Milan Montreal New Delhi San Juan
Singapore Sydney Tokyo Toronto

This is an  book.

McGraw-Hill

A Division of The McGraw-Hill Companies

Mosaic One
A Reading Skills Book
Third Edition

2 3 4 5 6 7 8 9 0   DOC DOC   9 0 9 8 7 6

ISBN 0-07-068997-0
ISBN 0-07-114511-7

This book was set in Times Roman by Monotype Composition Company, Inc. The editors were Tim Stookesberry, Bill Preston, and Karen Davey; the designers were Lorna Lo, Suzanne Montazer, Francis Owens, and Elizabeth Williamson; the production supervisor was Patricia Myers; the cover was designed by Francis Owens; the cover illustrator was Celia Johnson; the photo researcher was Cindy Robinson, Seaside Publishing; illustrations were done by Wayne Clark, Rick Hackney, and Lori Heckelman.

R. R. Donnelley & Sons Company, Crawfordsville, IN, was printer and binder.
Phoenix Color Corporation was cover separator and printer.

Library of Congress Catalog Card Number: 95-80832

Literary acknowledgments and photo credits

Literary acknowledgments: *Pages 2–4* Alison R. Lanier, *Living in the U.S.A.,* 4th edition. Reprinted with permission. Intercultural Press, Inc., Yarmouth, ME: 1988; *page 9* Cartoon by Ken Mahood. Reproduced by permission of *Punch,* from *Best Cartoons of the World II Atlas; pp. 10–13* Pierre Berton, "My Country." Reproduced by permission; *p. 18* Andrew A. Rooney, "In Praise of New York City." Reprinted with the permission of Scribner, an imprint of Simon & Schuster, Inc., from *A Few Minutes with Andy Rooney* by Andrew A. Rooney. Copyright © 1981 by Essay Productions, Inc.; *pp. 23–26* Bill Cosby, "How to Read Faster." Reprinted with permission of International Paper; *pp. 28–29* "Mark Twain." Reprinted with permission from "Twain, Mark" in *Encyclopaedia Britannica,* 14th edition, © 1972 by Enclopaedia Britannica, Inc.; *pp. 34–36* Eric Jensen, "How to Take Tests: Scoring What You're Worth" from *You Can Succeed* by Eric Jensen. Copyright © 1979 by Barrons Educational Series, Inc. Illustration copyright © 1979 by Charles McPherson; *pp. 44–45* Miki Prijic Knezevic, "The Changing American Family." Reprinted by permission of the author; *pp. 52–53* S. Kuzina, "70 Brides for 7 Foreigners," *World Press Review,* July 1993; *pp. 59–61* Ellen Goodman, "The Making of a Father" from *Close to Home.* Copyright © 1979 by the Washington Post

Contents

CHAPTER one

New Challenges   *1*

CHAPTER two

Looking at Learning   *21*

CHAPTER three

Relationships   *43*

Preface
to the Third Edition

The Mosaic One Program

The Mosaic One program consists of four texts and a variety of supplemental materials for intermediate to high-intermediate students seeking to improve their English language skills. Each of the four texts in this program is carefully organized by chapter theme, vocabulary, grammar structures, and where possible, language functions. As a result, information introduced in a chapter of any one of the Mosaic One texts corresponds to and reinforces material taught in the same chapter of the other three books, creating a truly integrated, four-skills approach.

The Mosaic One program is highly flexible. The texts in this series may be used together or separately, depending on students' needs and course goals. The books in this program include:

- **A Content-Based Grammar.** Designed to teach grammar through content, this book introduces, practices, and applies grammatical structures through the development of high-interest chapter topics. This thematic approach gives students motivation because they are improving their mastery of grammatical structures and vocabulary while expanding their own knowledge.

- **A Content-Based Writing Book**. This book takes students step-by-step through the writing process—from formulating ideas through the revision stage. Writing assignments progress from paragraphs to essays, and students write about interesting, contemporary subjects from the sciences, social sciences, and humanities that are relevant to their current or future academic coursework.

- **A Listening / Speaking Skills Book.** This book teaches study skills and language function while maintaining a strong focus on both listening and speaking. Each chapter includes a realistic listening passage about an interesting topic related to the chapter theme. Short conversations also provide comprehension practice, and a variety of speaking activities reinforce, in context, use of language functions.

- **A Reading Skills Book.** The selections in this book help students develop their reading skills in a meaningful rather than a mechanical way, enabling them to successfully tackle other academic texts. The three to four readings per chapter are from various authentic sources, such as textbooks, magazines, newspapers, and interviews, and are accompanied by pre- and postreading exercises, including questions, topics for library research, and group problem solving.

Supplemental Materials

In addition to the four core texts outlined above, various supplemental materials are available to assist users of the third edition, including:

Instructor's Manual

Extensively revised for the new edition, this manual provides instructions and guidelines for using the four core texts separately or in various combinations to suit particular program needs. For each of the core texts, there is a separate section with teaching tips, additional activities, and other suggestions. The testing materials have been greatly expanded in this edition.

Audio Program for Mosaic One: A Listening/Speaking Skills Book

 Completely rerecorded for the new edition, the audio program is designed to be used in conjunction with those exercises that are indicated with a cassette icon in the student text. Complete tapescripts for all exercises are now included in the back of the student text.

Audio Program to Accompany Mosaic One: A Reading Skills Book

 This new optional audio program contains selected readings from the student text. These tape selections of poems, articles, stories, and speeches enable students to listen at their leisure to the natural oral discourse of native readers for intonation and modeling. Readings that are included in this program are indicated with a cassette icon in the student text.

Video/Video Guide

New to this edition, the video program for Mosaic One contains authentic TV segments coordinated with the twelve chapter themes in the four texts. A variety of pre- and postviewing exercises and activities for this video are available in a separate Video Guide.

Mosaic One: A Reading Skills Book, Third Edition

Rationale

The main purpose of *Mosaic One: A Reading Skills Book*, third edition, is to develop in students a conscious attitude toward reading, along with skills that will enable them to read in a meaningful rather than a mechanical way. The great danger for intermediate students of a foreign language is to become blocked at this level and continue using the basic skills of memorizing vocabulary and grammar structures. The leap from highly structured, controlled texts to the real language as it is spoken and written must be made. Students must be shown how to find and decipher the clues that will allow them to perceive the author's general intent and to read for overall meaning, even when they are unfamiliar with many words and some grammatical structures.

In general, *Mosaic One: A Reading Skills Book* covers the reading skills for the intermediate to high-intermediate level as recommended by the guidelines of numerous universities throughout the country. This book emphasizes the mastering of these skills, rather than the content of the reading, (The chart at the end of the Preface summarizes the skills presented in this book.)

Nevertheless, the content of the reading selections is important for the achievement of the secondary purpose of the Mosaic One reader: to acquaint students with varied aspects of North American culture. Selections were chosen with a view to presenting in a challenging manner the representative customs, personalities, values, and ways of thinking of the American and Canadian people.

Chapter Organization

Every chapter begins with a brief introduction to the chapter theme. This introduction can be used to set the stage for later discussion and to give both teacher and students an idea of the class' knowledge of and prejudices toward the subject. The introduction is followed by three reading selections, each preceded by one or two prereading exercises and followed by comprehension and skill-building exercises. These readings are often accompanied by a Talking It Over section and occasionally by an activity such as group problem solving, debates or panel discussions, or a composition or library research assignment. These latter features are optional and are included primarily to give the book greater flexibility.

No set sequence of exercises is repeated chapter after chapter. Rather, the types of exercises vary according to each selection and the skill being emphasized. This organizational approach avoids tedium and helps lessen the chance of students relapsing into a mechanical, nonreflective way of reading. Previously presented skills are reinforced throughout, however, often by using different styles of exercises to review the same skill.

The principal aim of the prereading exercises is to condition students to stop and think before plunging into a reading, to become alert to clues from the title, pictures, source, layout, headings, or other factors that will help them gain an overall idea of the reading. At times, the prereading exercises are also used to teach the important skill of guessing the meaning of words from context or to highlight different types of vocabulary, such as slang, jargon, idioms, and figurative or pejorative language.

The skill-building exercises that follow each reading selection focus on reviewing basic skills such as skimming, scanning, finding topic sentences, using the dictionary, and identifying the main idea. These skills are reinforced throughout at the same time that more advanced skills are introduced, such as making inferences, separating fact from opinion, identifying slant or bias, summarizing, paraphrasing complex ideas, evaluating evidence, finding support for key ideas, distinguishing the general from the specific, comparing arguments, and reading critically. At times these exercises practice and reinforce skills introduced in the prereading exercises. A number of charts and graphs related to the selections are included with exercises to give students practice in this special type of reading.

Teaching Suggestions

The prereading exercises may be used in different ways, depending on the level of the students. At first, the teacher will probably do the exercises orally with the class as a means of introducing each selection and ascertaining class level. These exercises, especially the ones using direct quotations from the selection with vocabulary to be figured out from context, can act as a bridge, helping students over some of the difficult sections of the article. If, after a few weeks, the class seems to have little problem with the readings, these exercises can be assigned for homework and corrected quickly at the beginning of class.

It is a good idea at times to assign only some of the exercises to be done with the reading as homework. Then, if time permits, the other exercises can be done in class, adding an element of the unexpected. When an exercise aimed at reviewing a skill is used this way, you can ask one of the more extroverted students to play the role of the teacher (perhaps after having warned the student in advance). This is a sure way of gaining class attention because everyone wants to see if the new "teacher" will make a mistake, and it also challenges a confident, highly motivated student who might otherwise begin to lose interest.

The later chapters in the book are longer, and the harder readings are usually placed at the end of the chapters. This organization gives the teacher flexibility in choosing the selections that best correspond to the level of the class. The final chapter of the book is longer than the others and different in that it is more open-ended, containing a sampling of readings from various genres, with only comprehension exercises and discussion questions following each reading. The end of the term usually is such a busy time that it was decided to finish with this flexible approach. The teacher may choose from among the materials those best suited for reviewing the skills the class has still not mastered; or the teacher may use some selections for testing, for free reading, or even for supplementary assignments earlier in the term.

New to the Third Edition

1. **Streamlined Design.** The two-color design and revised art program make this edition more appealing to today's students. The book is also more user-friendly because many directions have been shortened and clarified, exercises and activities have been numbered,

and key information has been highlighted in shaded boxes and charts.

2. **New Chapter Theme on Crime and Punishment.** This timely theme provides the context for three new and very different types of readings: biography, historical fiction, and a sociological essay based on the analysis of scientific research. The second and third selections are considerably longer than most others in the book and are used to develop surveying and extended reading skills. In addition, many reading selections in other chapters are completely new, and many other sections of the book have been updated. Several chapter themes have been broadened to include new content.

3. **Audio Cassette.** This new optional tape includes selected readings from the text. Selections are read by skilled native readers to provide samples of oral reading style for imitation and modeling. Readings included on the cassette are indicated with a cassette icon in the student text.

4. **What Do You Think?** This entirely new boxed feature appears in every chapter near a thematically related section. This feature interests, amazes, amuses, or in some other way provokes a response and stimulates class discussion of popular culture that goes beyond the text.

5. **Focus On Testing.** These new boxed features present practical tips and strategies for maximizing a student's advantage in the vocabulary and reading sections of standardized exams for English, such as the TOEFL. Appearing in every chapter except the last one (which is devoted to open reading), Focus on Testing features are accompanied by an exercise designed to put the tips and strategies into immediate practice.

Acknowledgments

Our thanks to the following reviewers whose comments, both favorable and critical, were of great value in the development of the third edition of the Interactions/Mosaic series:

Jean Al-Sibai, University of North Carolina; Janet Alexander, Waterbury College; Roberta Alexander, San Diego City College; Julie Alpert, Santa Barbara City College; Anita Cook, Tidewater Community College; Anne Deal Beavers, Heald Business College; Larry Berking, Monroe Community College; Deborah Busch, Delaware County Community College; Patricia A. Card, Chaminade University of Honolulu; José A. Carmona, Hudson County Community College; Kathleen Carroll, Fontbonne College; Consuela Chase, Loyola University; Lee Chen, California State University; Karen Cheng, University of Malaya; Gaye Childress, University of North Texas; Maria Conforti, University of Colorado; Earsie A. de Feliz, Arkansas State University; Elizabeth Devlin-Foltz, Montgomery County Adult Education; Colleen Dick, San Francisco Institute of English; Marta Dmytrenko-Ahrabian, Wayne State University; Margo Duffy, Northeast Wisconsin Technical; Magali Duignan, Augusta College; Janet Dyar, Meridian Community College; Anne Ediger, San Diego City College; D. Frangie, Wayne State University; Robert Geryk, Wayne State University; Jeanne Gibson, American Language Academy; Kathleen Walsh Greene, Rhode Island College; Myra Harada, San Diego Mesa College; Kristin Hathhorn, Eastern Washington University; Mary Herbert, University of California-Davis; Joyce Homick, Houston Community College; Catherine Hutcheson, Texas Christian University; Suzie Johnston, Tyler Junior College; Donna Kauffman, Radford University; Emmie Lim, Cypress College; Patricia Mascarenas, Monte Vista Community School; Mark Mattison, Donnelly College; Diane Peak, Choate Rosemary Hall; James Pedersen, Irvine Valley College; Linda Quillan, Arkansas State University; Marnie Ramker, University of Illinois; Joan Roberts, The Doane Stuart School; Doralee Robertson, Jacksonville University; Ellen Rosen, Fullerton College; Jean Sawyer, American Language Academy; Frances Schulze,

College of San Mateo; Sherrie R. Sellers, Brigham Young University; Tess M. Shafer, Edmonds Community College; Heinz F. Tengler, Lado International College; Sara Tipton, Wayne State University; Karen R. Vallejo, Brigham Young University; Susan Williams, University of Central Florida; Mary Shepard Wong, El Camino College; Cindy Yoder, Eastern Mennonite College; Cheryl L. Youtsey, Loyola University; Miriam Zahler, Wayne State University; Maria Zien, English Center, Miami; Yongmin Zhu, Los Medanos College; Norma Zorilla, Fresno Pacific College.

We also wish to thank McGraw-Hill for its inspirational support and the innovative coordination of this edition, which began so propitiously in the multihued city of San Francisco. We are especially indebted to our publishing team of Thalia Dorwick, Tim Stookesberry, and Bill Preston for their astute and creative direction, encouragement, and unflagging patience and flexibility. Finally, a very special thank you to Elyane Steeves and Ivo Knezevic for their help in finding superb materials and to Jessica Wegmann for her insightful suggestions and assistance in proofreading the manuscript.

Summary of Reading, Vocabulary, and Test-Taking Skills

Chapter	Reading Skills	Vocabulary Skills	Focus on Testing
one	• reading without understanding every word • analyzing topic sentences • reading for a specific purpose • finding main ideas/topic sentences	• guessing word meaning from context • using an English dictionary • choosing correct definitions	• doing a close reading of a text
two	• selecting the main idea • describing an author by inference • using techniques for faster reading • guessing meaning from context • scanning for specific information	• recognizing slang and informal style • scanning for words from clues • guessing word meaning from context	• taking objective exams
three	• reading a statistical chart • scanning for facts • identifying general and specific statements • selecting the main idea • identifying sentence fragments	• understanding jargon • learning Latin roots • guessing word meaning from context • finding synonyms	• choosing the correct option in multiple choice
four	• using headings as guides • stating key ideas • paraphrasing • skimming for ideas • answering specific points of argument • identifying support for ideas • separating fact from opinion	• guessing word meaning from context • paraphrasing specialized vocabulary • paraphrasing idioms • applying definitions of medical terms • adding suffixes to form adjectives	• analyzing compound words
five	• skimming for the whole context • scanning for details • making inferences • identifying organizational clues • using key words to make a summary • inferring the author's purpose	• defining new words from context • coping with technical terms • scanning for abbreviations • guessing word meaning from context	• identifying restatements of ideas
six	• anticipating the contents • reading for speed • examining point of view • predicting the action	• scanning for word families • using the context to explain business terms • recalling idioms and expressions	• reading between the lines

Chapter	Reading Skills	Vocabulary Skills	Focus on Testing
seven	• skimming to identify "voices" • analyzing anecdotal evidence • analyzing the evidence in graphs • inferring point of view • paraphrasing the main idea • reading for speed • making comparisons	• guessing the meaning of expressions • scanning for words from clues • guessing the meaning of slang from context • identifying onomatopoeia • building a word description	• previewing the questions
eight	• reading for *who, what, why* • summarizing • making inferences and drawing conclusions • inferring the intended image of an interview • paraphrasing main ideas	• inventing definitions for technical terms • learning about word origins • checking knowledge of shapes and forms • scanning for words from clues • finding synonyms	• thinking twice about tricky questions
nine	• scanning for key definitions • making inferences • finding support for main ideas • making inferences about character • expressing the theme • hearing rhyme and rhythm in poetry	• scanning for words from clues • guessing word meaning from context • paraphrasing figurative language	• finding statements and implied ideas
ten	• skimming for organization in biography • finding support for character inference • surveying extended readings • understanding humor • finding the basis for inference • finding the point in long sentences • analyzing argument • drawing conclusions from a graph	• guessing word meaning from context • scanning for compound synonyms • classifying words as good or bad • scanning for words from clues	• judging between true and false
eleven	• separating fact from opinion • comprehending complex sentences • outlining as you read • comparing outlines • reading for speed	• learning about word origins • understanding acronyms • defining words from context	• doing the easy ones first
twelve	• open reading: application of all skills	• open reading: application of all skills	

CHAPTER one

New Challenges

in this chapter

It is difficult to define a "true" American or a "true" Canadian because both Canada and the United States are very large. Both have many different regions and citizens who come from varied backgrounds, as can be seen by looking at the names in any telephone directory. Here we discuss some common American customs and attitudes, examine one Canadian's view of the differences between the people of his country and their American neighbors to the south, and look at one view of New York City.

Customs Vary with Culture

Before You Read

Reading Without Understanding the Meaning of Every Word

The following article will probably contain a number of words you do not know. This is not surprising. Linguists tell us that, for various historical reasons, English has a larger vocabulary than any other known language. Later in this book you will learn more vocabulary and, more importantly, skills for guessing the meaning of new words from their context or form. Right now, practice the important skill of reading without knowing the meaning of every word by following these three steps:

1. Look over the entire article quickly, paying attention to the headings of the different sections and trying to get a general idea of the contents of each one.

2. Read the article for the main ideas. *Skip over* words and phrases you do not understand. Do *not* slow yourself down by looking words up in a dictionary. Keep going.

3. Do the postreading exercise called Recalling Information. If you have trouble with it, read the article (or parts of it) again. You will probably understand it better this time. Two or three quick readings are much better for understanding than one slow one. Once you have worked the exercise, you have read well enough for your present purpose.

The following selection is a chapter taken from a book called *Living in the U.S.A.* by Alison Raymond Lanier, author and lecturer on social change and behavior. What purpose do you think the author had for writing this book? Are you surprised by some American customs? Perhaps you will find an explanation for them in this selection.

Customs Vary with Culture

Many American customs will surprise you; the same thing happens to us when we visit another country. People living in varied cultures handle many small daily things differently. What a dull world it would be if this were not true!

5   Some differences are minor, and one soon becomes accustomed to them. At first, for example, some foreign women may be startled by having their hair cut and styled by men. Visitors may be amazed to see men wearing wigs or short shorts on women in downtown streets.

    The constant restless motion of Americans may be startling at first.
10   People in the flat Middle West think nothing of driving seventy-five to a

hundred miles just to have dinner with a friend; they go to a far-off city for an evening of theater or music or even a movie. Countless young people select a college thousands of miles away from their families "just to see another part of the country." Barely in their teens, they go off in droves to see what lies beyond.

People

Who are these people who are swirling around you? Some 245 million of them now call America home, but in fact they have their origins in every part of the world. The names you see over shop doors tell you so, as do the varied types of faces you pass on the streets. A roll call of school children will include such names as Adams, Ali, Bykowski, Capparella, Fujita, Gonzales, Mukerji, Nussiebeh, and Wong. Mostly, these diverse backgrounds have not been blended in the so-called American "melting pot." In fact, the idea that America is a melting pot is largely a myth. What exists more often is a kind of side-by-side living in which ethnic groups retain many of their own customs and social traditions. They merge into the American stream only in certain aspects of life—in schools, sports, business, and science, to name a few—but keep to many of their own customs and patterns socially and at home.

Because our people have come from so many nationalities, there is a far wider range of what is "acceptable" than in some countries where the inhabitants have grown up with a common heritage. As a result, no one needs to feel uncomfortable in following his or her own customs.

Informality

Although American informality is well known, many interpret it as a lack of respect when they first encounter it, especially in the business world. The almost immediate use of first names, for example, still jars nerves long accustomed to deference or respect from people of lower rank.

Americans have a minimum feeling for "rank," especially socially. Most do not themselves enjoy being treated with respect for age or position; it makes them uncomfortable. Many Americans find even the terms "Mr.," "Mrs.," or "Ms." stiff and formal. You hear people well beyond middle age say—even to quite young people—"Just call me Sally (or Henry or Don)." Being on first-name terms is taken as a sign of acceptance and friendliness. However, this need not bother you. If you are not comfortable in following the boss's immediate request to "Call me Andrew," it is quite all right. Just smile and say, "After a while perhaps, but thank you anyway" (meaning, for feeling that friendly!).

What we do use, however, are *occupational titles*. Occupations that

50　most frequently carry titles include: diplomats (Ambassador Jones), members of the Senate (Senator Smith), or certain other top government officials (Governor Rockefeller), judges (Judge Harley), doctors (Dr. Brown), professors (Dr. or Professor Green, Ph.D.), clergy (Reverend Gray), etc.

Personal Questions

55　Conversational questions may seem to you both too personal and too numerous—especially when you first arrive. "Where do you work?" "Are you married?" "How many children do you have?" "Have you taken your vacation yet?" are not personal questions by American standards. They are a search for common ground on which to build a relationship or base
60　a conversation. Understand that such questions are meant to be friendly; the questioner is interested in you. If you are asked questions that seem to you to be too personal, you need not answer them. You can simply smile or say pleasantly that you "do not know" or "In my country that would be a funny question," or turn the questions gently aside by some comment
65　such as "Isn't it interesting to see how different nationalities begin a conversation?" or something similar. The American will not be offended, but he or she will get the point.

Alison Raymond Lanier

After You Read
Recalling Information

After reading the article, tell which of these statements about Americans are true and which are false. Correct the false statements to make them true.

Americans . . .

1. _____ often drive long distances to go to a play or a movie.

2. _____ frequently send their children to colleges far away from home.

3. _____ live and work side by side but often observe different customs.

4. _____ are more informal than people from other countries.

5. _____ often call people by their first names as soon as they meet them.

6. _____ are very conscious of rank in business and usually call their boss by a title to show respect.

7. _____ use titles for certain occupations.

8. _____ like to pry into the affairs of foreigners and embarrass them by asking personal questions.

Analyzing Topic Sentences

An important skill for reading is finding the main idea. Often the main idea of a paragraph is stated directly. The sentence that states the main idea is called the topic sentence. The topic sentence is often (but not always) the first sentence of the paragraph. The other sentences can develop the paragraph in different ways: by giving examples or details to illustrate the main idea, by expanding upon it with related ideas, or by expressing an emotional reaction to the main idea.

 **exercise 2**   Practice analyzing the topic sentences of some paragraphs from the previous reading.

1. Look at the first paragraph. The first sentence is the topic sentence. How do the other two sentences develop the main idea?

2. Find the topic sentences of three other paragraphs in the reading selection and write them down.

3. Can you describe how each of these paragraphs is developed (with examples and details, by expanding, etc.)?

4. Are the topic sentences in these paragraphs always the first sentence?

Guessing the Meaning of Words from Context

It is often possible to guess the meaning of new words by reading past the word and finding clues in the context. Read to the end of the sentence and maybe even to the end of the paragraph. Then go back and read the word again.

 **exercise 3**   Practice this skill with the following words from the reading selection "Customs Vary with Culture." Choose the best definition for each context.

1. *accustomed to* (line 5)
   a. confused by   **b.** familiar with   **c.** pleased with

2. *countless* (line 12)
   a. many   **b.** few   **c.** unknown number of

3. *heritage* (line 32)
   a. amount of money   **b.** history and tradition   **c.** physical appearance

Using a Monolingual Dictionary

In general, you should not look up words in the dictionary as you read. You should guess their meanings from the context. But sometimes there will be one or two words that will seem especially important, will occur several times, or simply will bother you. Then you will want to use the dictionary. The trouble is that one word often has several meanings, and you must choose the correct one to fit the context. The following three points will help you find the correct definition.

1. A lot of information is given in a dictionary. Pay attention to only what you need.
2. The definitions are numbered. The most common meaning usually appears first, but that is not necessarily the one you want.
3. If a word can function as more than one part of speech (as a noun and verb, for example), you must first decide how it is functioning in the sentence. Then look at the definitions listed after the abbreviation for that part of speech.

 *exercise* These sentences from the reading selection each contain an italicized word that has several meanings. After the sentence, the word is given exactly as it appears in the dictionary. You should choose the definition that best fits the context.

1. "At first, for example, some foreign women may be *startled* by having their hair cut and styled by men. . . . The constant restless motion of Americans may be *startling* at first." You may not find the words *startled* and *startling* in the dictionary because they are adjectives made from the verb *startle,* but you will find *startle*. This should help you write a definition for *startled* and *startling*. (*Hint:* Add the endings *-ed* and *-ing* to synonyms of the verb.)

   Definition of *startled:*_____

   Definition of *startling:*_____

2. The word *rank* is used in two successive sentences. "The almost immediate use of first names, for example, still jars nerves long accustomed to deference or respect from people of lower *rank*. Americans have a minimum feeling for *rank,* especially socially."

   DICTIONARY
   rank (rangk), *n.* **1.** a number of persons forming a distinct class in a social hierarchy or in any graded body. **2.** a social or official position or standing: *the rank of vice-president.* **3.** high position or station in the social scale. **4.** a class in any scale of comparison. **5.** relative position or standing: *a writer of the highest rank.* **6.** a row, line, or series of things or persons. **7.** usually, **ranks.** the general body of any military or other organization apart from the officers or leaders. **8.** orderly arrangement; array. **9.** a line of persons, esp. soldiers, standing abreast in close-order formation (distinguished from *file*). **10.** a set of organ pipes of the same kind and tone quality. **11.** *Chess.* one of the horizontal lines of squares on a chess board. **12. pull rank,** *slang.* To make use unexpectedly of one's superior rank in demanding respect, obedience, etc. Also, **pull one's rank.**—*v.t.*

13. to arrange in ranks or in regular formation. **14.** to assign to a particular position, station, class, group, etc. **15.** to outrank. — *v.t.* **16.** to form a rank or ranks. **17.** to occupy a place in a particular rank, class, etc. **18.** to have a specified rank or standing. **19.** to be the senior in rank: *The colonel ranks at this camp.* [< F *ranc* (obs.). OF *renc, ranc, rang* row, line, Gmc; cf. OE hrinc RING¹] — **Syn. 3.** distinction, dignity. **6.** range, tier.

What two parts of speech are listed for *rank* in this dictionary entry? Which part of speech is *rank* in the sentences from the selection? Which definition is correct for these contexts?

Definition:_____

Can you find the synonyms given for rank?

_____

3. The word *deference* occurs in the same sentence as *rank:* "The almost immediate use of first names, for example, still jars nerves long accustomed to *deference* or respect from people of lower rank."

def.'er.ence (def′ər əns), *n.* **1.** submission or yielding to the judgment, opinion, will, etc., of another. **2.** respectful or courteous regard: *in deference to his wishes.* [< F *deference*]

Definition:_____

Can you find where it tells about the origin of the word *deference*?

What other words in the reading selection are new to you? Look up one of them in a monolingual dictionary and write down the correct definition. Compare words and definitions with your classmates.

More American Customs

activity 1

In small groups, look at the drawings below to find out more about American customs. What do you think of these customs? Are they similar in your country or are they different? Discuss your ideas.

1. To Shake Hands or Not to Shake Hands, That Is the Question

Don't be surprised if Americans do not always shake hands. They often just nod or smile instead. A casual "Hi" or "How are you doing?" or "Hello" often takes the place of a formal handshake, but it means the same thing. If a person extends her or his hand in greeting, then it is polite to shake hands.

2. Social Distance

The "comfort zone," or the distance people stand from each other when they talk, varies among different cultures. Greeks, Arabs, and South Americans stand quite close together when they talk. Often, they move closer as the conversation heats up. Studies show, however, that Americans feel most comfortable in conversation when standing about 21 inches apart from each other.

3. Blunt Speech

Don't think Americans are being rude if they tend to speak in monosyllables or answer with short answers. The brevity is not a personal insult: Americans are just not used to using long, gracious phrases in their language and often seem blunt.

4. Silence

Many Americans find silence uncomfortable. Some will babble on to fill any quietness if it lasts for more than a moment. Students often study with the radio blaring; people home alone will leave the television on as a "companion," even if they are not watching it.

What Would You Do?

In small groups, discuss the following four situations of foreign students studying at American universities. Decide what the student should do in each case.

1. Abdul is invited to supper at the home of an American family. The members of the family ask him many personal questions. He feels embarrassed by this. What can he do?

2. At a lecture, Graciela meets the professor she will work with in the laboratory. He is very friendly and tells her to call him "Bob." She feels confused. Does this mean she should always call him by his first name, or only at certain times?

3. Mark goes to dinner and is seated at a table with Americans. They are all talking a lot and trying to draw him into the conversation. He can't think of anything to say. Should he remain silent?

4. Rati enters the beauty parlor to get a haircut. A man comes to wash and cut her hair. This makes her uncomfortable because she prefers to have a woman fix her hair. Would it be rude for her to walk out?

Talking It Over

As a class, or in small groups, discuss the following questions.

1. What American customs seem strange to you?

2. What customs in your own country might seem unusual to visitors from the United States or Canada?

3. Do you agree with the common English proverb about travel: "When in Rome, do as the Romans do"? Why or why not?

Punch/London

"Oddly enough, language has proved no problem."

My Country

Before You Read
Reading for a Specific Purpose

Use the following selection to practice reading for a specific purpose. Do not be distracted by words or sentences you do not understand. Remember that many times an important idea will be repeated in different words. Read as quickly as possible to find out what differences there are, according to the Canadian author, between people from his country and Americans. Then test your comprehension by taking the quiz at the end of the reading.

What differences are there between Canadians and Americans? This question is of particular interest since the signing of NAFTA (North American Free Trade Agreement). Pierre Berton, one of Canada's leading writers and broadcasters (for both TV and radio), gives his thoughts on the subject in the following excerpts (sections) from his essay "My Country."

My Country (Excerpts)

*T*o a stranger, the land must seem endless. A herring gull, winging its way from St. John's, Newfoundland, to Victoria on the southern tip of Van-couver Island, will travel as far as the distance from London to Baghdad. It is the vastness that startles the imagination of all who visit my country.

5   Contrary to common belief, we do not live in snow-covered cabins far from civilization. Most of us inhabit cities that do not seem to differ greatly from those to the south of us. The observant visitor, however, will note some differences. The variety of our national makeup is, I believe, more pronounced than it is in the American melting pot. A newcomer in the United States quickly learns to cover up his or her origins and become an 10 American. A newcomer to Canada manages to keep something of the cul-ture and customs of his or her ethnic background.

    Traditionally, the stranger has thought of Canada as a mountainous, snow-swept land of Indians and Eskimos. It comes as a surprise to many to learn that there are hundreds of thousands of us who have never seen 15 an Eskimo, and some who have not even seen an Indian or a mountain. Most of us, as I have said, are city folk.

    Certainly it can get very cold in Canada. Few non-Canadians under-stand that it can also get very hot. In the Yukon, where I was born and 20 raised, I have worked in tropical conditions cutting survey lines through a

forest that was like a jungle. The eastern cities suffer in the humidity of July and August, and people actually die each year from the heat. In Victoria, roses bloom on Christmas Day. But, of course, we Canadians also know what it is like to be cold. In 1947, when the thermometer dropped to minus 65 degrees Celsius at a place called Snag in the Yukon, it was so cold that a bucket of water tossed into the air fell to the ground as ice.

Where temperature is concerned we are a country of extremes; and yet, as a people, we tend toward moderation and even conservatism. Non-Canadians think we are the same as our American neighbors, but we are not really like the Americans. Our temperament, our social attitudes, our environment, and our history make us a different kind of North American. Though these differences may not be easy for the newcomer to understand, they are very real to us.

First, there is the matter of our history. It has been called dull because it is not very bloody. Certainly we have no strong tradition of violence. We are, after all, the only people in all the Americas who did not separate violently from Europe. We have had three or four small uprisings but no revolution or civil war. We had no wild west and no wild Indians. Carrying a personal weapon is not our style: No Canadian feels he has a God-given right to carry a gun.

There are several reasons for this bloodlessness. First, there was the presence of those people who refused to fight against England during the American Revolution. They came, instead, to Canada. The influence of these United Empire Loyalists (my ancestor, Peter Berton, was one) has been great. Together with the Scots, who controlled the banks, railways, and educational institutions, they have helped give us our reputation as a conservative and cautious people. To a large extent it has been the American businessmen who have taken the financial risks in my country—and that explains why so much of Canada's manufacturing, industry, and natural resources are owned or controlled by Americans.

We were slow to give up our colonial ties to England. While the Americans chose freedom, we chose order. Our lawmen are appointed from above, not elected from below. The idea of choosing town marshals and county sheriffs by vote to keep the peace with guns never fitted into the Canadian scheme of things. Instead, we invented the North West Mounted Police. The Canadian symbol of the Mountie, neat and clean in his scarlet coat, contrasts with the American symbol of the lawman in his open shirt and gunbelt. The two differing social attitudes persist to this day. In the United States the settlers moved across the continent before law—hence the "wild" west. In Canada the law came first; settlement followed. Drinking saloons were unknown on the Canadian prairies. So were gambling halls, gunmen, and Indian massacres.

Outward displays of emotion are not part of the Canadian style. We are after all a northern people. We do not live in the street as southern races do. We are an interior people. The Americans are far more outgoing than we are. One reason for this, I think, is the very real presence of nature in our lives. Although it is true that we are city folk, most of us live within a few hours' drive of the wilderness. We escape to the woods whenever we can. No Canadian city is far removed from those mysterious and silent places which can have such an effect on the human soul.

Changing times: Today women are part of the Royal Canadian Mounted Police

There is another aspect of my country that makes it unique in the Americas, and that is our bilingual and bicultural makeup. (Canada has two official languages, English and French, and in its largest province a majority of the inhabitants speak French almost exclusively.) It gives us a picturesque quality, of course, and that certainly helps tourism: Visitors are attracted to the "foreignness" of Quebec City, with its twisting streets and its French-style cooking. But there is also a disturbing regional tension. Quebec has become a nation within a nation, and the separatist movement is powerful there.

Canadians are not anti-American. We watch American television programs. We read American magazines and the American best-selling novels. We tend to prefer American-made cars over the European and Asian products. We welcome hundreds of thousands of American tourists to our country every year and don't complain much when they tell us that we're exactly the same as they are.

Of course, we're *not* the same. But the visitor may be pardoned for thinking so when he or she first crosses the border. The buildings in our cities are designed in the international styles. The brand names in the supermarkets are all familiar. The chicken palaces, hot dog stands, gas stations, and motels along our superhighways are American-franchised operations. It is only after several days that the newcomer begins to sense a difference. He cannot put his finger on that difference, but then, neither can many of my countrymen. The only thing we are really sure of is that we are not Americans.

Pierre Berton

After You Read

Comprehension Quiz

Tell whether each of the following statements is true or false, according to Pierre Berton. Correct the false statements to make them true.

1. _____ Most Canadians live in snow-covered cabins far from civilization.

2. _____ In Canada, newcomers keep more of their original country's customs and culture than do newcomers in the United States.

3. _____ Many Canadians have never seen an Eskimo.

4. _____ Canada is a very cold country, even in the summertime.

5. _____ The history of Canada is more bloody and violent than the history of the United States.

6. _____ Generally speaking, Canadians are more conservative and cautious than Americans.

7. _____ Canadians have taken most of the financial risks in their country, but Americans have taken control of much of Canada's industry.

8. _____ The "wild west," with its guns, saloons, and constant battles between whites and Indians, was an important part of American and Canadian history.

9. _____ Canadians express their emotions more openly than Americans do.

10. _____ The United States has only one official language, but Canada has two.

11. _____ In general, Canadians are anti-American, and Americans are anti-Canadian.

12. _____ Canadian buildings, food, and business are very different from those in the United States.

Talking It Over

activity

In small groups, discuss the following questions.

1. Does a newcomer to your native culture have to cover up his or her origins? Do different groups keep some of their own culture or customs?

2. In your opinion, is there a connection between climate and national character? Between geography and national character? Do these connections exist in your native country?

Doing a Close Reading of a Text

To succeed in many standardized tests of vocabulary and reading comprehension, you must do a close reading of the texts. This does not mean reading slowly because in a test situation you must work under time pressure. A close reading means looking for clues in a whole part of the text in order to understand the meaning of particular words, ideas, or expressions.

In most texts, the different paragraphs or sentences are interrelated, so they provide contexts for understanding individual words and ideas. To help understand the meaning of a particular word or words, look for clues in the surrounding words or sentences, or in the word itself.

The following two steps will help you to do a close reading:

1. Look through the whole paragraph—or at least the sentences before and after the target word—for clues to its meaning.
2. Look at the word itself to see if it is made up of smaller words, or if it has a prefix or suffix that hints at its meaning.

exercise   Do a close reading of the indicated paragraphs from the reading selection "My Country." For each word or phrase in items 1 to 8, write down clues that you find in the indicated paragraph that help you understand the meaning of the word(s). Then circle the letter **a, b, c,** or **d** of the word(s) that best keeps that meaning.

example: vastness (paragraph 1)
    a. variety
    b. movement
    c. large size
    d. small size

Clues: _endless, comparison with distance from London to Baghdad, -ness ending suggesting a quality_

1. ethnic (paragraph 2)
    a. business
    b. ethical
    c. educational
    d. nationality

Clues: _____

_____

2. where I was born and raised (paragraph 4)
    a. where my life began
    b. where I grew up
    c. where my family comes from
    d. where I worked

Clues: _____

_____

3. conservatism (paragraph 5)
   a. traditional attitudes
   b. extreme attitudes
   c. conservation of the environment
   d. emotionalism

   Clues: _____

   _____

4. uprisings (paragraph 6)
   a. difficulties
   b. misunderstandings
   c. rebellions
   d. wars

   Clues: _____

   _____

5. ancestor (paragraph 7)
   a. relative from the past
   b. childhood friend
   c. countryman
   d. cousin

   Clues: _____

   _____

6. scheme of things (paragraph 8)
   a. business plan
   b. clever plan
   c. situation
   d. trick

   Clues: _____

   _____

7. settlement (paragraph 8)
   a. agreement between
      two groups
   b. families coming to a
      place to live
   c. calming down of people at war
   d. separating for political or social
      reasons

   Clues: _____

   _____

8. picturesque quality (paragraph 10)
   a. artistic image
   b. French style
   c. air of being older and different
   d. interest in culture and language

   Clues: _____

   _____

In Praise of New York City

Before You Read

Choosing the Correct Definition for a Context

 *exercise*   The italicized words in the sentences in column A are important for understanding the next reading selection. Practice the skill of recognizing the correct definitions of new words. Choose the definition from the list in column B that best fits the meaning of each italicized word.

COLUMN A

1. _____ People do not like to work in that office because there is so much *ill will*.

2. _____ Most religions teach that we should feel *compassion* for the poor, the weak and the unfortunate.

3. _____ The boy *resented* the cruel treatment of his father

4. _____ She was studying so hard that she was *oblivious* to all the noise around her.

5. _____ The soldier felt *remorse* after the bombing of the village of innocent people.

6. _____ The indifference and carelessness of the teenagers *dismayed* the older residents of the neighborhood.

7. _____ Native Americans have a *heritage* that extends back over 1,000 years.

8. _____ The tourists did not get to know Chicago because they were only there *in transit* from Minneapolis to Boston.

COLUMN B

a. unmindful, unaware

b. culture or traditions handed down from the past

c. moving from one place to another; passing through

d. harsh, unfriendly attitude

e. made unhappy, disheartened

f. felt displeasure at something that seemed unjust

g. strong regret; guilt for one's actions

h. sorrow for the suffering of others; pity

New York is one of the largest and best-known cities in the world. People tend either to love it or hate it. The following selection is from an article by Andy Rooney, a popular American journalist and TV commentator who knows New York very well. From the title, what can you tell about his attitude toward the city? About his purpose in writing the article? What are some points that you expect he will include in his description? Can you also think of some negative points that people often associate with New York City? Do you think Mr. Rooney will mention those or avoid them? Why?

 # *In Praise of New York City (Excerpt)*

*I*t might appear to any casual visitor who may have taken a few rides about town in a taxicab that all New Yorkers are filled with a loudmouthed ill will toward each other. The
5 fact of the matter is, though, that however cold and cruel things seem on the surface, there has never been a society of people in all history with so much compassion for its fellow man. It clothes, feeds, and houses 15
10 percent of its own because 1.26 million people in New York are unable to do it for themselves. You couldn't call that cold or cruel.

Everyone must have seen pictures at least of the great number of poor people who
15 live in New York. And it seems strange, in view of this, that so many people come here seeking their fortune or maybe someone else's. But if anything about the city's population is more impressive than the great
20 number of poor people, it's the great number of rich people. There's no need to search for buried treasure in New York. The great American dream is out in the open for everyone to see and to reach for. No one seems to
25 resent the very rich. It must be because even those people who can never realistically believe they'll get rich themselves can still dream about it. And they respond to the hope of getting what they see others having. Their
30 hope alone seems to be enough to sustain them. The woman going into Tiffany's to buy another diamond pin can pass within ten feet of a man without money enough for lunch. They are oblivious to each other. He
35 feels no envy; she no remorse.

There's a disregard for the past in New York that dismays even a lot of New Yorkers. It's true that no one pays much attention to antiquity. The immigrants who came here came for something new, and what New
40 York used to be means nothing to them. Their heritage is somewhere else.

Old million-dollar buildings are constantly being torn down and replaced by new
45 fifty-million-dollar ones. In London, Rome, Paris, much of the land has only been built on once in all their long history. In relatively new New York, some lots have already been built on four times.

50 Because strangers only see New Yorkers in transit, they leave with the impression that the city is one great mindless rush to nowhere. They complain that it's moving too fast, but they don't notice that it's getting
55 there first. For better and for worse, New York has *been* where the rest of the country is going.

Andy Rooney

After You Read

Finding Main Ideas: Stated Directly vs. Implied

To review, an important skill for reading is finding the main idea. Remember that the sentence that states the main idea is called a topic sentence. Remember too that the topic sentence is often, but not always, the first sentence in a paragraph.

Often the main idea of a paragraph is stated directly. This is true in paragraph 1 of the previous reading selection. Sometimes, however, the main idea is not stated directly; it is only implied or suggested. This is true in paragraphs 2 and 5 of the reading.

 *exercise*

Answer these questions about paragraphs from the reading selection "In Praise of New York City."

1. Which sentence in paragraph 1 expresses the main idea? (*Remember:* It may not be the first sentence.)

2. Which words in paragraph 1 act as a cue or indicator to you that the main idea is coming soon?

3. Which of the following statements in paragraph 2 best expresses the main idea? Explain your choice.
   a. There are many more rich people than poor people in New York.
   b. The rich and poor both have a place and seem to get along in New York.
   c. In New York, the poor resent the rich, and the rich feel remorse about their wealth.

4. Which of these statements in paragraph 5 best expresses the main idea? Explain your choice.
   a. New York is moving fast and is getting nowhere.
   b. New York is a leader among American cities.
   c. New York seems to be in transit, but it is really changing for the better.

Talking It Over

In small groups, discuss the following questions.

1. What points in the article give you a negative impression of New York? Why do you think that the author included these?

2. What points about New York seemed positive to you?

3. According to the author, why are there few older buildings in the city? How do New Yorkers feel about this?

4. Have you ever been to New York City? Would you like to go there? From what you know about it, would you like to live there or not? Why?

5. Looking at the photograph of New York City on page 17, what would you tell a friend about New York in two or three sentences?

WHAT DO YOU THINK?

Panhandling

Recently, posters appeared in New York City subway cars as a part of a campaign to discourage riders from giving money to panhandlers (people begging for money in public places). Across North America, there's a concern that public spaces are being taken over by homeless beggars. In many big cities, people who live and work in these areas say they have a right to be left alone. They do not want to be constantly bothered by panhandlers. Advocates for the homeless quickly denounced the posters and the campaign. What do you think? Should there be laws against begging in public places? Why or why not?

CHAPTER **two**

Looking at Learning

The first selection explains three ways to read faster and comprehend more of what you read. The second selection is a timed reading that gives you an opportunity to test those methods. The third selection presents techniques for taking tests that improve your scores, even though your knowledge of the subject stays the same. Next is a sample test in which you can practice these techniques and analyze the results.

How to Read Faster

Before You Read

Recognizing Informal Style and the Use of Slang

exercise

Even without knowing about the author's background, you can tell that the article is written in an informal style because of the use of slang. Slang refers to words that are not accepted in standard usage but are often used in conversation or in popular writing because they are more vivid, colorful, or humorous than ordinary language. What word is used in the very first sentence instead of the more ordinary word *child*? In the third and fourth sentences, there are two other examples of slang: the word *zipped* and the phrase *a snap*. Can you guess the meaning of these from context and replace them with more ordinary words? How many other words or phrases can you find in the first section (before the heading marked 1. Preview . . .) that seem conversational and informal? Which kinds of paragraphs—long or short—seem more characteristic of informal style? What about the length of sentences? As you read, try to decide why the author chose an informal style to present this kind of information.

The following article was written by the well-known African American comedian and TV star Bill Cosby. He grew up in poor circumstances at a time when opportunities for African Americans in the United States were very limited. (This situation improved significantly after the Civil Rights Movement of the 1960s.) Despite these limitations, Mr. Cosby was successful. After becoming rich and famous, he returned to college and earned a doctorate in education so he could help others survive in academic life. Do you have any practical questions about reading that might be answered in the article? From what you know about the author's background, how do you think he will present the information?

How to Read Faster

When I was a kid in Philadelphia, I must have read every comic book ever published. (There were fewer of them then than there are now.)

I zipped through all of them in a couple of days, then reread the good ones until the next issues arrived.

Yes, indeed, when I was a kid, the reading game was a snap.

But as I got older, my eyeballs must have slowed down or something! I mean, comic books started to pile up faster than my brother Russell and I could read them!

It wasn't until much later, when I was getting my doctorate, I realized it wasn't my eyeballs that were to blame. Thank goodness. They're still moving as well as ever.

The problem is, there's too much to read these days, and too little time to read every word of it.

Now, mind you, I still read comic books. In addition to contracts, novels, and newspapers; screenplays, tax returns, and correspondence. Even textbooks about how people read. And which techniques help people read more in less time.

I'll let you in on a little secret. There are hundreds of techniques you could learn to help you read faster. But I know of three that are especially good.

And if I can learn them, so can you—and you can put them to use *immediately.*

They are commonsense, practical ways to get the meaning from printed words quickly and efficiently. So you'll have time to enjoy your comic books, have a good laugh with Mark Twain, or a good cry with *War and Peace.* Ready?

They'll give you the *overall meaning* of what you're reading. And let you cut out an awful lot of *unnecessary* reading.

1. Preview—If It's Long and Hard

Previewing is especially useful for getting a general idea of heavy reading like long magazine or newspaper articles, business reports, and nonfiction books.

It can give you as much as half the comprehension in as little as one-tenth the time. For example, you should be able to preview eight or ten 100-page reports in an hour. After previewing, you'll be able to decide which reports (or which *parts* of which reports) are worth a closer look.

Here's how to preview: Read the entire first two paragraphs of whatever you've chosen. Next read only the first sentence of each successive paragraph. Then read the entire last two paragraphs.

Previewing doesn't give you all the details. But it does keep you from spending time on things you don't really want—or need—to read. Notice that previewing gives you a quick, overall view of *long, unfamiliar* material. For short, light reading, there's a better technique.

2. Skim—If It's Short and Simple

Skimming is a good way to get a general idea of light reading—like popular magazines or the sports and entertainment sections of the paper.

You should be able to skim a weekly popular magazine or the second section of your daily paper in less than *half* the time it takes you to read it now.

Skimming is also a great way to review material you've read before.

Here's how to skim: Think of your eyes as magnets. Force them to move fast. Sweep them across each and every line of type. Pick up *only a few key words in each line.*

Everybody skims differently.

You and I may not pick up exactly the same words when we skim the same piece, but we'll both get a pretty similar idea of what it's all about.

To show you how it works, I circled the words I picked out when I skimmed the following story. Try it. It shouldn't take you more than ten seconds.

My brother Russell thinks monsters live in our bedroom closet at night. But I told him he is crazy.

"Go and check then," he said.

I didn't want to. Russell said I was chicken.

"Am not," I said.

"Are so," he said.

So I told him the monsters were going to eat him at midnight. He started to cry. My Dad came in and told the monsters to beat it. Then he told us to go to sleep.

"If I hear any more about monsters," he said,

"I'll spank you."

We went to sleep fast. And you know something? They never did come back.

Skimming can give you a very good idea of this story in about half the words—and in less than half the time it'd take to read every word.

So far, you've seen that previewing and skimming can give you a *general idea* about content—fast. But neither technique can promise more than 50 percent comprehension, because you aren't reading all the words. (Nobody gets something for nothing in the reading game.)

To *read faster and understand most*—if not all—of what you read, you
need to know a third technique.

3. Cluster—To Increase Speed *and* Comprehension

Most of us learned to read by looking at each word in a sentence—*one at a time.*

Like this:

My—brother—Russell—thinks—monsters . . .

You probably still read this way sometimes, especially when the words are difficult. Or when the words have an extra-special meaning—in a poem, a Shakespearean play, or a contract. And that's O.K.

But word-by-word reading is a rotten way to read faster. It actually *cuts down* on your speed.

Clustering trains you to look at *groups of words* instead of one at a time—to increase your speed enormously. For most of us, clustering is a *totally different way of seeing what we read.*

Here's how to cluster: Train your eyes to see *all* the words in clusters of up to three or four words at a glance.

Here's how I'd cluster the story we just skimmed:

(My brother Russell) (thinks monsters) (live in)
(our bedroom closet) (at night.) (But I told him) (he is crazy.)
("Go and) (check then,") (he said.)
(I didn't want to.) (Russell said) (I was chicken.)
("Am not,") (I said.)
("Are so,") (he said.)
(So I told him) (the monsters) (were going to) (eat him)
(at midnight.) (He started to cry.) (My Dad came in)
(and told the monsters) (to beat it.) (Then he told us)
(to go) (to sleep.)
("If I hear) (any more about) (monsters," he said,)
("I'll spank you.")
(We went) (to sleep fast.) (And you) (know something?)
(They never did) (come back.)

Learning to read clusters is not something your eyes do naturally. It takes constant practice.

Here's how to go about it. Pick something light to read. Read it as fast as you can. Concentrate on seeing three or four words at once rather than one word at a time. Then reread the piece at your normal speed to see what you missed the first time.

Try a second piece. First cluster, then reread to see what you missed in this one.

When you can read in clusters without missing much the first time, your speed has increased. Practice fifteen minutes every day and you might pick up the technique in a week or so. (But don't be disappointed if it takes longer. Clustering *everything* takes time and practice.)

So now you have three ways to help you read faster. Preview to cut down on unnecessary heavy reading. Skim to get a quick, general idea of light reading. And cluster to increase your speed and comprehension.

With enough practice, you'll be able to handle more reading at school or work—and at home—in *less* time. You should even have enough time to read your favorite comic books—and *War and Peace*!

Bill Cosby

After You Read
Selecting the Main Idea

 Circle the number of the statement that you think best expresses the main idea of Bill Cosby's article. Why is it better than the other two?

1. Moving your eyes fast across each line will give you a general idea of the content of reading material in much less time than it would take to read every word.

2. It is necessary to choose your method of reading according to the kind of material you have to read and the amount of comprehension you need.

3. You should preview long and heavy readings, skim simple ones, and read in groups or clusters when you have to understand most of the material quite well.

Comprehension Quiz

 Answer the following questions about the article.

1. Is previewing a useful technique for all kinds of reading? Why or why not?

2. How many 100-page reports should you be able to preview in an hour?

3. Exactly how do you preview?

4. When is it better to skim rather than preview?

5. How do you skim?

6. Why is it better at times to use the technique of clustering instead of previewing or skimming?

7. How do you cluster?

8. What do you think the author means by "heavy" reading and "light" reading? Can you give examples of each of these?

Word Detective

Can you remember (or find by a quick scanning of the article) the following words or phrases, using the clues given?

1. A humorous way of saying *eyes*: _____ (lines 6 to 10)

2. The name of an animal that is used commonly as slang to mean *afraid*:

   _____ (lines 60 to 64)

3. A verb beginning with the letter *c* meaning "to pay attention, to put one's

   thoughts (on)": _____ (lines 113 to 116)

4. A three-word verb meaning "to reduce or decrease," as in the sentence,

   "You can _____ the amount of reading":

   _____ (lines 123 to 125)

Describing a Person

When an author uses an informal style, he or she often "opens up" to the reader, giving information about his or her personal life or feelings. After reading the article, what descriptions can you give of Bill Cosby as a person?

Giving and Receiving Directions and Other Information

Working in small groups, each person should take a turn talking in an informal manner about one of the following five topics. The speaker can use ideas from the article and from his or her own experience. The other members of the group should ask the speaker questions.

1. How to read a scientific article

2. How to read a long book

3. How to reread a lot of material the night before a test

4. Some good books I have read in English

5. My favorite newspaper or magazine and how I read it

Mark Twain

Before You Read

Timed Reading

exercise

Did you recognize the three references that Bill Cosby made to literature: Mark Twain, *War and Peace,* and Shakespeare? Learn more about one of them as you practice the techniques described in Cosby's article by taking the following timed reading.

The selection is taken from the *Encyclopaedia Britannica* entry for Mark Twain. Read quickly to find out something about the early life of and about one of the most famous books by this great author. Then do the comprehension quiz that follows. Try to finish both in eight minutes. (*Hint:* Look at the quiz first to see what it covers.)

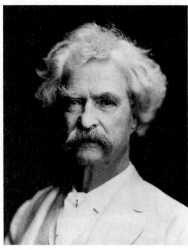

Twain, Mark, was the pen name of Samuel Langhorne Clemens (1835–1910), the United States' most famous humorist and the author of popular and
5   outstanding autobiographical works, travel books, and novels. The first thirty-six years of Clemens' life gave him experiences—as a boy in a little town in Missouri, as a steamboat pilot, as a reporter
10   on the far western frontier, and as a traveler abroad—which he thereafter used as materials for his best and most successful writings.

    He was born November 30, 1835, the . . . fifth child of John Marshall
15   and Jane (Lampton) Clemens, both descendants of Virginians. His birthplace was Florida, Missouri, a village to which the family had moved the previous June. The boy's father, a storekeeper and at times a lawyer, had little talent for moneymaking and failed there as he had elsewhere. The Clemenses therefore moved in the fall of 1839 to Hannibal, Missouri.

20   Hannibal was the town of Sam Clemens' boyhood, destined to figure importantly in several of his finest books. Almost in the geographical center of the United States, it had the wide Mississippi River rolling past it on the east, and on the other sides were forests, farmlands, and prairie. The

river was the route from and to the rest of the nation, bringing as it did all sorts of exciting visitors—river men, (religious) revivalists, circus troupes, . . . migrants to points as far westward as California. The steamboats which Sam and his gang of boyhood friends watched wheeling past or docking at the wharf were endlessly fascinating. So, too, were the steamboat men and the townspeople, many of whom were prototypes of characters in Twain's books. The river, an island nearby, and the woods around the town were wonderful places for boys to play. In the summer Sam ordinarily paid a vacation visit to the farm of his uncle John Quarles, near Florida. Some of his happiest and most vivid memories were to be of his play around Hannibal and of his visits to the farm. . . .

The Adventures of Tom Sawyer (1876) was one of Twain's best books, certainly his best for a juvenile audience. The setting was St. Petersburg,

which was Hannibal made idyllic by the passage of time; the characters were the grownups and the children of the town in the 1830s, also for the most part viewed sympathetically. Twain once characterized the book as "simply a hymn put into prose form to give it a worldly air." The nostalgic attitude was typical of the period when in every section of the country writers such as Edward Eggleston, Harriet Beecher Stowe, and George Washington Cable were writing local-color stories wistfully re-creating pre–Civil War life. The happenings were shaped by American humor, which for some time had been making fun of the Sunday-school story—its prematurely moral children who were rewarded and its prematurely immoral children who came to grief. Tom, says the first chapter, "was not the Model Boy of the village. He knew the model boy very well though—and hated him." Tom was by contrast "the normal boy," the book implied, mischievous and irresponsible but goodhearted; and the subplots in which he figured showed him again and again winning triumphs. These happy endings endear the book to children; the lifelike picture of a boy and his friends is enjoyed by both young and old. . . .

Encyclopaedia Britannica

After You Read

Comprehension Quiz

Circle the correct answer to finish each of the following statements about Mark Twain's life and his most famous book.

1. Mark Twain's real name was
   a. John Marshall.
   b. Sam Clemens.
   c. Tom Sawyer.

2. He lived about
   a. 50 years ago.
   b. 100 years ago.
   c. 200 years ago.

3. Twain spent his boyhood in the state of
   a. Missouri.
   b. Virginia.
   c. Pennsylvania.

4. His early life could be characterized as
   a. quiet and scholarly.
   b. active and adventurous.
   c. sad and difficult.

5. Twain based most of his successful writings on
   a. pure fantasy.
   b. facts he learned from school.
   c. true-life experience.

6. An important element in this author's childhood was the
   a. Mississippi River.
   b. Boston Art Museum.
   c. Pacific Ocean.

7. As a child, he had a great deal of contact with
   a. wealthy people.
   b. music.
   c. nature.

8. His famous book *The Adventures of Tom Sawyer* contains
   a. religious hymns and prayers.
   b. accounts of the Civil War.
   c. happenings from small-town life.

9. The general tone of the book is
   a. humorous.
   b. tragic.
   c. critical.

10. The book tells the story of a boy who was a
    a. prematurely immoral child.
    b. model of kindness and virtue.
    c. normal mixture of good and bad.

WHAT DO YOU THINK?

Censorship

In the United States and Canada, some groups of parents and religious and community leaders are trying to censor books from schools and libraries. They object to certain books because of a negative presentation of women or minority groups. They object to other books because of the violence, harsh language, or sexual scenes that are included. In some places, a number of classics have been challenged and sometimes prohibited. Examples are *Huckleberry Finn* by Mark Twain, *Catcher in the Rye* by J. D. Salinger, *Of Mice and Men* by John Steinbeck, *Romeo and Juliet* by William Shakespeare, and even the traditional fairy tale *Snow White and the Seven Dwarfs*. Some educators think it is good to censor books. Others believe that censorship is bad and goes against the basic right of freedom of expression. What do you think? Is it good to censor the books used in libraries and schools? Why or why not?

How to Take Tests: Scoring What You're Worth

Before You Read

Guessing the Meaning of Words from Context

Nine words or expressions that will be important to your understanding of the next reading selection are presented below in contexts that should help you guess their meaning. Circle the one word or phrase that would best keep the meaning of each sentence if it were substituted for the underlined word or phrase.

1. Words and phrases such as *often, usually, sometimes, in part,* or *on occasion* are <u>qualifiers</u> that change or limit the meaning of a sentence.
   a. synonyms
   b. prepositions
   c. objects
   d. modifiers

2. Of all the candidates, Jack is the <u>least likely to win</u> because he does not know many voters.
   a. one who will probably win
   b. one who will probably not win
   c. one who would like to win
   d. one who would not like to win

3. A teacher sometimes will <u>give a hint</u> to aid students with a difficult exam question.
   a. tell the answer
   b. explain the reason
   c. make a suggestion
   d. offer comfort

4. The students <u>assembled</u> their notes from the whole semester before beginning their study session for the final exam.
   a. brought together
   b. took apart
   c. questioned
   d. memorized

5. Her essay was excellent because she presented her <u>thesis</u> very clearly and gave so much evidence that any reader would have to be convinced.
   a. fact
   b. description
   c. expression of personal feelings
   d. main idea

6. From the sad expression on Sheila's face, the teacher could see that she <u>was totally stumped by</u> the question.
   a. was pleased about
   b. was trying to comprehend
   c. had finally seen
   d. did not understand

7. The flood itself was terrible, but the next day we saw the <u>aftermath</u>, which was even worse.
   a. resulting situation
   b. time before
   c. number of problems
   d. earlier condition

8. When he saw that half of the test was on word definitions, he knew he would <u>cash in on</u> the many hours he had spent studying vocabulary.
   a. get money for
   b. receive benefit from
   c. forget completely
   d. totally explain

9. Your clear knowledge of math <u>paid off</u> when you were interviewed for the bookkeeping job.
   a. was worthwhile
   b. was useless
   c. gave you confidence
   d. caused you to fail

What are objective tests? Which words often indicate a true answer in true/false tests? Which words can indicate a false answer? What should you do before answering multiple-choice questions? The answers to these and other practical questions concerning tests are in the following selection from Eric Jensen's book *You Can Succeed.* This book belongs to a genre (kind) that is popular with Americans, the "how-to" book. In it, Mr. Jensen explains test-taking techniques that he has taught successfully to more than 3,000 students. As you read, pay attention to the headings (titles of sections) and try to remember the specific suggestions that could help you do well on each type of test.

How to Take Tests: Scoring What You're Worth

Taking Objective Tests

Objective tests are those that include questions in a true/false, multiple-choice, matching, or fill-in format. Usually the answer is provided but the student must decide among several possibilities.

5　1. True/False Questions

True/false questions are the easiest test questions for the obvious reason that you have at least a fifty-fifty chance of getting the right answer. First, be sure you have read the question correctly. Look for words such as *always* or *never*; these words often indicate a false answer. Words such as
10　*often, usually, rarely,* or *sometimes* can indicate a true answer. Decide if the statement is totally true before you mark it true. Answer what the tester intended, not what you read into the question. For example, the statement "General Motors produces compact cars" is true. If the question had read "General Motors *alone* produces compact cars," then it
15　would be false. On true/false questions, stick with your first impression. Studies have shown over and over that your first impression is usually right, so be slow to change your answer, if you change it at all. A statement is more likely to be true if it is a fairly long statement; it takes more qualifiers to make a true statement than a false one.

Preparation means *confidence*!

2. Multiple-Choice Questions

An important rule to remember when answering multiple-choice questions is to read the answers first. This way, you'll view each answer separately and equally, without "jumping" on the first and easiest one. Look for an answer that not only seems right on its own but completes the question smoothly. If the question asks why something occurs, then your answer must be a cause. Try to eliminate any obviously poor answers. Suspect as a possible right answer phrases such as "all of the above," "none of the above," or "two of the above." Check the wording of questions to notice qualifying phrases such as "all of the following are true *except...*" or "which two of the below are *not...*" Statistically, the least likely correct answer on a multiple-choice question is the first choice. When in doubt, pick the longer of two answers. But, just as in true/false sections, always put something down. Even an educated guess is better than leaving the question blank and getting it wrong for sure.

3. Sentence Completion or Fill-in Questions

These generally ask for an exact word from memory. They don't allow for much error, so make sure your answer is a logical part of the sentence as a whole. Use the length and number of blanks given as a hint. Make sure the grammar is consistent. When in doubt, guess. Even if it's a generalized guess, you may get partial credit. If you are unsure of two possibilities, include both and hope for half credit.

Taking Essay Tests

When answering questions on an essay test, begin by making an outline on a piece of scratch paper. Assemble and organize the main points. Check the wording of the question to make sure you are interpreting the question correctly. For example, if the question asks you to compare and contrast, do not give a description or a discussion. Begin your essay by using the same words in your answer that are in the question. Keep your answer to the point. Always write something in answer to a question, even if you don't have much to say. Think and write by using this format:

1. *Introduction.* Introduce your topic.
2. *Background.* Give historical or philosophical background data to orient the reader to the topic.
3. *Thesis and Arguments.* State the main points, including causes and effects, methods used, dates, places, results.
4. *Conclusion.* Include the significance of each event, and finish up with a summary.

When totally stumped for an answer on an essay, think about book titles, famous names, places, dates, wars, economics, and politics. Usually
something will trigger some ideas. If you know nothing about the essay
question, invent your own question on the subject and answer it. You'll
usually get at least partial credit. That's better than nothing.

The Aftermath

When you complete a test, be sure to reread all your answers. Check the
wording of the questions again. Eliminate careless errors, and you can
save a lot of disappointment later. This is the time when you can cash in
on your brief encounters with your professor. Write your name in large,
visible letters. If you have made a positive impression on your professor
from personal contact, it will pay off now. Sometimes just a good impression can give you the higher grade in a borderline situation. Take as much
time as you need. When you think you have finished the test, turn it up-
side down on your desk. Think about it for a few minutes, giving your
mind some time to relax and come up with some answers. If you still
agree with what you have written, then turn it in. But sometimes those few
moments spent just thinking about the questions will bring back the answer that gives the A.

Once your corrected test is returned, look it over. Check your errors and
find out not what they were but what kind of errors they were. Was it from
answering questions too quickly, poor organization, a missed assignment,
or incorrect notes? Understand why you made errors and avoid the problem on the next test.

Eric Jensen

After You Read
Scanning for Specific Information

Fill in the blanks with the correct information from the article. If you do not
remember a specific point, find the appropriate heading and scan that section for
the answer.

1. The two main kinds of tests are _____ tests and essay tests.

2. On true/false tests, words such as *often*, _____ ,

_____ , or _____ can indicate a true statement.

3. On true/false tests, a fairly long statement is more likely to be

_____ because it takes more qualifiers to make a

_____ statement than a _____ one.

4. Before answering multiple-choice questions, you should

_____

5. Phrases such as *all of the above*, _____ _____

_____ _____ , or _____ _____

_____ _____ should be suspected as possible

_____ answers on multiple-choice tests.

6. According to statistics, the least likely correct answer on a multiple-choice

test is the _____ one.

7. On completion, or fill-in, tests, use the _____ and

_____ of blanks as a hint; if you are unsure of two possibilities,

_____ .

8. When answering questions on an essay test, begin by making an

_____ on a piece of scratch paper.

9. When writing the answer to an essay question, use the following format:

(1) Introduction, (2) _____ , (3) Thesis and Arguments, and (4)

_____ .

10. If you know nothing about the essay question, _____

_____ _____ _____ on the subject and

answer it in order to get partial credit.

Talking It Over

In small groups, discuss the following questions.

1. The author suggests that it is better to make an "educated guess" than to leave a question blank. What do you think he means by an educated guess?

2. When is it *not* a good idea to guess on a test?

3. Do you find it hard to answer multiple-choice questions with qualifying phrases such as "all the following are true *except* . . ." or "which of the below is *not* . . ."? Will the correct answer to such a question be something that is true or false?

4. Do you prepare differently for different types of tests? Explain your answer.

5. What type of test do you find the most difficult? Why?

6. Which pieces of advice in the article do you think are the most helpful?

7. How do you prepare yourself for taking an important exam? Do you go to sleep early the night before, or do you study up to the last minute? What can you do to avoid getting nervous?

8. When is it correct to ask a teacher to give you a hint about the type of exam that he or she is going to give? How can you do this in a polite way?

Taking an Objective Test

The following test is a sample exam on vocabulary and reading comprehension. The first two sections of it are based on the Test of English as a Foreign Language (TOEFL), an exam many American and Canadian universities require entering foreign students to take. Before beginning the sample test, review in your mind or with your classmates the suggestions from the article about taking objective tests. Then try to apply these as you take the exam. (Do not be discouraged if you don't do well on this test. It is difficult, as is the TOEFL. Take it again in one or two months and note how your score improves.)

Sample Test on Vocabulary and Reading Comprehension— Total Time 22 minutes (25 questions)

Part A *Directions:* In questions 1–8, each sentence has an underlined word or phrase. Below each sentence are four other words or phrases, marked (A), (B), (C), and (D). Circle the *one* word or phrase that *best keeps the meaning* of the original sentence if it is substituted for the underlined word or phrase.

1. The police suspect that the culprit might still be at large.
   - **(A)** innocent bystander
   - **(B)** unlucky victim
   - **(C)** guilty person
   - **(D)** helpful witness

2. It was a decisive victory for medicine when the disease of smallpox was finally eradicated.
   - **(A)** treated by radiation
   - **(B)** removed to other areas
   - **(C)** watered down
   - **(D)** gotten rid of

3. Cassius loathed Julius Caesar because Caesar was so rich and powerful.
   - **(A)** hated
   - **(B)** accused
   - **(C)** admired
   - **(D)** undermined

4. The scientist reluctantly announced that the experimental results were ambiguous.
   - **(A)** completely negative
   - **(B)** unable to be measured
   - **(C)** modestly successful
   - **(D)** open to interpretation

5. The candidate declined to comment on the proposed tax increase.
   - **(A)** changed his mind with regard to
   - **(B)** said less than usual concerning
   - **(C)** refused to speak about
   - **(D)** mentioned in passing

6. Some critics think that Mark Twain's autobiography should be ranked with the great autobiographies of the world.
   - **(A)** eliminated from
   - **(B)** considered equal to
   - **(C)** put on a level below
   - **(D)** edited to the standards of

7. The brave hero faced all <u>hazards</u> without flinching.

   (A) villains   **(C)** chances

   (B) dangers   **(D)** goals

8. <u>Prior to</u> the appointment, it is advisable to obtain an application form.

   (A) after   **(C)** rather than

   (B) before   **(D)** because of

Part B   *Directions:*   In questions 9–15, you will read two passages. Each one is followed by several questions about it. Circle the <u>one</u> best answer, (A), (B), (C), or (D) to each question. Answer all questions following a passage on the basis of what is <u>stated</u> or <u>implied</u> in that passage.

QUESTIONS 9–12

An Augustinian monk named Gregor Mendel was the first person to make precise observations about the biological mechanism of inheritance. This happened a little over 100 years ago in an Austrian monastery, where Mendel spent his leisure hours performing experiments with pea plants of different types. He crossed them carefully and took notes about the appearance of various traits, or characteristics, in succeeding generations. From his observations, Mendel formed a set of rules, now known as the Mendelian Laws of Inheritance, which were found to apply not only to plants but to animals and human beings as well. This was the beginning of the modern science of genetics.

9. The importance of Gregor Mendel is that he was the first person to

   (A) imagine that there existed a precise mechanism to inheritance.

   (B) approach the problem of inheritance scientifically.

   (C) think about why animals and plants inherit certain characteristics.

   (D) invent the word *genetics.*

10. When did Mendel perform his experiments?

   (A) in ancient times   **(C)** in the 1860s

   (B) in the 1680s   **(D)** at the beginning of this century

11. Why did Mendel do this work?

   (A) It was part of his duties.   **(C)** He lived in Austria.

   (B) He enjoyed it.   **(D)** He was paid for it.

12. The Mendelian Laws of Inheritance describe the transmission of biological traits in

   (A) plants.   **(C)** human beings.

   (B) animals.   **(D)** all the above.

QUESTIONS 13–15

The magnificent warship *Wasa,* which sank after a maiden "voyage" of some 1,500 yards, was salvaged and restored, after lying at the bottom of Stockholm's harbor for over 330 years. The ship now rests in the National Maritime Museum of that city.

13. The *Wasa* sank around the year
- **(A)** 1330.
- **(B)** 1500.
- **(C)** 1650.
- **(D)** 1950.

14. Which of the following statements about the *Wasa* is probably *not* true?
- **(A)** It met with a catastrophe shortly after being built.
- **(B)** It carried many soldiers and cannons.
- **(C)** It was a veteran of many hard-fought battles.
- **(D)** It was raised by modern salvaging techniques.

15. The *Wasa* ship appears to be
- **(A)** Swedish.
- **(B)** Dutch.
- **(C)** American.
- **(D)** British.

Directions: In questions 16–19, circle the answer that is closest in meaning to the original sentence. Note that several of the choices may be factually correct, but you should choose the one that is the closest restatement of the given sentence.

16. No hour is too early or too late to call Jenkins Plumbing Company.
- **(A)** Jenkins Plumbing Company does not answer calls that are too early or too late.
- **(B)** Jenkins Plumbing Company accepts calls at any hour of the day or night.
- **(C)** Whether you call early or late, Jenkins Plumbing Company will come in one hour.
- **(D)** If you call at a good hour, Jenkins Publishing Company will never be late.

17. When TV first became available to large numbers of Americans in the 1950s and 1960s, most producers ignored its possibilities as a tool for education.
- **(A)** In the 1950s and 1960s, there were not many educational programs on American TV.
- **(B)** Until the 1950s and 1960s, most of the TV programs in the United States were tools for education.
- **(C)** After the 1950s and 1960s, most American producers did not see the educational possibilities of TV.
- **(D)** During the 1950s and 1960s, educational programs first became available to Americans.

18. In spite of the high interest rates on home loans, the couple did not change their plans to buy a new house.
- **(A)** High interest rates caused the couple to change their plans about buying a house.
- **(B)** The couple did not buy the house because of the high interest rates.
- **(C)** Since interest rates were no longer high, the couple bought the house.
- **(D)** Although the interest rates were high, the house was bought by the couple.

19. Had more young people voted, Mr. Wilkes would have won the election.
- **(A)** The election was won by Mr. Wilkes with the help of the young voters.
- **(B)** Mr. Wilkes did not win because there were not many young people who voted.
- **(C)** Since the young people voted in the election, Mr. Wilkes did not win.
- **(D)** Most young people would have liked to vote for Mr. Wilkes.

Part C In questions 20–25, you will be given reading materials followed by true/false questions about the meaning. For each question, circle T (*true*) or F (*false*) according to what is stated or implied in the passage.

QUESTIONS 20–23

Legal Secretary Wanted Our legal department requires a mature, versatile secretary who will report to one senior counsel and one assistant counsel. The successful candidate will have a solid background in organizational work, advanced skill in shorthand and data processing, combined with at least three years of legal secretarial training. Some experience in real estate could be an asset. Sunham Life offers excellent opportunities for personal advancement. Compensation will be in accord with qualifications, beginning at a minimum of $2,000 per month. A superior benefit package and an attractive incentive program are included. Begin at once. Interviews will be held Monday through Friday, May 12th to 16th. Applicants are requested to mail detailed resumes to:

Sunham Life Insurance Company
P.O. Box 210
Hamilton, Ontario L50 2X8

20. Maturity and versatility, proficiency in data processing, and extensive experience in real estate are all requirements for the advertised position.   T F

21. Salary will be at least $2,000 per month to start.   T F

22. In order to apply for the position, a person should send in a summary of previous experience.   T F

23. An appropriate applicant for the job would be an older, experienced secretary.   T F

QUESTIONS 24 AND 25

Adults: one or two tablets, with water, one to three times in twelve hours. *Children's dosage:* 10 to 14 years, one tablet, one to three times in twelve hours; 5 to 10 years, one-half tablet one to three times during a twelve-hour period.

24. In one period of twelve hours, an adult should not take more than six tablets.   T F

25. An 11-year-old boy has just taken a tablet; he should wait two hours before taking another.   T F

CHAPTER three

Relationships

in this chapter

In the United States, the 1970s and 1980s led to dramatic changes in families and personal relationships in general. The first reading selection is an overview of recent changes in family structure in the United States, along with some statistics. The second article gives a new twist to an old phenomenon, "mail-order" brides. The third selection is the story of one father's relationship with his children before and after divorce.

The Changing American Family

Before You Read

Understanding the Use of Jargon

Many articles on current topics use jargon: words or phrases that have been taken from a particular branch of study or work. The use of a great deal of jargon is considered bad style because it makes communication difficult. However, some jargon is often useful, especially to discuss changes and new aspects of life that are not easily described with other vocabulary. The following article uses three terms taken from popular sociology. These terms describe different types of families: the extended, the nuclear, and the blended. Scan the article for the definitions and write them below.

extended family: _____

nuclear family: _____

blended family: _____

Which of the terms is set off by punctuation to show that it is not yet in common usage?

With all the recent changes and the stress in modern society, many people wonder if the traditional structure of the family can survive. How do you think the family has changed in the past several decades? The following article discusses new trends and presents some statistics about the American family of today.

The Changing American Family

The American family unit is in the process of change. In the first half of the twentieth century, there were mainly two types of families: the extended and the nuclear. An extended family includes mother, father, children, and some other relatives, such as grandparents, aunts, uncles, or

5 cousins, living in the same house. A nuclear family is composed of just parents and children living under the same roof.

As the American economy progressed from agricultural to industrial, people were forced to move to different parts of the country to get good jobs. These jobs were mainly in the large cities. Now, in fact, three-quar-

10 ters of Americans live in urban areas, a mere 2.5 percent of the nation's

total land mass. Of the 118 million in the civilian labor force, only 3 million still work on the farm.

Since moving for better jobs often split up the extended family, the nuclear family became more prevalent. At present, 55 percent of the families in the United States are nuclear families. But besides these two types of traditional family groupings—extended and nuclear—the word *family* is now being expanded to include a variety of other living arrangements.

15

American families today are made up of many diverse combinations. With one in two marriages ending in divorce, there is an increase in single-parent homes: a father or mother living with one or more children. About one household in ten is headed by a single parent. Divorce has also led to more "blended families." Blended families occur when previously married men and women marry again and combine the children from former marriages into a new family. Some married couples are deciding not to have any children at all, so there is an increase in two-person childless families. Many couples are also deciding not to get married legally, and so there is an increase in couples just living together. There are also more people living alone: single, widowed, divorced. About one in five Americans lives alone.

20

25

M. Prijic

After You Read
Recalling Information

 **exercise 1** Circle the correct word or phrase to complete the following sentences about the article.

1. In the past, many American families included parents, grandparents, or other relatives who were living with the parents and children; this was called the (extended/nuclear/blended) family.

2. With the industrialization of American society, the (extended/nuclear/blended) family became more common.

3. At present, nearly one out of every (two/three/four) marriages in the United States ends in divorce.

4. A family composed of parents with children from previous marriages is called (an extended/a nuclear/a blended) family.

5. Currently there is (an increase/a decrease) in the number of childless marriages.

6. At the same time, there is (an increase/a decrease) in the number of people who live alone.

Reading a Statistical Chart

The statistical chart on page 47 gives you an idea of some of the big changes that occurred in the American family from 1960 to 1990. A chart presents information to us in a clear and compact way. Often, however, a chart contains much more information than we need. This can make it hard to understand. When reading a chart for information, follow these three steps:

1. Skim for a general idea of what the chart shows.
2. Focus clearly on each question you want to answer.
3. Scan the chart for the information.

Households and Families: Growth and Change, 1960–1990 (numbers in thousands)

type of unit	1960	1970	1980	1985	1990	percent change 1970–1980	percent change 1980–1990
Households	52,799	63,401	80,776	86,789	93,347	27.4%	15.5%
Average size	3.33	3.14	2.76	2.69	2.63	—	—
Family households:	44,905	51,456	59,550	62,706	66,090	15.7	10.9
Married couple	39,254	44,728	49,112	50,350	52,317	9.8	6.6
Male householder*	1,228	1,228	1,733	2,228	2,884	41.1	66.4
Female householder*	4,422	5,500	8,705	10,129	10,890	58.3	25.1
Nonfamily households:	7,895	11,945	21,226	24,082	27,257	77.7	28.4
Male householder	2,716	4,063	8,807	10,114	11,606	116.8	31.8
Female householder	5,179	7,882	12,419	13,968	15,651	57.6	26.0
One person	6,896	10,851	18,296	20,602	22,999	68.6	25.7
Families	45,111	51,586	59,550	62,706	66,090	15.4%	11.0%
Average size	3.67	3.58	3.29	3.23	3.17	—	—
Married couple	39,329	44,755	49,112	50,350	52,317	9.7	6.5
Male householder*	1,275	1,239	1,733	2,228	2,884	39.9	66.4
Female householder*	4,507	5,591	8,705	10,129	10,890	55.7	25.1
Unrelated subfamilies	207	130	360	526	534	176.9%	48.3%
Married couple	75	27	20	46	68	N.A.†	N.A.†
Father-child*	47	11	36	85	45	N.A.†	N.A.†
Mother-child*	85	91	304	395	421	234.1	38.5
Related subfamilies	1,514	1,150	1,150	2,228	2,403	0%	109.0%
Married couple	871	617	582	719	871	−5.7	49.7
Father-child*	115	48	54	116	153	N.A.†	183.0
Mother-child*	528	484	512	1,392	1,378	5.8	169.1

*No spouse present.
†Not shown; base less than 75,000.
Sources: U.S. Bureau of the Census. *Household and Family Characteristics: March 1990* (1991) and *The Statistical History of the U.S.* (1976).

Find the following information in the chart. Look for the answers to the questions by following the three steps described in the box on page 46.

1. In general, what kinds of changes does the chart show?

2. Did the average size of the American household (group of people living together in a house) go up or down between 1960 and 1990?

3. Was there a greater or a smaller percentage of the American population living alone in 1990 as compared with 1960?

4. Which parent—the mother or the father—was more common in a single-parent home in 1990? Was this situation the same in 1960?

Filling in a Family Tree

The United States and Canada are lands of immigrants, except for the Native Americans, who are the only true natives. Many people have a "family tree" like the one in the illustration on page 49, which they construct with the help of elderly relatives and old documents to show who their ancestors were and where they came from. How well do you know the names for relatives and family members in English? Check your knowledge by answering the questions below about Mary Smith's family, using the illustration on the facing page as a guide.

1. How many nieces does Mary have? How many nephews?

_____

2. Does she have more uncles or more aunts? _____

3. What is the name of her maternal grandmother?

_____

4. What is her brother-in-law's name? Her paternal grandfather's?

_____

5. How many first cousins does her son have? Are they male or female? What is their relationship to Mary?

_____

6. What nationalities would you say that Mary has in her background?

_____

Now answer the following questions about yourself.

1. How many uncles and aunts do you have? How many first cousins?

_____

Family Tree of Mary O'Grady Smith

2. Do you have any nieces or nephews? Why or why not?

_____

_____

3. Do you know the names of your great-grandfathers? Do you know where they were born?

_____

4. What nationalities are in your background?

_____

5. Who is the newest member on your family tree? How old is he or she?

_____

6. Does your family know the names of many of its ancestors? How many generations could you put on your family tree?

_____

Talking It Over

In small groups, discuss the following questions.

1. In North American slang, a husband and wife who both work and have no children are called DINKS. DINK is an acronym for Double Income No Kids. Some people think that these couples are selfish. What do you think of DINKS?

2. What kinds of families are most common in your country?

3. Do you know of any marriages that were arranged by the families? Some people say that these arranged marriages are better and last longer than marriages in which the spouses have chosen each other. Do you agree?

4. What do you think of the following "rules for a successful marriage"?
   a. A wife should be younger than her husband.
   b. A husband should earn more money than his wife.
   c. The families of the husband and the wife should get along well with each other.
   d. A couple should live together for at least a year before marrying.

5. Think of a question related to marriage or family life that you would like to discuss in class. Write it here.

Two Old Jokes

activity **2**

To understand the following two jokes, you must see that the last words (written in italics) have more than one meaning. In small groups, talk about the jokes. Are they funny? Why or why not? Take turns telling other jokes you may know about marriage, families, or children.

Confirmed Bachelor: "I believe that marriage is a great institution. But who wants to live in an *institution*?"

A Common Toast at Weddings: "May you both have health, wealth, and happiness, and may all your troubles be *little ones*!"

70 Brides for 7 Foreigners

Before You Read

Scanning for Facts

You already have used the technique of skimming, or reading quickly for main ideas. Another useful technique is scanning. Scanning is reading quickly for specific information. You skim for the gist, or general idea. You scan for a fact or a particular bit of information. To scan, follow these three steps:

1. Think of what you are looking for.
2. Move your eyes quickly until you find it.
3. Stop and record the information.

exercise  Scan for the following information in the article "70 Brides for 7 Foreigners" and write the answers on the lines. Items are listed in order of their appearance. The first one is done as an example.

1. The percentage of Russian mothers wanting their daughters to marry foreigners: ___23 percent___

2. The name of the Russian prince whose daughter became queen of France:

   _____

3. The number of phone calls an Australian man received within two days of placing his personal ad:_____

4. The number of Russian women who go each day to the Alliance dating agency in Moscow: _____

5. The percentage of Russian women from the agency's files who actually get married: _____

6. The three countries of origin of most of the foreign men applying for Russian wives: _____ , _____ , _____

7. The number of marriages involving a foreigner that are registered in Moscow each year: _____

Many years ago, there was a popular American musical called *Seven Brides for Seven Brothers.* The title of the following article contains an "echo" of that earlier title, but the numbers are different. The article is about Russian women who marry foreign men. Why do you think they want to do that? Why do you think some men from other countries want to marry Russian women?

70 Brides for 7 Foreigners

Russia seems to be turning into a major exporter of brides. Almost 1,500 marriages with foreigners are registered in Moscow every year. Another 10,000 women go to the international marriage agency *Alliance* each year, according to a poll, and 23 percent of Russian mothers would like their daughters to marry foreign citizens.

Russian brides have always been prized by foreigners—ever since the time of Yaroslav the Wise [an 11th-century grand prince of Kiev], whose daughter became the queen of France. But during Joseph Stalin's time, the attitude toward marriages to foreigners was intolerant.

In the 1960s, the registration of foreign marriages was resumed, and since then the trickle of Russian brides abroad has turned into a powerful torrent. Tens of thousands of Russian women dream of an advantageous marriage and look for foreign husbands. How? One way is through personal ads in newspapers. One ad read: "Man from Australia (37, 5 feet 5, 132 pounds) seeks short (5 feet 1 to 5 feet 5), slender woman 22–29 for marriage." The man is from Sydney. His mother advised him to marry a Russian woman because Australian women are very liberated, change men like gloves, and do not do housework. Russian women, in the opinion of the placer of the ad, love to clean, cook, stay home, and have children. In two days, he got 100 calls.

Many women are not shy about going to dating agencies. *Alliance* is one of the largest in Moscow, with branches in Russia's large cities and abroad. It has been flourishing for more than five years. The director, Tamara Alckseyevna Shkunova, is an academician and director of the Russian Institute of the Family at the International Academy of Information Systems and editor in chief of *Moskovskaya Brachnaya Gazeta* [the *Moscow Marriage Gazette*].

Each day about 10 women go to the agency, but only two to three of them are put in the files. There are criteria for selection. First, you must be successful in your professional milieu. Second, you must know a foreign language. And third, you must meet a standard of "European looks": blond with blue eyes, slender with long legs. Of the 2,000 women a year who get into the files, only 10 percent get married. Of the 200 who have married recently, one was lucky enough to become the wife of a millionaire.

For a 25-year-old woman without children, the service costs $5.30; for 30- to 40-year-old women with children, the service costs $8.00

There are 700 foreign men in the files, mostly from the United States, Germany, and Britain. Up to 300 men apply annually. They must meet only one requirement—that they be well-to-do. The information on the man's passport is checked, and a call is made to his place of work.

Once a husband is found, the next stop is Wedding Palace Number 4, the only place in Moscow that registers marriages to foreigners. Each year, 1,200 couples get married there. In 1992, the bridegrooms came from 96 countries. The greatest number came from the United States; in second place was Israel, followed by Turkey and Bulgaria.

Registration requires a passport and a guarantee from the groom's embassy that there are no obstacles to his getting married. The French Embassy, for example, takes a very serious attitude toward marriages to foreign women. It requires that the French groom obtain certification of his "legal capacity for marriage." If an embassy official registers a couple that has not passed the requisite medical tests, the official is fined. Stiff requirements are also imposed by Germany.

The Wedding Palace requires confirmation that, in the given country, a marriage to a citizen of another state is valid. After all, in a number of countries a foreign wife and her children could find that they have no property rights. In Syria, for example, marriage to a foreigner is considered invalid without special permission.

Many countries are trying to erect barriers to the marital migration from Russia. For example, one Moscow woman tried for nine months to get permission to go to the United States, where her fiancé was waiting for her. Another couple wanted to get registered in Canada. The fiancée was called to the Canadian Embassy for an interview, but an entry visa was never granted. "Prove that this isn't a fictitious marriage," they said.

Many Russian women who marry foreigners quickly get divorced and come back. The reasons are well known: a sense of second-class status, a language barrier, financial difficulties. Deceptions are frequent: One "sweetheart" described his home as a palace with a fountain, but, in reality, it turned out that he lived in a small cottage without a bathtub.

S. Kuzina

After You Read
Identifying General and Specific Statements

 **exercise 1**   Which one of the following two columns contains *general* statements related to the article and which contains *specific* examples? Match each general statement to the specific example that illustrates or supports it.

1. _____ About 10,000 women go to the international marriage agency in Moscow every year.

2. _____ One husband described his home as a palace with a fountain, but it was really a cottage without even a bathtub.

3. _____ The Russian fiancée of a Canadian man was told at the Canadian embassy to "prove that this isn't a fictitious marriage."

4. _____ An Australian man said that his mother advised him to marry a Russian woman because they love to clean, cook, stay home, and have children.

5. _____ Each day about 10 women go to the agency, but only 2 or 3 of them are selected.

a. Certain countries are trying to stop or slow down the influx of brides from Russia.

b. Many Russian women are looking for foreign husbands.

c. It is not easy in Moscow for a woman to get in the files of a dating agency.

d. Traditionally, Russian women have the reputation of being good wives.

e. Many Russian women who marry foreigners get disappointed and come back to their homeland.

focus on testing

Eliminating the Incorrect Choices

As you know, the Vocabulary and the Reading Comprehension sections of the TOEFL use a multiple-choice format; that means that you are given four possible answers and asked to choose the best one. The items on multiple-choice vocabulary tests often follow a pattern. One of the words is completely wrong and may even have the opposite meaning. One is a sort of "decoy," similar in form but different in meaning; and one is close in meaning but not quite right.

example: Ten thousand women go to the international marriage agency Alliance each year, according to a poll.

    (A) custom   **(C)** survey

    (B) policy   **(D)** list

exercise Each sentence has an underlined word or phrase. Below each sentence are four other words or phrases. You are to circle the *one* word or phrase that *best keeps the meaning* of the original sentence if it is substituted for the underlined word or phrase. Do the exercise with the pattern described above in mind. What examples do you find that fit these descriptions? *Note:* The words and phrases all come from the reading selection "70 Brides for 7 Foreigners."

1. During Joseph Stalin's time, the attitude toward marriages to foreigners was <u>intolerant</u>.
   (A) close-minded   **(C)** generous
   (B) indifferent   **(D)** open

2. Tens of thousands of Russian women dream of an <u>advantageous</u> marriage.
   (A) beneficial   **(C)** costly
   (B) distressful   **(D)** outrageous

3. In the 1960s, the registration of foreign marriages was resumed, and since then the <u>trickle</u> of Russian brides abroad has turned into a powerful torrent.
   (A) large number   **(C)** entrance
   (B) small number   **(D)** trickery

4. There are <u>criteria</u> for selection. First, you must be successful in your professional milieu.
   (A) payments   **(C)** standards
   (B) criticisms   **(D)** problems

5. Up to 300 men apply annually. They must meet only one requirement—that they be <u>well-to-do</u>.
   (A) healthy   **(C)** well-meaning
   (B) wealthy   **(D)** employed

Selecting the Main Idea

 The article uses both general and specific information to present one main idea. Here and on page 56, circle the number of the statement that you think best expresses the main idea of the article. Why is it better than the other two?

1. Each year 1,200 couples get married at Wedding Palace Number 4, the only place in Moscow that registers marriages to foreigners; in 1992, the bridegrooms came from 96 different countries.

2. Following an old tradition, a large number of Russian women are marrying foreign men, and, despite some obstacles and disappointments, this seems to be a trend that will continue.

3. Many foreign embassies take a very serious attitude toward the increasing number of brides who are leaving Russia to marry citizens from other nations.

Talking It Over

In small groups, discuss the following questions.

1. What does the mother of the man from Sydney think about Australian women? Why do you think she feels this way?

2. In your opinion, are women from certain cultures generally better wives than the women from other cultures? Why or why not?

3. In your opinion, do men from some cultures make better husbands than those from other cultures? Why or why not?

4. What do you think about the criteria for selection of the dating agencies? Are they fair? Explain.

5. Would you consider marrying someone from a different culture? What advantages and disadvantages are there to such a marriage?

6. Nowadays, some people choose not to marry at all. What do you think about that idea?

Outside Assignment: Getting Personal

Find some ads from the *Personals* section of a newspaper or magazine and bring them to class. In small groups, discuss the following questions.

1. What is your opinion of these personal ads as a way to find a marriage partner?

2. Would meeting people this way be safe and effective?

3. Would it be better to go to an agency that uses computers to match possible partners?

Now compare your ads and write a group opinion to read to the class about this topic.

SELECTION three

The Making of a Father

Before You Read
Learning Words Through Their Latin Roots

 Many English words originally came from the Latin language and still have Latin roots (parts). Becoming familiar with Latin roots can help you remember the meaning of some English words. Study the meanings of the following Latin roots; then fill in the blanks with words made from them.

COMMON LATIN ROOTS	
pater-, patr-	father
mater-, matr-	mother
frater-, fratr-	brother
homo-	man
geno-	race, kind
sui-	self

SUFFIXES DERIVED FROM LATIN	
-al	of, like, or suitable for
-ity	state, character, condition
-cide	killing

1. A woman who acts like a mother toward someone treats that person in a *maternal* way. A man who acts like a father to someone is said to have a _____ attitude toward that person. The city of Philadelphia was founded by a religious group called the Quakers, who believed in brotherly or _____ love.

2. In hospitals, there are special sections for women who are in the condition of being or becoming mothers; these are called *maternity* wards. On college campuses, there are often groups of male students who live together like brothers; these associations are called _____ .

3. A person who kills his father commits *patricide.* If he kills his mother, this act is called _____ .

4. Can you guess the meaning of the following words?

   homocide: _____

   genocide: _____

   suicide: _____

5. Two words used in the next reading selection are *fratricide* and *paternity*. Can you give their definitions? _____

_____

Guessing the Meaning of Words from Context

 Read the following excerpts from the next selection and the commentaries for each. Circle the correct meaning for each italicized word.

1. "At the smallest sign of crankiness [bad temper] or illness, [the children] had been promptly sent back to the kitchen, and to the mother who had been held more or less responsible for such a *lapse*."

The words *crankiness* and *illness* tell us that there was something wrong with the children. Because of this, they were sent back to the mother, the person considered responsible for this *lapse*. The implication is that the mother had not prepared the children correctly. Therefore, *lapse* means a small

a. success.　　　　**b.** error.　　　　**c.** help.

2. "So instead, at thirty-five years of age, he chose paternity. Ten years earlier he had been more or less *drafted*. This time he really chose it."

A contrast is made between a man at thirty-five who chooses to be a father and the same man at twenty-five who had not chosen it, who had been *drafted*. Therefore, *drafted* means

a. accepted.　　　　**b.** invited.　　　　**c.** forced.

3. ". . . The visited father finally established a *rapport* with his children. He spent more time with them in ten months than he had in ten years."

The words *finally established* and *spent more time* tell us that a *rapport* is something that a person establishes with someone else over a period of time. So, a *rapport* is a

a. home.　　　　**b.** relationship.　　　　**c.** job.

4. "It was his daughter who pointed out the *absurdity* of the sign on the corner that read: Go Children Slow. 'That doesn't make sense.'"

The words *that doesn't make sense* show us that *absurdity* means

a. difficulty.　　　　**b.** nonsense.　　　　**c.** cleverness.

5. "Sometimes he was jealous. Of men who had *custody* of their children. Of live-in fathers."

The words *of live-in fathers* tell us that the fathers who have *custody* of their children

a. take care of them most of the time.

b. get along well with them.

c. can visit them when they choose.

What do you think about divorce? Is it common in your country? Do you think it is harmful to the children involved or do you think at times it is beneficial to them?

The following essay by the well-known journalist Ellen Goodman describes how one man changes after his divorce. In the first paragraph, Goodman uses a comparison to show what the man was like before his divorce, when he lived with his family. She compares him to a visitor in his own home and speaks about him having his children "brought in on a tray at cocktail hour." This is an example of *figurative* language (language that uses a figure or symbol to show something). It does not mean, of course, that the children were literally (really, actually) carried in on a tray. It means that the father's distant, formal attitude toward his children was similar to the attitude of a guest toward the snacks and drinks that are offered to him on a tray before dinner. Can you show how this comparison is extended in the first two paragraphs by the use of more figurative language? Why do you think the author begins like this instead of saying directly what she means?

The Making of a Father

When he lived with them, he had been a visiting father. The sort who has his children brought in on a tray at cocktail hour and collected before dinner is served. The sort who prefers his children to come shiny-clean, cheerful, and in small doses.

5 He had sniffed them as if they were corks from a new wine bottle.* At the smallest sign of crankiness or illness, they had been promptly sent back to the kitchen, and to the mother who had been held more or less responsible for such a lapse in the quality of the wine cellar. It's true. He'd always wanted them perfect, 98.6 degrees[†] and in full repair.

10 But things were different now. He was no longer a live-in visiting father. He had signed on the dotted line of a very formal agreement, full of clauses and subclauses, one of which read: "The father shall have reasonable visitation rights."

But now that he was officially, legally, the visiting (or visited) father, 15 something remarkable happened. He had made his first full connections with the small people in his life. In a peculiar way he knew this was his first Father's Day.

In the last ten months he had become a father, not just a name on a birth certificate. He discovered that this transition wasn't unique with him, 20 but he wasn't entirely sure why it happened to so many divorced fathers.

When first apart, he thought he would be a "swinging"[‡] bachelor, with a high-rise studio apartment and a mirror over his bed. But somehow he'd felt rather silly.

---

*People often smell the corks of wine bottles to get an idea of how the wine will taste.
[†]Normal human temperature on the Fahrenheit scale.
[‡]In quotation marks because it is slang for going out with many members of the opposite sex.

"Good! Now we can go back to watching television."

So instead, at thirty-five years of age, he chose paternity. Ten years earlier he had been more or less drafted. This time he really chose it. Out of loneliness and guilt at first, and out of pleasure at last, the visited father finally established a rapport with his children. He spent more time with them in ten months than he had in ten years.

They were with him through Wednesdays, weekends, and vacations, through the flu and sunburn and carsickness and various attempts at fratricide.

Alone with his children, he took intensive on-the-job training. The mother who had been designated the expert by all of them wasn't around for consultations. He had to cram. Indeed, the father developed a repertory of attitudes on subjects like these: Should his daughter have dessert if she refused to eat the vegetables? What was the appropriate punishment for a ten-year-old boy who spread honey all over the cat?

He became the kind of parent who knew how to braid hair and limit junk food and tuck in tired bodies—and yell. He learned what his children liked to eat, that they hated to wash, and where they were likely to have left the other tennis shoe. He learned that even when they'd seen each other at their worst, they liked each other.

Alone with his children, he'd found them to be remarkably interesting. That was an odd word to use, but there it was: interesting. It was his son who explained to him quite clearly why there was no such thing as nothing, "because then nothing has to be something." It was his daughter who pointed out the absurdity of the sign on the corner that read: Go Children Slow. "That doesn't make sense. It should read: 'Go Slow, Children.'"

50 The visiting father who had never had time for his children made time. Period. He met both teachers. He had seen one child play basketball and the other play hockey.

Sometimes he was jealous. Of men who had custody of their children. Of live-in fathers. He wondered why he had waited so long.

55 But at least he had learned. When he couldn't take them for granted,* he discovered that you can't take them for granted. What he had with his children was what they created. They had made him, at last, a father.

Ellen Goodman

After You Read

Finding the Sequence of Events: Before and After

**exercise 1**

There is a contrast throughout the essay between the father's situation before and after his divorce. Write *before* in front of sentences that describe the man's relationship with his children before his divorce and *after* in front of sentences that describe his relationship after his divorce.

1. _____ He talked with them a lot and learned interesting things from them.

2. _____ He never spent much time with them.

3. _____ He took them for granted.

4. _____ He went to watch them participate in sports.

5. _____ He sent them to their mother when they were ill or cranky.

6. _____ He fed them and put them to bed.

7. _____ He lived all the time in the same house with them.

8. _____ He yelled at them.

9. _____ He established a rapport with them.

Can you explain why the past perfect tense (*had* + participle) is used in the second paragraph of the reading?

_____

*Count on them always to be there.

Finding Synonymous Vocabulary

 exercise 2 Find the words from the story that are close in meaning to the italicized words. The words are given in order of their appearance.

1. At the smallest sign of *irritability* or illness . . .

2. . . . they had been *immediately* sent back to the kitchen . . .

3. . . . and to the mother who had been held more or less responsible for such a *fault*.

4. At thirty-five years of age, he choose *fatherhood*.

5. The father finally established a *relationship* with his children.

6. He took *thorough* on-the-job training.

7. The mother had been *named* the expert by all of them.

8. Now she wasn't around for *advice*.

9. He had to *study intensively.*

10. Indeed, the father developed a *collection* of attitudes on certain subjects.

Identifying Sentence Fragments

> Writers of popular essays or magazine or newspaper articles often like to use short sentences. Sometimes they even use sentence fragments, groups of words that are written as sentences but lack a main subject or a main verb or both. It is not good to imitate this usage for general academic writing. You should recognize sentence fragments and avoid using them.

 exercise 3 Answer the following questions.

1. How many complete sentences are there in the first paragraph of the essay "The Making of a Father"? How many sentence fragments are there? Why are these fragments rather than complete sentences?

2. Toward the end of the reading, what two sentence fragments can you find that lack both a main subject and a main verb?

Talking It Over

In small groups, discuss the following questions.

1. Why do you think the father in the story found his children interesting after his divorce but not before?

2. In your opinion, what is meant by the last two lines of the essay: "What he had with his children was what they created. They had made him, at last, a father."

3. The author tells us that the father experiences several different feelings after his divorce. At one point he feels silly. Do you remember why? How does he change his actions because of this? Later, he feels loneliness, guilt, pleasure, and jealousy. Explain when and why he felt each of these emotions. In what other situations might someone feel each of these?

4. Americans often talk about their feelings, usually with close friends. If they are happy, they want to share their happiness with someone. If they are sad or angry, they usually feel better if they discuss the reasons with another person. Is it also the custom in your country to discuss feelings with others? Which of the emotions mentioned in question 3 do you think would be most difficult to talk about? Why?

Proverbs

In small groups, discuss your interpretation of the following proverbs. Which two contradict each other? Which one of those two do you think is correct? Think of a proverb about love and marriage in your native language and write it down as well as you can in English. Share it with the class.

1. Marriages are made in heaven.

2. Love is blind.

3. Absence makes the heart grow fonder.

4. Look before you leap!

5. Out of sight, out of mind.

6. Love and marriage go together like a horse and carriage.

WHAT DO YOU THINK?

Adoption

In the foster care system (where people take care of children who are not their own) in the United States, over 100,000 children are waiting to be adopted. In the past, there have been rigid qualifications concerning race, marital status, and age for parents planning to adopt children. Now, people who have been restricted from adopting children are applying for rights to adopt. This group includes single people, gay couples, people of a race different from that of the child, older couples. Whom do you think should be allowed to adopt children? What qualifications would you apply for adoptive parents if you were running an adoption agency?

CHAPTER four

Health

in this chapter

Many Americans and Canadians are becoming increasingly health-conscious. Exercise centers and health-food stores are everywhere. Numerous books on health become instant best-sellers. Here we examine three aspects of health. The first is diet, the effects that the foods we eat have on our bodies. The second is smoking, a devastating health hazard. The third is surprising and beyond our control: the relationship between our physical condition and the weather.

SELECTION **one**

Eat Like a Peasant,
Feel Like a King

Before You Read

Using Headings as Guides in an Extended Reading

The following article is longer—more extended than the ones you have read so far. After the introduction, there are three headings. List them in the spaces below.

1. Introduction

2. _____

3. _____

4. _____

Picking out the headings in a long article helps you see the organization and major ideas. Headings are usually of two kinds: They tell the main topic of a section, or they simply give a small detail to catch the reader's interest. The ones that tell the main topic are the most helpful for comprehension. Which two of the headings are of this kind? In your own words, tell what you think you will read about in the sections that follow these headings.

Guessing the Meaning of Words from Context

Follow the instructions in each of the following items.

1. The only uncommon word in the title is *peasant*. To infer its meaning, notice how it is in a parallel construction with the word *king*: "Eat Like a _____, Feel Like a _____." A parallel construction is used either for comparison or for contrast. So *peasant* means either something very similar to *king* or something very different. With this clue in mind, read the sentence on lines 50 to 53, and tell what you think is meant by a "peasant diet." How does this relate to the title?

_____

_____

2. Words (often in italics) sometimes follow the title of an article and give a brief summary of its main idea. In this case, the word *elite* is used at the end of the summary. Do you know its meaning? If not, notice the context: "Eat simple foods, not *elite* treats." The word *not* tells you that *elite treats* are the opposite of *simple foods*. *Elite* is also used in line 125 to describe a group of people. Look at this context, too; then, in your own words, explain the meaning of *elite*.

_____

_____

3. Look at the second word of the second paragraph: *eclectic*. It describes the menu that makes up the entire first paragraph. Read that paragraph and think about what is special and unusual about the grouping of foods described here. Then explain the meaning of the word *eclectic*.

_____

_____

4. Scan the first two sections of the essay for the noun *affluence* and its related adjective *affluent*, which are used four times. From the contexts, guess its meaning and write it below. Can you also find in the fifth paragraph a synonym for *affluence*, beginning with the letter *p*?

_____

_____

5. The word *cuisine* is used five times in the essay. Scan for it and, using the contexts, explain what you think it means.

_____

_____

"You are what you eat" is a popular American saying, and what you eat can contribute to destroying your health. According to modern research, certain cultures have healthier diets than others. Which cultures are these? What foods should you choose in order to avoid cancer, hypertension, and heart disease? Read the following article from *American Health* magazine to find out.

Eat Like a Peasant, Feel Like a King

Research around the globe points to a recipe for well-being: Eat simple foods, not elite treats.

Start with miso soup, a classically simple Japanese recipe. For an appetizer, try a small plate of *pasta al pesto*. On to the main course: grilled chinook salmon, with steamed
5 Chinese cabbage on the side. End with a Greek salad, sprinkled with olive oil, and a New Zealand kiwi fruit for dessert.

An eclectic menu, to be sure. But it could contain some of the world's healthiest dishes.
10 Miso soup, according to recent Japanese research, may help prevent cancer, as may cabbage. Salmon, olive oil, and the garlic in your pesto can all help fight heart disease. Even the kiwi is rich in fiber, potassium, and vita-
15 min C.

In the last few years, nutritionists have been studying such international super-foods—dishes from around the globe that may hold the key to healthy eating. They're
20 building on research that began in the '40s and '50s, when researchers first realized that a country's diet is intimately connected to the health of its people.

Since then, an explosion of medical stud-
25 ies has produced a flood of information on diverse human diets—from the Eskimos of the Arctic to the Bushmen of Africa's Kalahari Desert. But the globe-trotting researchers have done more than discover the best fea-
30 tures of each country's cuisine. They've also demonstrated broad nutritional principles that apply to people all over the world. And their clearest finding is a sobering one.

In many countries, they've found, the
35 healthiest diet is simple, inexpensive, traditional fare—precisely the diet that people abandon as they move into affluence. Japanese immigrating from the high-carbohydrate Pacific to high-fat America have a greater
40 risk of heart disease the more westernized their diet becomes. The same pattern holds for developing nations that emerge from poverty into prosperity. Poor people who can't get enough to eat are at risk, of course,
45 whatever their diets. But as a country's food

becomes richer, the scourges of poverty (infectious disease and malnutrition) are replaced by the "diseases of civilization" (arteriosclerosis, certain cancers, obesity).

50 The simple, ideal diet—often called the "peasant diet"—is the traditional cuisine of relatively poor, agrarian countries such as Mexico and China. It's usually based on a grain (rice, wheat, corn), fruits and vegeta-

55 bles, small amounts of meat, fish, eggs or dairy products, and a legume.

The advantages are obvious: low fat and high fiber, with most calories coming in the grains and legumes. "A low-fat, high-fiber

60 diet is a preventive diet for heart disease, certain cancers, hypertension, adult onset diabetes, obesity," says Dr. Wayne Peters, director of the Lipid Consultation Service of Massachusetts General Hospital.

65 Early Diets: Nuts and Plants

According to Peters, "We evolved eating a low-fat diet, and that's what our genetic composition is really designed to handle."

70 Studies of one of the world's most primitive diets—and one of the healthiest ones—back him up. In southern Africa's Kalahari Desert, some tribes still eat as early humans did, hunting and gathering. Anthropologists

75 say the foods of the Bushmen are probably closest to foods that, over two million years, shaped our intestines, our cutting and grinding teeth, our churning stomachs.

"Hunting and gathering may not have

80 been such a bad way of life," says Richard Lee, an anthropologist at the University of Toronto who has studied the !Kung tribe since the 1960s. "The main element for the !Kung is the mongongo, a superabundant

85 nut eaten in large quantities. They routinely collect and eat more than 105 edible plant species. Meat is secondary."

Another student of the !Kung—Stewart Truswell, a professor of human nutrition at

90 Australia's University of Sydney—says their eating schedule is really continual "snacking" (the gathering) punctuated by occasional feasts after a successful hunt. They are nutritionally healthy, the only shortfall being

95 fairly low caloric intake. And Bushmen show few signs of coronary heart disease. Those who avoid accidents or other calamities, says Lee, often live to "ripe old age."

Few people, though, would choose a

100 !Kung diet—or even a simple peasant diet from western Europe. . . . In an affluent society, it takes willpower to keep fat intake down to the recommended maximum: 30% of total calories. (The average American gets

105 more than 40% of his calories from fats.) When a country reaches a certain level of affluence, as the U.S. . . . and Japan . . . , grains and beans give way to beef and butter. And animal protein—in meat and dairy prod-

110 ucts—usually comes packaged with artery-clogging saturated fats and cholesterol.

In India, for example, many middle-income people are now gaining weight on a rich diet—even though the poor half of the

115 population still can't afford enough to eat. As the middle class has become more affluent, they've been able to indulge, and Indian doctors are reportedly seeing more obesity, hypertension, and heart disease. Many In-

120 dian dishes are soaked in ghee (clarified butter) or coconut oil, one of the few vegetable oils that is virtually all saturated fat. Very recently, though, Indians have gone in for the diets and aerobics classes that are popular

125 among the rest of the world's elite.

If it's just too difficult to stay with a really low-fat "peasant" diet, the alternative is to rehabilitate high-calorie dishes. Cut down on overall fat intake and substitute, in the words of one researcher, "nice fats for nasty fats." Americans have already been following this advice. In the past 20 years the consumption of "nasty" saturated fats has declined, while we've taken in more of the polyunsaturated fats, such as corn and safflower oils, that can help lower blood cholesterol. This change may help explain the simultaneous 20% to 30% drop in heart disease in the U.S.

Why Socrates* Loved Olive Oil

An even better strategy for changing our fat intake may come from studying diets in the Mediterranean—Spain, Greece, and southern Italy. With some regional variation, people in these cultures eat small amounts of meat and dairy products (although consumption has increased steadily since World War II) and get almost all of their fat in the form of olive oil, says physiologist Ancel Keys, professor emeritus at the University of Minnesota School of Public Health and leader in international dietary studies.

Keys has noted that farmers sometimes quaff a wineglass of the oil before leaving for the fields in the morning. Elsewhere in the Mediterranean, bread is dipped in olive oil. Salads are tossed with it. Everything's cooked in it.

Though people in some of these countries eat nearly as much total fat as Americans, they are singularly healthy, with very little heart disease. Now laboratory studies of olive oil help explain why. Unlike most other vegetable oils common in the West, olive oil consists mainly of "monounsaturated" fats. Recent research indicates that monounsaturates do a better job of preventing heart disease than the more widely touted polyunsaturates.

Some healthful foods from around the world. Can you identify them?

---

*Socrates was an ancient Greek philosopher. He is often used to represent a wise man.

As Americans become ever more concerned with healthy eating, we're likely to pay more and more attention to world cuisines. The polyglot among nations, we've started to seek out ethnic flavors from everywhere. "Foreign" ingredients, from seaweed and bean curd to tortillas and salsa, are now readily available in large supermarkets. And Mexican and Asian restaurants have become more widespread than any other eateries except ice cream parlors, hamburger stands, and pizzerias, according to the National Restaurant Association.

But the trick to finding healthy food, wherever it comes from, is to look carefully at each dish. No single cuisine is all good or all bad. Each has something to teach us.

The moral is simple: Whether you're eating an American beef stew or a French cassoulet, you need to know what's in it. With a little nutritional knowledge, you can sample some of the world's tastiest foods and know you're also eating some of the best.

Healthy Diets from Around the World

China: The Chinese eat a diet that's about 69% carbohydrate, 10% protein, and only 21% fat. That's remarkably close to the mixture that western nutritionists recommend. Rice, noodles, Chinese cabbage, and mushrooms, along with other vegetables and small portions of fish and meat, are staples of Chinese diets. Recent medical research suggests that oriental mushrooms help boost the immune system and also have qualities that may help prevent heart disease. The downside of Chinese cookery, as in Japan, is the excess of salt and the use of monosodium glutamate (MSG). MSG is as bad as salt if you're fighting high blood pressure, and it can also cause allergic reactions. For many people, when dining in Chinese restaurants it is best to ask for the MSG to be cut out.

Mexico: What Mexican dishes are best for health-conscious diners? Though it's high in fat, guacamole is a surprisingly good bet. Most of the fat in avocado is monunsaturated, like the fat in olive oil. Seviche (fish marinated in lime juice) is low in fat overall; so are some chicken dishes like chicken tostadas, if they're not fried. And in case you're wondering, the hot chili peppers of Mexican cuisine could actually be good for you, if you can take the heat. Chili peppers are an excellent source of vitamins A and C. They may even help you fight a cold, asthma, bronchitis, and sinusitis.

Eskimo: The tremendous amount of fish that Eskimos eat helps to prevent heart disease. Fish oil is beneficial in that it lowers blood pressure, cholesterol, and the blood's capacity to clot. A recent Dutch study showed that eating as few as two fish meals a week cut the death rate from coronary heart disease by half.

Italy: In southern Italy, age-old staples —such as pasta, olive oil, garlic, whole-wheat bread—provide a true gift of health: protection from cancer and heart disease. Like oriental mushrooms, garlic is good for the heart and the immune system.

Japan: Two products of the lowly soybean—miso and tofu—are healthy staples. Miso soup may fight cancer; tofu gives low-fat protein. Seaweed, the Japanese lettuce, is high in many nutrients. On the other hand, Japan's smoked, salted, and pickled foods lead to a high incidence of stroke and stomach cancer.

Andrew Revkin

After You Read

Recalling Information

exercise **1** Based on what you read, match each item of food to its effects.

FOODS

1. _____ MSG
2. _____ garlic and oriental mushrooms
3. _____ Mexican chili peppers
4. _____ miso soup
5. _____ fish oil
6. _____ smoked, salted, and pickled foods

PROBABLE EFFECTS ON HEALTH

a. seems to lower blood pressure, cholesterol, and the blood's capacity to clot
b. rich in vitamins A and C and possibly a help in fighting colds and asthma
c. contributes to high blood pressure and may cause allergic reaction
d. may help fight cancer
e. probably lead to strokes and cancer of the stomach
f. good for the heart and the immune system

Formulating the Key Ideas

exercise **2** Follow the instructions in each of the following items.

1. The main idea of the article is given in simple terms in the title and the italicized sentence that follows it. In your own words, what is the main idea?

_____

_____

2. Another key idea is the relationship between affluence, diet, and health. The article illustrates this by referring to several different societies. In your own words, explain how affluence changes diet and health, and refer to at least two cultures that illustrate it.

_____

_____

_____

_____

_____

_____

Paraphrasing Material with Specialized Use of Vocabulary

> Sometimes a particular word is used in a very special way that depends on the meaning of the entire sentence or paragraph. For example, the most common use of the word *sober* is as an antonym of the word *drunk*. A *sober person* is one who is not under the influence of alcohol or drugs, one who is clear-headed, in full control of his or her senses. Note the specialized use of this word in lines 30 to 33.
>
> *examples:*   "But the globe-trotting researchers have done more than discover the best features of each country's cuisine. They've also demonstrated broad nutritional principles that apply to people all over the world. *And their clearest finding is a sobering one.*"
>
> The italicized sentence can be paraphrased (put into clear and direct words) like this: <u>The main conclusion of the researchers makes us face a serious fact</u>.

exercise 3

First read the vocabulary hints. Then paraphrase the italicized parts of the excerpts.

1. The usual meaning of the word *punctuate* is to put punctuation marks into a piece of writing so as to separate it into meaningful chunks. Think about what it means in the following excerpt from lines 88 to 93 and paraphrase the italicized part.

   "Another student of !Kung . . . says *their eating schedule is really continual 'snacking' (the gathering) punctuated by occasional feasts after a successful hunt.*"

   _____

   _____

2. The word *quaff* is quite unusual, but its meaning can be guessed simply by looking at the two words that follow it and making the obvious inference. Read the following sentence (lines 153 to 155) and tell what common word is usually used in place of *quaff*.

   "Keys has noted that farmers sometimes *quaff* a wineglass of the oil before leaving for the fields in the morning."

   _____

Talking It Over

activity

In small groups, discuss the following questions.

1. What are your favorite cuisines? After reading this article, which cuisine do you think is the most healthful? Why?

2. What kind of restaurant do you like to go to? At what time of day? Why?

3. What do you think of "fast food"? Is it healthful? Why do you think it is so popular?

4. Can you explain what "junk food" is? Give some examples. Do you ever indulge in it?

5. Besides diet, what other factors are important for our health? In your opinion, what is the key to a long and healthy life?

Last night, Maurice ate food that disagreed with him.

focus on testing

Analyzing Compound Words

Many English words are made up of two shorter words. These are called compound words, and they are usually adjectives or nouns. Some compound words are written with a hyphen between them, such as *low-fat*; others, such as *wineglass*, are written as one word, while others, such as *grocery store*, are written as two separate words. Breaking apart compound words can help you understand their meaning. For example, look at the word *well-being* in the introductory quote in the reading selection "Eat Like a Peasant, Feel Like a King." What do you think it means? When taking vocabulary tests, try breaking apart the compound words to help understand their meaning.

exercise   Circle the word or phrase that best explains the meaning of the underlined word or phrase. Refer back to the context in the selection "Eat Like a Peasant, Feel Like a King" if necessary.

1. globe-trotting researchers (line 28)
    a. professors and students of geography
    b. investigators who travel around the world
    c. people who study the movement of the earth
    d. experts in the benefits of exercise

2. shortfall (line 94)
    a. help
    b. turn
    c. shift
    d. lack

3. intake (lines 95, 102)
    a. interference
    b. planning
    c. consumption
    d. disease

4. widespread (line 179)
    a. large in size
    b. open to the public
    c. present in many locations
    d. complicated with new rules

5. downside (line 206)
    a. negative part
    b. good news
    c. lower section
    d. deep mystery

6. health-conscious (line 215)
    a. smart and strong
    b. bright and informed
    c. interested in not getting sick
    d. aware of patterns of thought

Thou Shalt Not Smoke

Before You Read

Skimming for the Main Idea

> An article usually contains several important ideas, illustrated and supported by facts and examples. However, there is always one main idea. It is often presented in partial form near the beginning, expanded upon in the middle, and stated more directly at the end.

 **exercise**

To practice the skill of identifying the main idea, skim the next article, "Thou Shalt Not Smoke." (For Bill Cosby's explanation on how to skim, see pages 23 to 26.) Then come back to this page, look at the list of statements that follow, and tell:

a. _____ which statement expresses the *main idea.*

b. _____ which two statements express *secondary ideas.*

c. _____ which statement expresses a *specific fact used to support an idea.*

d. _____ which statement is *not true at all* with relation to the article.

1. In the United States, the personal smoking habits of the top executives determine to a large degree the policy toward smokers in a company.

2. In general, large American firms will not hire a person unless he or she signs a pledge promising not to smoke for at least five years.

3. More and more American companies are banning or restricting smoking in different ways, and this is producing varied reactions among workers.

4. At one newspaper in the eastern part of the United States, the employees who smoke were the ones who voted to ban smoking from the premises.

5. At present, many employees of American firms feel they are being unfairly discriminated against because of their smoking habit.

Now read the article again more carefully.

Would you like a cigarette? If you say yes and smoke one, would you be infringing on the rights of others? Could you be endangering their health along with your own? In a few short years, the rights of smokers on airplanes, at restaurants, and in the workplace, versus the rights of nonsmokers, has become a very controversial topic. Before reading the following article on this issue, think about your own opinion. Do both groups have equal rights? If you were the boss of a firm, would you allow your employees to smoke or not? Explain your answer.

Thou Shalt Not Smoke

Companies restrict the use of tobacco in the workplace.

In the newsroom of the *Denver Post*, reporters and editors cope with a company ban on smoking by gnawing on licorice roots and chewing on unlit cigars. Broward Davis &
5 Associates, a surveying and consulting firm in Tallahassee, refuses to hire anyone who smokes. New England Telephone employees can take a puff in only half the company's rest rooms, and workers at United Technolo-
10 gies' Hartford headquarters must refrain from lighting up in any public work area.

As corporate America comes to terms with the antismoking fervor that has gripped much of the public, more and more firms are
15 regulating the use of tobacco in the workplace. According to a study by the Bureau of National Affairs, about 35% of all U.S. companies restrict smoking (only 2% ban it outright) and an additional 20% are studying
20 the issue. In many cases, companies have no choice: 17 states and hundreds of localities outlaw smoking in offices and other workplaces. The surgeon general's report last year asserting that smokers create health
25 risks for nearby nonsmokers has encouraged companies to promote smoke-free work environments. Finally, firms are increasingly aware of the cost of having smokers on staff: higher insurance expenses and increased ab-
30 senteeism.

Most companies try to accommodate their nonsmoking workers without alienating their tobacco-dependent colleagues. Many firms begin to formulate a policy by
35 polling their staffs. When New England Telephone discovered that 70% of its 27,000 employees did not smoke, it decided to take a strong stand against tobacco. Smoking is now permitted only in certain hallways and
40 rest rooms and in a small section of the cafeteria. Eastman Kodak has democratized the decision-making process. Employees vote on whether common work areas should be smoke-free. While smoking is generally
45 banned in conference rooms, exceptions can be made if there are no objections from anyone present.

A company's policy often reflects its top executive's personal attitude toward smok-
50 ing. Says Cynthia Ferguson, acting executive director of the American Lung Association: "We see this very clearly. Management support means everything." Ted Phillips, chairman of New England Telephone, a
55 Boston-based company, is an ex-smoker who strongly believes smoking on the job should be limited to private offices in order to safe-

guard the health of all workers. That is precisely the policy of his firm. At Frosty Acres
60 Brands, a Georgia canned-goods packager, a smoking ban is unlikely because President Louis Dell smokes almost two packs a day. But Dell acknowledges that the rights of nonsmokers should be protected. As a result,
65 smoking is not allowed in the firm's executive conference room, and employees are free to ban smoking in their private offices.

No matter how well intentioned their bosses may be, many smokers feel perse-
70 cuted by their firms' antismoking policies. "Just call me Sneaky Pete," says a salesman of novelty items who would face being fired if his smoking habit was discovered. Says he: "It's incredibly unfair. I was a smoker
75 when they hired me, and then, out of the blue, I'm supposed to stop just because the boss says so." Some employees fear their chances for advancement may be choked off by their smoking habit, though favoritism
80 toward nonsmokers is rarely explicit. Len Beil, director of human resources at Pacific Northwest Bell, says a bias against smoking "could be in the back of a manager's mind when making decisions on a promotion."

85 Job seekers are discovering that smoking can endanger their careers. Newspaper classified advertisements frequently specify that employers are looking for "nonsmokers only." One of the first questions asked of job
90 applicants at Vanguard Electronic Tool in Redmond, Washington, is "Do you smoke?" If the answer is yes, the interview is over. That is perfectly legal. On the other hand, federal laws forbid an employer to discrimi-
95 nate on the basis of race, sex, religion, or marital status.

Many smokers may secretly welcome the corporate crusade against smoking. Says Robert Rosner, executive director of the
100 Seattle-based Smoking Policy Institute, a consulting firm that advises companies on how to formulate smoking policies: "The fact is, most smokers want to quit." Many of them embrace the new corporate activism as
105 an incentive to give up tobacco once and for all. At Rhode Island's *Newport Daily News,* it was the smokers who unanimously voted to ban smoking from the premises, although taking a drag is not a cause for dismissal.

110 More and more companies that have imposed restrictions on smoking are attempting to help their employees kick the habit. BMC Software, a Texas company that prohibits smoking on the job, has sent employees to
115 antismoking hypnosis sessions. Abbott Laboratories hires smokers but strongly urges them to sign a pledge to take a company-sponsored workshop that teaches people how to stop smoking. The five sessions cost em-
120 ployees $30, but if they stay off cigarettes for four months, Abbott refunds the money.

Despite the changes taking place, anti-smoking lobbyists continue to press for stricter limitations on smoking in the workplace. Last week the American Public Health Association and Ralph Nader's Public Citizen Health Research Group petitioned the Occupational Safety and Health Administration to impose an emergency rule that would eliminate or restrict smoking in virtually all indoor work sites. While the government is not expected to take any immediate action, the pressure is sure to grow. Smokers, after all, make up a shrinking minority. Nonsmokers, like any other large majority, know the numbers—and the clout—are increasingly on their side.

Barbara Rudolph

After You Read

Paraphrasing Idioms to Show Their Meaning

> An idiom is an expression whose meaning cannot be understood simply by knowing the sense of each of its words. An example is the expression *to hit the ceiling,* which means "to get very angry." Idioms can often be understood from the context.

 **exercise 1**

Read the following excerpts from the article "Thou Shalt Not Smoke" and paraphrase (explain in different words) the meanings of the idioms in italics.

1. "... *more and more* firms are regulating the use of tobacco in the workplace."

2. "When New England Telephone discovered that 70% of its 27,000 employees did not smoke, it decided to *take a strong stand* against tobacco."

3. "Says he [a salesman who smokes]: 'It's incredibly unfair. I was a smoker when they hired me, and then, *out of the blue,* I'm supposed to stop just because the boss says so.'"

4. "Many of them [the smokers] embrace the new corporate activism as an incentive to give up tobacco *once and for all.*"

5. "More and more companies that have imposed restrictions on smoking are attempting to help their employees *kick the habit.*"

Countering the Specific Points
of an Argument with Facts

 Find facts from the article "Thou Shalt Not Smoke" that counter (argue against) the specific points presented in the following paragraph.

A SMOKER'S DEFENSE

"All I want is fair treatment and equal rights. I feel I have a right to smoke while I work. Right now most companies are concerned only with the rights of nonsmokers and make no provisions at all for employees who smoke. Of course, I know that smoking is bad for my health but, after all, that is my problem. My smoking does not hurt anybody else but me. Smoking is also expensive, but I am the one who must pay the cost, not the company. Other people have different bad habits, such as eating junk food or drinking too much alcohol. Besides, smoking is an addiction. Everybody knows that it is very hard to quit, yet companies never offer any help to their employees to show them how to kick the habit. So, why don't they stop discriminating against smokers and just leave us alone?"

Talking It Over

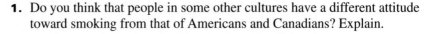 In small groups, discuss the following questions.

1. Do you think that people in some other cultures have a different attitude toward smoking from that of Americans and Canadians? Explain.

2. What is your opinion on smoking in the workplace? In hospitals? In airplanes?

3. Some people say that cigarette manufacturers should be forbidden to advertise their product in the developing countries of Africa, Asia, and Latin America. Do you agree or disagree with this idea? Why?

4. In your opinion, is hypnosis a good way to quit smoking or not? Why? What is the best method?

"I didn't ask for smoked meat!"

SELECTION **three**
The Cruel Winds

Before You Read
Learning Some Common Medical Terms

 *exercise*

The next reading selection contains a number of terms for illnesses and disorders. Study the definitions of those given below. Then "play doctor" by making a diagnosis (medical judgment about what is wrong with someone) for each of the imaginary patients on the list. When you've finished, compare answers with your classmates.

MEDICAL TERMS

1. *anginal pains*   discomfort produced by angina pectoris, a heart disease in which there are spasms of pain in the chest, with feelings of suffocation (being without air, being unable to breathe)
2. *asthma*   a chronic disorder characterized by coughing, difficulty in breathing, and a suffocating feeling
3. *high blood pressure*   too much pressure produced by the blood pressing against inner walls of the blood vessels (veins and arteries)
4. *dehydration*   weak condition caused by a rapid loss of water
5. *hemorrhaging*   heavy bleeding; rapid loss of blood
6. *insomnia*   inability to sleep; excessive wakefulness
7. *leukemia*   a cancer of the blood-forming tissues
8. *depression*   an emotional condition characterized by discouragement and negative feelings
9. *migraine*   a severe headache usually limited to one side of the head and often accompanied by dizziness and nausea (upset stomach)
10. *neurosis*   a mental disorder characterized by worries, fears, obsessions, and other symptoms that seem to have no physical cause. A person suffering from this is said to be neurotic.

PATIENTS AND THEIR SYMPTOMS

1. Mary Wong: "I went to bed early but stayed awake all night long. I was completely unable to relax, and in the morning I was very tired."

   diagnosis: _____

2. Abdul James: "My head kept hurting intensely on the right side, and after a few hours I could no longer keep down my food."

   diagnosis: _____

3. Vindu Gopal: "My six-month-old baby took almost no liquids yesterday, and by evening he seemed too quiet and looked pale. He was so different from his usual active self."

   diagnosis: _____

4. Miguel Garcia: "My seventy-three-year-old father complains of sharp pains in his chest that come and go and of respiratory (breathing) troubles."

diagnosis: _____

5. Peter Kahn: "I am concerned about eating because so many foods contain harmful ingredients. For this reason I never eat in restaurants, and I spend three to four hours a day cleaning my kitchen and food supplies.

diagnosis: _____

Biometeorology is said by some to be a new science that researches the effect weather has on people and their health. Perhaps you have an aunt who can predict the weather by some ache or pain, or a cousin who suffers from migraine headaches or depression when the humidity is high. Julius Fast, bacteriologist, hematologist, and author of *Weather Language,* says that one out of every three persons is "weather sensitive." This means that he or she reacts physically to winds, humidity, hot and cold weather. Read the following selection from Fast's book and see what you think of biometeorology.

The Cruel Winds

Some four hundred years ago the great Swiss physician and alchemist*
Paracelsus stated, "He who knows the origin of the winds, of thunder, and
of the weather also knows where diseases come from." He could have
added, "And why weather-sensitive people shudder when the winds
5   blow," for they do. Some winds can put weather-sensitive people through
every agony known to biometeorology. In fact, these same winds can also
affect people who usually are not weather sensitive.

Winds blow hot and cold, and it's a toss-up which is worse. Statistics
show that when cold polar winds sweep down on the land, there is an in-
10   crease in the number of heart attacks. Anginal pain gets worse and blood
pressure shoots up because the heart must work harder to keep the body
warm.

Psychological tests given while hot winds were blowing have turned
up some good news and some bad news about the relations among
15   winds, personality, and ability. The bad news first: Hot winds make people
more neurotic and irritable, and then they do worse on intelligence tests.
They can't understand mechanical instructions as well as they can in
cooler weather.

The good news: Hot winds won't keep you from doing your best in
20   math and clerical work, nor will they affect your visual perception.

_____

*A practitioner of the chemistry of the Middle Ages, which was a mixture of science and magic

Dust storms in the United States in the 1930s—in some areas, fertile land was turned into desert.

Some winds are lovely, cool, and refreshing—poets' winds, warm west winds. But others are terrible—veritable monsters. Europe's *foehn* is one of these. In medieval times, people thought the *foehn* blew in from Phoenicia, and they named it the "Phoenicias," then shortened that to *foehn*. This hot, dry terror is deadly not only in the biometeorological sense but in a physical sense as well. It blows in from Italy loaded with wet, humid air, drops its moisture on the Swiss Alps, and then, warm and dry, sweeps down into the northern reaches of the land. As it blows, it warms the mountain snow and causes avalanches.

Albert is a resident of Bad Tolz, a town in Germany in the foothills of the Alps. I talked to him about the *foehn*, and he shook his head sadly. "Some reporters from Munich came here a few years ago to talk about the *foehn,* and they told us it was all in our heads. But they didn't understand. They weren't here while it was blowing. Everyone in the village was upset. You couldn't talk to your neighbor, or if you did, you snapped at him. We were all on edge.

"Every night while the *foehn* was blowing, I'd have trouble sleeping—the nightmares. And I'd wake up with a headache. My sister—she hemorrhaged the day before it started.

"It seems to go on forever, day after day. It's so dry. You sweat, and the sweat is just pulled out of you by the wind. We were all thirsty. My God, the beer we consumed!"

"How does it start?" I asked.

"It starts with warm air over the cold ground. At first it's wet before the real blowing begins, and once it comes it goes on for weeks. In our street there was one suicide, and I put it down to that devil wind. And it's not only sickness and upset. My cousin who works in a factory in Munich told me there were more accidents during the weeks of the *foehn* than for months and months before or after."

Albert's report had the ring of truth, and I had additional scientific confirmation of the *foehn*'s deadly quality from other sources. A psychiatrist told me that in mental institutions there were almost one-quarter more patients with problems when the *foehn* struck. An internist in another Alpine town told me that he had at least one-third more complaints during *foehn* days.

Why the *foehn* affects people is still not clear. Some researchers believe the hot, dry wind creates an enormous number of positive ions* because of the friction of its descent down the Alps. Positive ions have been held to be the cause of many upsets, and Dr. W. Morikofer tried to test this with ion-testing apparatus. He reported, however, that he couldn't duplicate the *foehn*'s action.

Other researchers feel that certain people have nervous systems particularly vulnerable to hot, dry winds—that, in fact, these are our weather-sensitive people.

Other European winds are hard on people in their paths. The warm, dry *autan* blows along the Rhone Valley in France, and it is accompanied by low-pressure systems.† Babies are usually the first to react: They run high temperatures and suffer dehydration, become restless, and can't sleep. Some children don't do well in school when the *autan* blows, and others suffer respiratory troubles, colds, and asthma.

Weather-sensitive adults react strongly to the *autan,* almost as strongly as they do to the *foehn.* Quarrels, insomnia, heart attacks, and migraines are typical *autan* symptoms.

The *mistral* is another Rhone Valley wind, but unlike the *autan,* it is cold and dry. This strong wind, however, is still ugly in its effects. Like the *foehn,* the *mistral* causes migraine and insomnia and is dreaded by weather sensitives.

There are other "killer winds" around the world; in Africa and Asia the *simooms* are hot, dry, desert winds. In India there is the *bhoot.* In the Mediterranean countries there is the *sirocco*; in Spain, the *solano.* And so

---

*An atom, group of atoms, or molecule with a net electrical charge
†Weather system characterized by unsettled weather (generally cloudy with rain or snow)

it blows all through Europe, Asia, and even Australia, where they have the *brickfielder.* This wind earned its colorful name by blowing clouds of dust from the brickfields. After a while it was renamed the *southerly buster.*

Israel has its own killer wind, the *sharav.* It is heated up by the desert sands, and it brings with it depression, headache, irritation, and respiratory upset.

Here in the United States we have few natural deadly winds, perhaps because of the geography of our country. Winds on the Pacific Northwest Coast blow wet against the Rockies, then dry and sometimes hot down the landward side. The *chinook* is one such wind, and it causes almost as many problems as its European cousin, the *foehn.* In southern California, the Santa Ana wind has a deadly reputation. When it blows across Los Angeles, its heat and dryness seem to cause an enormous increase in crime.

Many winds are given names to personify them, and perhaps as an ancient way of pacifying them. You can plead with a named object, wind, or mountain or storm god, and you can ask it to spare you. The *chinook* was named after an Indian tribe, and in the United States we name our hurricanes. But the old practice of giving them women's names has been replaced, after protest, by naming them alternately for men and women.

Hurricanes are killer winds, but their destructive power lies in the physical damage they can do. They will lift houses, turn over cars, and destroy entire communities. We respect them for this, but we may have winds that are just as dangerous and, for some, even more dangerous. Because they are gentle winds or soft winds, we ignore them.

Dr. H. B. Schultz studied the disposal of agricultural wastes in northern California and found that the "monsoonlike inflow of oceanic air" cleaned the air over the nearby cities. However, in the fall, when 1.5 million tons of rice straw have to be burned for pest control, these same winds can blow the burning pollutants over the nearby cities. This cleansing wind then becomes a deadly one.

In Colorado, there is a vast nuclear installation at Rocky Flats. A gentle wind blows from Rocky Flats toward Denver, and an area near the city in the path of the wind has recorded twice as many cases of leukemia and lung cancer as one would normally expect. Here another harmless wind has been turned into a killer by our own efforts.

When nature fails to provide us with the winds like the *foehn* and the *mistral,* we seem to create our own.

Julius Fast

After You Read

Identifying Support for Ideas

exercise 1  Most pieces of factual writing contain a number of general ideas that are supported by details and examples. Tell which details on the right give support to each of the general ideas listed on the left. (You might find some details that you feel do not really support any of the ideas, or that may support more than one general idea.)

GENERAL IDEAS

1. _____ European winds are hard on the people in their paths.

2. _____ Besides the European winds, there are other "killer winds" around the world.

3. _____ Many winds are given names to personify them.

4. _____ When nature fails to provide us with destructive winds, we seem to create our own.

SUPPORTING DETAILS

a. the American wind *chinook,* named after an Indian tribe

b. the higher number of accidents at a factory in Munich during the weeks of the *foehn*

c. the colorful name *brickfielder* given to a wind in Australia

d. the doubling of the number of cases of leukemia and lung cancer in areas in the path of a wind near a nuclear installation

e. the existence of a wind called *bhoot* in India

f. the quarrels, insomnia, and migraines that people suffer when the *autan* blows

g. the custom in the United States of calling hurricanes by people's names

h. the depression and headaches said to accompany the *sharav* in Israel

Separating Fact from Opinion

The distinction between fact and opinion often is not clear. Events taken to be common knowledge or statements supported by scientific evidence are generally considered to be facts. Beliefs expressed by only one person are often considered just opinions, unless the person is judged to be an authority on the matter.

Which of the following statements in the reading do you think are facts and which ones are opinions? Why? The line numbers are given so that you can examine the context if you wish.

1. "He who knows the origin of the winds, of thunder, and of the weather also knows where disease comes from." (lines 2 to 3)

2. "Statistics show that when cold polar winds sweep down on the land, there is an increase in the number of heart attacks." (lines 8 to 10)

3. "Hot winds make people more neurotic and irritable, and then they do worse on intelligence tests." (lines 15 to 16)

4. "My cousin who works in a factory in Munich told me there were more accidents during the weeks of the *foehn* than for months and months before or after." (lines 47 to 49)

5. "A psychiatrist told me that in mental institutions there were almost one-quarter more patients with problems when the *foehn* struck." (lines 51 to 53)

6. "Other researchers feel that certain people have nervous systems particularly vulnerable to hot, dry winds—that, in fact, these are our weather-sensitive people." (lines 62 to 64)

7. "When [the Santa Ana wind] blows across Los Angeles, its heat and dryness seem to cause an enormous increase in crime." (lines 92 to 93)

Expanding Your Vocabulary: Adding Suffixes to Form Adjectives from Verbs or Nouns

Many adjectives are formed by adding a suffix to the root of a related verb or noun. Fill in each of the following blanks with an adjective used in the article "The Cruel Winds." Each adjective will be related to the word in bold type preceding it. The first blank is filled in as an example.

WINDS AROUND THE WORLD

Everyone knows that many winds do not cause any apparent **harm.** In fact, these ___harmless___ winds often **refresh** us. After a hot day, a
_____ breeze in the evening can be very welcome. Winds
sometimes **clean** the air over cities. For example, the _____ action
of winds from the Pacific Ocean makes life more pleasant in certain areas of California.

Some winds, however, sweep down from the North or South **Poles.** These cold _____ winds seem to produce adverse physical symptoms in
<u>4</u>
many people. Hot winds also cause troubles. Two warm, dry winds in Europe, the *foehn* and the *autan,* can cause an increase in heart attacks, migraines, and difficulties with **respiration.** These _____ problems are particularly
<u>5</u>
serious for asthma sufferers, but there may also be psychological symptoms, such as **neurosis** and irritability. People often find that they feel irritable, on edge, or even _____ when the *foehn* comes to certain towns in the
<u>6</u>
Alps. The inhabitants of these _____ towns are not alone, however,
<u>7</u>
for people all over the world suffer as a result of winds. Canadians who live in Calgary, Alberta, a city on the side of the Rocky Mountains facing away from the ocean and toward the **land,** sometimes experience amazing temperature changes of 40 degrees in one hour as a result of the *chinook,* a wind that sweeps down the _____ side of the mountains. Even more serious
<u>8</u>
is the great physical damage caused by hurricanes, the **monsoons** of Asia, and _____ winds in other places. These winds kill people and **destroy**
<u>9</u>
property; their _____ power is greatly feared.
<u>10</u>

Comprehension Quiz

 *exercise* **4**   Answer the following questions about the article "The Cruel Winds."

1. What beneficial actions can winds have?

2. Is it hot or cold winds that cause the problems?

3. What are the names of two harmful European winds? What adverse symptoms can they produce?

4. Where is Calgary located? What inconvenience do Calgarians sometimes experience as a result of the *chinook*?

5. What is the name of an Asian wind famous for the destruction that it causes?

Talking It Over

In small groups, discuss the following questions.

1. Are there destructive winds in your country that cause damage or make people sick? Have you ever been in a strong windstorm?

2. Besides winds, what other kinds of weather affect people? Can certain weather conditions make you sleepy or happy? On edge? Depressed?

3. In your opinion, what is the best way to predict the weather?

4. If you take this article as an example, do you think that biometeorology is a real science? Explain why or why not.

5. Why do you think that hurricanes in the United States used to be called by women's names? How and why has this custom changed? What do you think of this custom?

6. Does climate affect human behavior? How are the people who live in colder climates different in customs and character from people who live in warmer lands?

WHAT DO YOU THINK?

Choosing Medical Care

Suppose you have terrible back pain. Whom would you see? What would you do? In the United States and Canada, most people probably would see an orthopedic surgeon. This doctor might suggest surgery or complete bed rest. Since alternative medicine is now becoming more popular, however, other choices for treatment are available. Some people might choose to see a chiropractor, a massage therapist, or an acupuncturist. Some might even see an herbalist and seek help through herbs and teas. What do you think? What would you do? Whom would you see? What could be the positive and negative effects of each of the above treatments?

CHAPTER five

High Tech, Low Tech

Technology keeps transforming our world. The first article describes the Internet, a new communication and research tool used by millions and gaining thousands of new users each month. The second article discusses the laser, an older invention that is finding amazing new applications, from medicine to art. But some people think that the price of technology is too high. The third selection examines the dark side of technology: the negative effects of high tech on personal privacy.

First-Time Tourists Need a Pocket Guide to Downtown Internet

Before You Read

Skimming for the Whole Context

exercise 1

Before reading about something complex, skim the whole selection for the general idea. This will give you a context to help with understanding new vocabulary. The first article is written in a question-and-answer format, with Q standing for question and A for answer. Skim the article. Then circle the most appropriate ending to the following statement.

> The questions and answers in the article deal mostly with
> **a.** technical and mathematical problems of the Internet.
> **b.** practical information on how and why to use the Internet.
> **c.** social and political implications of the Internet.

Defining New Words from Context

exercise 2

Use the context and the clues in parentheses to find or make up simple definitions of the following technical terms. Add examples if helpful.

1. e-mail (The article tells what the *e* stands for. Can you guess how people

communicate this way?) _____

_____

_____

2. network (This word is used a lot nowadays for different types of systems.

Find the specific definition for this context that is given in the article.)

_____

3. The Internet (Find the definition given in the article.)_____

_____

4. prototype (The prefix *proto* means "first," or "earliest form of." Adding

this to the second part of the word, invent a definition.) _____

_____

5. service provider (This one you have to guess from context.) _____

_____

6. modem (The article gives you the first word of the definition. Continue by adding its use and, if you want, one of its characteristics that is mentioned later.) _____

_____

_____

The 1990s have brought on a revolution in the electronic media. This revolution is the result of the computer, telephone, fax, and television. These technologies can be combined to bring many conveniences into the school, home, and office. People talk about "information superhighways" that will soon offer services such as movies on demand, shopping without leaving your living room, picture phones, conversations with friends via computer, a push-button choice of 500 TV programs, bill payments from home, and access to databases (computerized collections of information) from around the world. Which of these services would you like to have?

The following selection is part of an informative article from the Apr. 5, 1994 edition of the *New York Times* newspaper that talks about the Internet, a new tool for communication and research used by millions of people around the world. The title of the article contains the words *tourist, downtown,* and *pocket guide.* There is an implied comparison between using the Internet and visiting a new and exciting city. In what ways do you think these two experiences are similar?

First-Time Tourists Need a Pocket Guide to Downtown Internet

Q: *What is the Internet?*

A: When two or more computers are linked together to share files, and electronic mail (e-mail), they form a network. Some individual networks consist of thousands of computers. The Internet is a network of thousands of networks, linking schools, and universities, businesses, government agencies, libraries, nonprofit organizations and millions of individuals. The Internet is much smaller in size, however, than the worldwide telephone network, but because the Internet links computers instead of telephones it has vastly more power.

Q: *Is the Internet the same thing as the "information superhighway" everyone is talking about?*

A: The Internet is a sort of early model for the data highway. Originally designed as a high-speed communications network for universities and military research, the Internet has now expanded to include private and commercial clients. It may eventually be a backbone for the so-called data superhighway, or it may become the equivalent of Route 66,* bypassed by newer and wider roads. The highway will probably consist of computer networks, cable TV, interactive phone services and other technologies.

Q: *What can I find on Internet?*

A: If you can imagine it, you can probably find it. You can check the card catalogue of the Library of Congress, retrieve free software, get the latest news, send and receive electronic mail, complain about the Mets† with fellow sufferers, view NASA satellite images, reach the world's leading authorities on kangaroos, and so on. There are literally thousands of "interest groups" on the net.

Finding things in such a vast supply of data is not easy. There is no complete road map or directory. Part of the fun is exploring.

Q: *What do I need to get onto the Internet?*

A: For now, the requirements are a personal computer, a device called a modem, a communications program, access to a telephone line and an account with an Internet service provider. The computer does not have to be too fancy, although the ability to use Windows software or the Macintosh operation system is a definite plus. The modem should have a speed of at least 9,600 bits per second; 14,400 bits is better.

Q: *What is my first step in getting onto the Internet?*

A: Go to the bookstore and get an Internet introductory guide. There are at least two dozen of them out there now.

Q: *Who owns the Internet?*

A: Nobody owns it. It is a cooperative but often chaotic federation of independent networks. Some regulatory groups set standards for the way the information flows over the Internet, but they are not too effective at present.

Peter H. Lewis

*Route 66 is an old highway system that used to handle lots of traffic moving east to west across the United States. It has now largely been replaced by interstate highways.

†The New York Mets are a major-league baseball team that had little success in the late 1980s and early 1990s.

After You Read
Scanning for Details

exercise Use your scanning technique to quickly find the following facts.

1. The communications network that is larger than the Internet but less powerful: _____

2. The two groups that originally used the Internet when it was first designed:

a. _____

b. _____

3. Three of the "interest groups" mentioned in the article:

a. _____

b. _____

c. _____

4. The five requirements to get onto this new technology:

a. _____

b. _____

c. _____

d. _____

e. _____

5. What you should buy first: _____

6. The name of the owner of the Internet: _____

Making Inferences

exercise **2** Some ideas are not directly stated, but they can be inferred or concluded from what is stated. These are called *inferences*. Which of the following statements express inferences that can be made from the article? Write Yes in front of them. Which statements do not express inferences that can be made from the article? Write No in front of them. (If you are not certain, skim the whole article again.)

1. _____ At the present moment, nobody knows exactly what the information superhighway will be like.

2. _____ It takes some computer knowledge or some practice to work effectively on the Internet.

3. _____ The Internet is a carefully controlled system with definite rules and regulations.

Talking It Over

As a class or in small groups, discuss the following questions.

1. Do you use a computer, or do you prefer a typewriter? Which is better? Why?

2. In your opinion, what is the hardest part of working with a computer?

3. Do you use e-mail? If not, would you like to? Why or why not?

4. Which of the Internet uses mentioned in the article appeals to you the most?

5. Do you think that the Internet should be made easier or changed in some other way? Explain.

Coping with a Mean Machine

How many machines are important for your daily living? Do you use a typewriter or a computer? A car, a fax machine, a bank machine, a Walkman, or an electric can opener? What machines do you use for transportation, for dealing with money, for music, food, clothing, health, communication? Make a list of the above categories (and any others that are relevant). Underneath each category, put all the machines you use. Then, in small groups, take turns telling how you feel about them. Tell which ones are "mean machines," machines that seem to hinder instead of help. Would you prefer *not* to use some of these? Why or why not? Compare your lists with those of your classmates. Do you use more or fewer machines than most people? Is your lifestyle "high tech" or "low tech"?

Using an Illustration to Learn Terminology

 *activity* **3**

Are you computer literate? This illustration gives you an idea of the components that make up a personal, or "home," computer. Study it for five minutes. Then check your comprehension by answering the questions that follow on the next page. It will help if you scan the illustration and note the terms that seem obvious or that you already know; then concentrate your efforts on the other terms.

Parts of the Personal Computer and What They Do

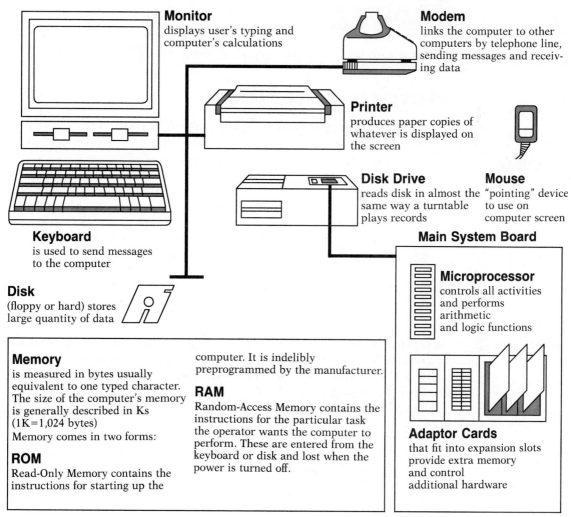

Monitor
displays user's typing and computer's calculations

Modem
links the computer to other computers by telephone line, sending messages and receiving data

Printer
produces paper copies of whatever is displayed on the screen

Disk Drive
reads disk in almost the same way a turntable plays records

Mouse
"pointing" device to use on computer screen

Keyboard
is used to send messages to the computer

Main System Board

Disk
(floppy or hard) stores large quantity of data

Microprocessor
controls all activities and performs arithmetic and logic functions

Memory
is measured in bytes usually equivalent to one typed character. The size of the computer's memory is generally described in Ks (1K=1,024 bytes)
Memory comes in two forms:

ROM
Read-Only Memory contains the instructions for starting up the computer. It is indelibly preprogrammed by the manufacturer.

RAM
Random-Access Memory contains the instructions for the particular task the operator wants the computer to perform. These are entered from the keyboard or disk and lost when the power is turned off.

Adaptor Cards
that fit into expansion slots provide extra memory and control additional hardware

1. How do you tell your computer something?

2. What do the disks* do?

3. Which part of the computer is like a record player? Why?

4. What is the difference between RAM and ROM? Which one is lost when you turn the computer off?

5. How many Ks do you need to store 2,000 words (assuming an average word is five letters)?

SELECTION two

Laser: Supertool of Our Time

Before You Read

Identifying Organizational Clues

 **exercise 1**
Preview the next article. List the six headings in the spaces below.

1. _____

2. _____

3. _____

4. _____

5. _____

6. _____

exercise 2
Skimming over the headings in a technical article helps you see the organization and main ideas. Look at the headings you wrote in Exercise 1. Which of the sections discuss what a laser is? Which discuss its economic importance? Which discuss its uses? Now you can answer this question: What does most of the next reading selection deal with?

_____

---

*Many new computers have hard disk drives inside the computer, so external disks are not needed.

Coping with Technical Terms

 The following article uses four technical terms to describe the quality of laser light. As is common in technical articles, the definition of these terms is given near the first appearance of the word, in either the same sentence, the one before, or the one after. In the first section, find the definitions for the following technical terms.

1. *intensity:* _____

_____

_____

2. *directionality:* _____

_____

_____

3. *coherent:* _____

_____

_____

4. *monochromatic:* _____

_____

_____

As you read the article, use the same method to help you learn other technical terms that are new to you. Stop, look around for the definition, and then reread the sentence a few times until you understand it.

In the 1990s, we find that the laser, like the computer, has become a commonplace item in our society. Still, how many of us really know what a laser is and what it is used for? The word itself is an acronym, a word formed from the first letters of other words. (Acronyms are discussed more fully in Chapter Eleven, pages 232 to 233.) In the following blanks, fill in the words that the five letters of *laser* stand for.

_____ _____ _____ _____ _____

(If you don't know the answer, you can find out in any good English dictionary.) Understanding the acronym gives you some idea of what a laser is. To find out more, read the following chapter that presents many facts about laser technology.

Laser: Supertool of Our Time

*T*hink of a laser simply as a tool. One that uses light instead of mechanical energy. And a tool that allows its user to control the form and amount of energy directed at a particular place. The laser can cut through a two-inch-thick sheet of steel or detect a single atom. It can perform a task as dramatic as igniting a thermonuclear fusion reaction or as seemingly mundane as drilling a hole in a baby-bottle nipple.

What Is a Laser?

A laser is a device that produces a very special kind of light. You can think of it as a super flashlight. But the beam that is emitted by the laser differs from the light that comes out of a flashlight in four basic ways:

- Laser light is *intense.* Yet only a few lasers are *powerful.* That's not the contradiction you might think. Intensity is a measure of power per unit area, and even a laser that emits only a few milliwatts can produce a lot of intensity in a beam that's only a millimeter in diameter. In fact, it can produce an intensity equal to that of sunlight. An ordinary lightbulb emits more light than a small laser like this, but that light spreads out all over the room. Some lasers can produce many thousands of watts continuously; others can produce trillions of watts in a pulse only a billionth of a second long.

- Laser beams are narrow and will not spread out like ordinary light beams. This quality is called *directionality.* You know that even the most powerful flashlight beam will not travel far. Aim one at the sky, and its beam seems to disappear quickly. The beam begins to spread out as soon as it leaves the flashlight, eventually dispersing so much as to be useless. On the other hand, beams from lasers with only a few watts of power were bounced off the moon, and the light was still bright enough to be seen back on the earth. One of the first laser beams shot at the moon—in 1962—spread out only two and a half miles on the lunar surface. Not bad when you consider that it traveled a quarter of a million miles!

- Laser light is *coherent.* This means that all the light waves coming out of a laser are lined up with each other. An ordinary light source, such as a lightbulb, generates light waves that start at different times and head in different directions. It's like throwing a handful of pebbles into a lake. You cause some tiny splashes and a few ripples, but that's about all. But if you take the same pebbles and throw them one by one, at exactly the right rate, at the same spot, you can generate a more sizable wave in the water. This is what a laser does, and this special property is useful in a variety of ways. Put another way, a lightbulb or a flashlight is like a shotgun; a laser is like a machine gun.

- Lasers produce light of only one color. Or, to say it in a more technical way, the light is *monochromatic.* Ordinary light comes in all the colors of visible light (that is, the *spectrum*). Mixed together, they come out white. Laser beams have been produced in every color of the rainbow (red is the most common laser color), as well as in many kinds of invisible light, but each laser can emit one color and one color only. There are such things as tunable lasers, which can be adjusted to produce several different colors, but even they can emit only one color at a time. A few lasers can emit several monochromatic wavelengths at once—but not a *continuous* spectrum containing all the colors of visible light as a lightbulb does. And then there are many lasers that project invisible light, such as infrared and ultraviolet light.

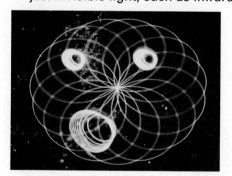 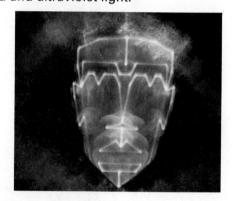

Laserium images

What Are Lasers Good For?

The range of uses for the laser is striking, going far beyond the original ideas of the scientists who developed the first models.

The wide variety of lasers is also striking. At one end of the scale there are lasers made from tiny semiconductor chips similar to those used in electronic circuits, no larger than grains of salt. At the other end, building-size laser weapons are being tested by the military.

The tasks that lasers perform are usually difficult or impossible with any other tool. Lasers are relatively expensive tools and are often brought in to do a job only because they can deliver the required type and amount of energy to the desired spot. Charles H. Townes, one of the inventors of the laser and a Nobel Prize winner, said recently that he believes the laser "is going to touch on a very great number of areas. The laser will do almost anything. But it costs. That is the only limitation."

The $50,000 Scalpel and Television Fibers

A typical surgical laser, for example, costs from $30,000 to $50,000 and up, or about a thousand times more than a good conventional scalpel. And to be honest, for many operations a scalpel may be better than a laser. But if you have a detached retina, a condition that could lead to blindness, you may be happy that these expensive scalpels exist. A laser can do what a knife can't: weld the retina back to the eyeball. No incision is required for this delicate surgery, which can be performed right in the doctor's office. The laser beam shines through the lens of the patient's eye and is focused on the retina, producing a small lesion that helps hold it to the eyeball. Exotic as this sounds, a similar laser treatment has become a standard way of curing blindness caused by diabetes.

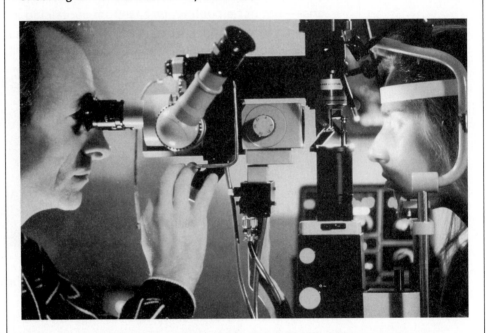

Lasers are commonly used in medicine, where they can often do what standard surgery can't.

Laser medicine probably hasn't touched you personally (you'd know if it had), but laser communication has undoubtedly served you already. If you watched the Olympics or some of the major football games on television recently, you probably saw signals that were transmitted part of the way to your home by lasers. Lasers carry telephone signals in dozens of places around the country. In both cases, light from the lasers is carried through hair-thin fibers of glass—*fiber optics*—a technology that could ultimately bring a multitude of new communication services into your home.

Death Rays, Drills, Nuclear Fusion

Lasers are already commonplace items among our military, but probably not in the way you think. Their main function in the business of war is that of range finder and target designator, not ray gun. Lasers are used to measure the distances to targets or pinpoint them with a "bull's-eye," helping either guns or missiles to home in on the enemy. And yes, in an offshoot of H. G. Wells's idea, the U.S. military is also spending about $300 million a year trying to build lasers able to destroy targets ranging from helicopters to ballistic missiles and satellites.

In factories around the world, lasers are now used routinely to drill holes in diamonds, label automotive parts, and weld battery cases for heart pacemakers. Laser quality-control "inspectors" sit ever-vigilant on assembly lines, making sure that the sizes of parts do not deviate from an acceptable range.

One of the hopes for ending our energy problems is *thermonuclear fusion,* the process by which energy is generated by the sun. One way of creating fusion here on earth is to heat and compress pellets containing hydrogen to the temperatures and pressures needed to fuse the nuclei of the hydrogen atoms together, creating tiny hydrogen bombs and thus generating incredible power. What can compress these pellets? Lasers, of course.

Three-Dimensional Images and Super Readers

Lasers are what make holograms possible—those three-dimensional images that seem to float before you, suspended in space. But holography has many seemingly mundane applications as well, from testing the quality of aircraft tires to measuring heat flow to aiding in the design of such things as hair dryers.

Lasers have made new art and new entertainment forms possible, even beyond holography. Laser light shows, the best known of which is *Laserium*, have been seen by millions of people around the world. A laser is also at the heart of one type of videodisk player, which plays back movies and television programs prerecorded on phonographlike disks.

Lasers can read. Those cryptic bar codes on food packages in supermarkets are read by scanning them with a laser beam. The pattern of reflected light is decoded to tell a computer in the back of the store what the label says. This not only tabulates the price on the cash register but automatically registers it in the computer's inventory memory. Lasers also read special typewriter faces, so that manuscripts can be typeset automatically, without human aid.

And lasers can write. It's simple for a computer to control a laser, making it write on film, special paper, or the drum of a copying machine, for later transfer to paper. Lasers expose printing plates for newspapers and print statements for insurance companies and mutual funds.

A Billion Dollars a Year

Lasers also serve the interests of pure scientific research, aiding in numerous and complicated experiments. Lasers can cause and control chemical reactions and someday might even propel rockets and aircraft.

The laser's catalogue of wonders is growing larger each day, as is the thriving laser industry. The market for lasers and related equipment hit $1 billion for the first time in 1980. But the laser has a long way to go. Its potential is only just beginning to be exploited.

There are still many problems to be overcome regarding the use of the laser. These obstacles demand sophisticated and elaborate techniques—or the simple, brilliant insight that leads to breakthroughs. However, similar obstacles have been faced and overcome before. That's how we got to where we are now.

Jeff Hecht and Dick Teresi

After You Read

Filling in Key Words to Make a Summary

exercise

Fill in the blanks with the appropriate key words from the article. In some cases, more than one word may be correct.

LASERS AND THEIR USES: A SUMMARY

Basically we can think of a laser simply as a _____ that
1
produces a very special kind of _____ . The beam from a laser is
2
_____ even if it is not powerful because it emits a lot of power per
3
_____ _____ _____ . Laser beams are
4
narrow and do not spread out; this quality is known as _____ . Light
5
waves from a lightbulb start at different times and go out in different

_____ , but laser light is _____ because the light waves
6   7
are lined up with each other. Laser light is monochromatic, which means it is

all of one _____ . Big and small lasers perform many jobs effec-
8
tively, but their one important limitation is that they _____ a lot.
9

Lasers are used in certain medical operations instead of a _____ .
___10___
They are used by the _____ as range finders or target designators
___11___
more than as _____ . They are used in _____ to drill
___12___   ___13___
holes in diamonds and label auto parts and for many other types of work. In
the future they might be used to compress pellets that contain hydrogen to
solve our _____ problems through the process of
___14___
_____ . Lasers make the three-
___15___
dimensional images known as _____ possible. They have produced
___16___
new forms of _____ that have been seen by millions. In supermar-
___17___
kets they _____ the bar codes on food packages. When controlled
___18___
by _____ , they can also _____ on film, special paper, or
___19___   ___20___
the drum of a copying machine. These and many other uses have caused lasers
to become a $_____ -a-year business that is still growing rapidly.
___21___

Talking It Over

In small groups, discuss the following questions.

   1. What is the difference between a laser beam and ordinary light?

   2. What are some uses of large lasers? Of small lasers?

   3. How are you affected by lasers in your daily life?

   4. Have you ever seen a laser light show? If so, what was it like?

Hi and Lois, reprinted with special permission of King Features Syndicate, Inc.

WHAT DO YOU THINK?

Taking the Chunnel

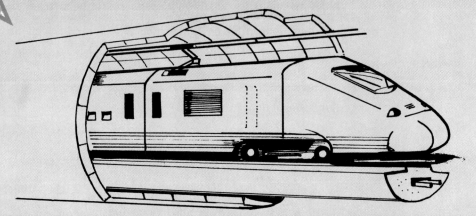

Over $30 billion was spent on a tunnel across the English Channel connecting England and France. A train that carries cars, trucks, and passengers speeds through the underwater "chunnel" at rates of 90 to 180 miles per hour. The cost of a round-trip ticket is $150 to $300. The ride under the channel lasts 35 minutes; this is about 40 minutes less than the much cheaper ferry boat ride on top of the channel. The French like the idea of "le grand project" and think it is progressive. The British think it will encourage terrorism and sabotage and bring unwanted animal species with diseases such as rabies from mainland Europe to Great Britain. What do you think? Is the chunnel a waste of money? Is it progressive and helpful? Are the fares too expensive? Would you take it, or would you be afraid?

Privacy Loses to Computers

Before You Read
Scanning for Abbreviations

 **exercise 1**   Use your scanning technique to quickly find the following abbreviations.

1. The old way of abbreviating the U.S. state of Massachusetts:

_____ (The correct abbreviation at present is MA. Some writers

prefer to use the old way.)

2. The abbreviation for the U.S. state of North Carolina: _____

3. The short way of referring to the Chief Executive Officer of a company:

_____

4. The abbreviation of *corporation*: _____

5. The common short form for the word *condominium* (an apartment owned

by the person living in it: _____

6. The slang term for *husband*: _____

Guessing Meaning from Context

exercise 2   Learn some important vocabulary that will help you read the article. Read each
sentence and circle the one word or phrase that is closest in meaning to the underlined word.

1. Unfortunately, he lives in a part of town where few services are <u>accessible</u>.
   a. far away   **c.** organized
   b. within reach   **d.** understandable

2. The little boy cried when his sister <u>punctured</u> his balloon.
   a. broke   **c.** inflated
   b. made   **d.** described

3. If he keeps on <u>harassing</u> them, they will call the police.
   a. amusing   **c.** ignoring
   b. bothering   **d.** hurrying

4. The king was <u>usurped</u> by his brother and sent into exile.
   a. warned   **c.** urged
   b. joined   **d.** overthrown

"How much money do you make each year?" "How much money do your mother and father make?" Do you consider these questions rude? In the United States and Canada, many people would think these questions were very rude. A person's income is thought of as private information, and privacy is considered important. However, the following article shows that a person's income and a lot of other information is available today to almost anybody. The article describes an experiment by the *Boston Globe* newspaper that set out to discover exactly what kind of information it could get about people's private lives.

Privacy Loses to Computers

*F*ormer Boston Celtics player M. L. Carr is no stranger to millions of basketball fans.

Or is he?

You may remember Carr as the hard-driving, towel-waving player for the Celtics. But did you know he lives in a nine-room house in Weston, Mass., worth $687,500, three times what he paid; his neighbors' median income is $131,900 and most are doctors, lawyers, or executives; he owns a 1983 Mercedes 300SD and a 1985 Chevrolet truck and has been stopped twice since 1989 for speeding; during the last decade, he helped start six businesses, three of which have survived; and as a teenager he was arrested after a fight to defend the honor of a black girl in Wallace, N.C., his hometown, and was sentenced to six months' probation?

Carr didn't tell us all that.

Computers did.

Computers with files on Carr that he never knew existed but that are part of an invisible electronic network of information assembled by credit companies, direct marketing businesses, and many federal and state bureaucrats. Part of that network is accessible from a reporter's computer terminal or from that of anyone who rents the files; the rest is open to thousands—maybe hundreds of thousands—of people Carr has never met.

And for a few dollars and a willingness to push the law to its limits, even unpublished phone numbers and bank records tumble open. In under an hour, for $69, a Florida firm dug up Carr's unlisted number in Weston.

There's comparable data out there on nearly all the rest of us, puncturing the privacy that is as basic to most Americans' sense of well-being as liberty and happiness.

Arnold Hiatt, former chairman and CEO of Stride Rite Shoe Corp., never worried much about privacy—until he realized how easily his could be violated. Hiatt and Carr were two volunteers in a *Boston Globe* experiment to illustrate how the electronic era threatens to make privacy a thing of the past.

We learned that Hiatt's 11-room house in Weston is valued at $664,900. He drives a modest 1988 Cutlass wagon but drives fast enough to have been stopped for speeding three times since 1988. He bought a downtown Boston condo for $1.025 million in 1988 and sold it three years later for $205,000 less. Over the last 20 months, he sold 307,895 shares of Stride Rite stock, worth $4,122,018. He has charge accounts at Brooks Brothers, Saks, Cherry Webb, Bloomingdale's, Filene's, Jordan Marsh, Lord & Taylor, Nieman-Marcus, and Sears. And two years ago, after receiving harassing calls from a former Stride Rite worker, he got a judge to order her to keep away.

"Privacy is something that everyone in this country likes to feel they have a right to," Hiatt said. "To have that right so easily usurped by the electronic data-collection apparatus is just counter to everything this democracy stands for."

Carr agreed, adding that he's especially upset by the ease with which his unlisted phone number was obtained: "I'm a very public person, and when I go home, that's my refuge, the place where I can kick back and just be daddy and hubby. . . . If you can't have refuge in your house, where can you have it?"

Scene from the movie *1984*.

High-Tech Piracy

For a half-century, science fiction writers have been forecasting a society in which intimate information is available everywhere and personal privacy is in danger of disappearing. Aldous Huxley called it a "Brave New World." George Orwell predicted its arrival in "1984."*

Their timing may have been wrong, but a four-month investigation by the *Boston Globe* makes it clear that America today is well into the kind of troubling new world the fiction writers predicted, a world in which the most basic principles of privacy are under attack.

You can see it as companies take information given for one purpose, such as a death certificate, and use it for another, such as selling the surviving spouse a membership in a dating service.

All via computers.

You can sense it as employers quietly read employees' electronic mail.

*The novels *Brave New World* and *1984* were written in the 1930s and 1940s and predicted the emergence of totalitarian states and the control of information by centralized governments.

Some call it high-tech piracy or the passing away of privacy.

Whatever the label, this new electronic listening is claiming victims who can be counted and named, such as the California actress murdered by an obsessive fan who tracked her down using motor vehicle records.

"Technology is developing so fast that the violations of privacy are ahead of the protections," said former New York Mayor Edward Koch, who was a leading advocate for privacy protections when he was in Congress nearly 20 years ago.

Concerns like that weren't much concern to the men who drafted the U.S. Constitution or those who wrote our laws for the first 100 or so years of our history.

It wasn't that they didn't care. They simply took for granted people's right to be left alone. And with society's limited capacity to collect and communicate information—and its almost limitless elbow room—there wasn't much risk of strangers' finding out too much about us.

Progress vs. Privacy

All that began to change about this time last century.

The population was expanding and frontiers were contracting. Government was getting bigger, with more people to serve and more data to collect. And new telephone and telegraph technologies, along with more publishing, meant that any information gathered could be shared quickly and widely.

While those changes substantially improved the quality of life for most Americans, they also put in jeopardy their ability to keep their affairs private.

Information Market

Consider the ease with which we learned intimate details about our *Globe* volunteers.

The investigation began in the convenience of the newsroom. This paper, like many other businesses, buys data. So, with the push of a computer key, the data told us about Carr's Mercedes and his Chevrolet, about Hiatt's phone number, those of his neighbors and how he sold his remaining Stride Rite stock last year.

Each nugget of information we dug up helped us dig up more.

We took the names and addresses to three of America's biggest data-collection companies, as well as to county and state agencies and to John DiNatale, a seasoned private detective in Boston. Using files available to anyone who can pay, they produced nearly 200 pages on Hiatt's and Carr's activities.

Larry Tye

After You Read

Making an Inference about the Author's Purpose

The author never tells you why he wrote this article. Is it to describe or inform? Is it to persuade the readers to take some action? Remember that an *inference* is an idea that is not directly stated but that you infer from what is stated. Think about the whole article. Skim it if necessary. Then make an inference about the author's purpose and write it here. Compare your inference with those of your classmates.

The author wrote this article in order to _____

_____

_____

Talking It Over

In small groups, discuss the following questions.

1. In your culture, is privacy considered as important as it is in the United States? What does privacy mean to you?

2. Were you surprised by any of the facts that the *Boston Globe* found out? Which of these facts should be kept secret?

3. What do you think of the following actions? Would you do them or not? Under what circumstances?
   a. Read someone else's e-mail.
   b. Listen to another person's phone conversation (use a scanner, e.g.).
   c. Hire a private detective to get information about someone.
   d. Find out an unlisted phone number.
   e. Try to find out the income of a co-worker.

The arrows in the picture on the next page show how various types and sources of personal information about Ed Wong (an imaginary person) were used by other people for many different purposes. As a class or in small groups, discuss the following questions:

1. Do you think Mr. Wong's privacy has been invaded?

2. What surprised you about the information that companies found out?

3. Do you think there should be laws to protect your privacy? What kind of laws?

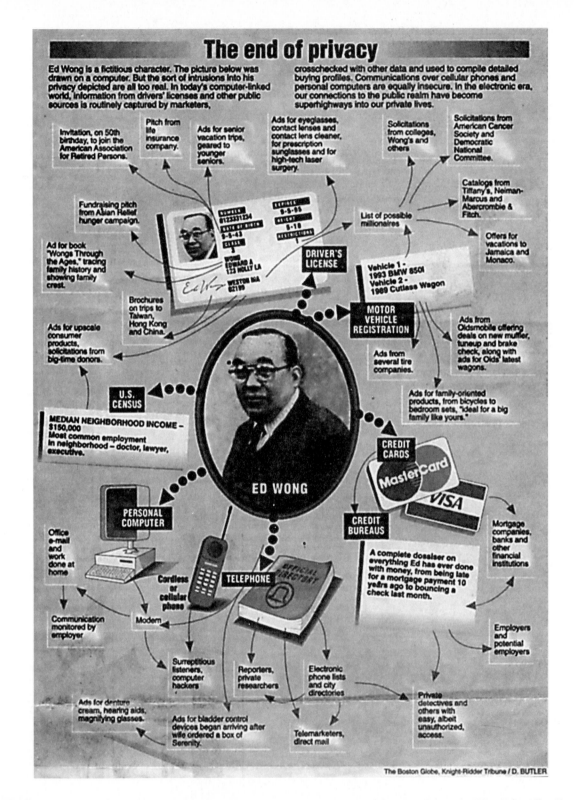

The Boston Globe, Knight-Ridder Tribune / D. BUTLER

Identifying Restatements of Ideas

In many reading-comprehension tests, you are asked to read a passage (a section of a reading selection) and choose the best answers to questions about it. Often these tests are tricky because all the answers will seem partly true. The word *partly* is important. Remember that if any small part of the answer is wrong, the whole answer is wrong. Do not be fooled into selecting an answer just because it uses words from the passage. Many times the correct answer is a restatement, or a paraphrase, of an important idea from the passage, but it is usually expressed in other words. Read the passage and each question carefully. Remember that what you are looking for is the one item that really answers the question.

exercise   Here and on the next page are several passages from the article "Privacy Loses to Computers." Each passage is followed by one or two questions about it. Circle the *one* best answer, a, b, c, or d, to each question.

QUESTIONS 1 AND 2

For a half-century, science fiction writers have been forecasting a society in which intimate information is available everywhere and personal privacy is in danger of disappearing. Aldous Huxley called it a *Brave New World.* George Orwell predicted its arrival in *1984.*

Their timing may have been wrong, but a four-month investigation by the *Boston Globe* made it clear that America today is well into the kind of troubling new world the fiction writers predicted, a world in which the most basic principles of privacy are under attack.

1. What did Aldous Huxley and George Orwell do?
    a. They forecast the arrival of personal privacy.
    b. They wrote about a society that had little privacy.
    c. They produced science fiction for a half century.
    d. They predicted the disappearance of information.

2. According to the passage, what is the best description of America today?
    a. A country that is more like fiction than the real world
    b. A society with troubles caused by investigations
    c. A nation without principles or correct timing
    d. A place without respect for people's private lives

Concerns like that weren't much concern to the men who drafted the
U.S. Constitution or those who wrote our laws for the first 100 or so years
of our history.

It wasn't that they didn't care. They simply took for granted people's
right to be left alone. And with society's limited capacity to collect and
communicate information—and its almost limitless elbow room—there
wasn't much risk of strangers' finding out too much about us.

3. Why didn't the authors of the U.S. Constitution and the early
   lawmakers write laws to protect personal privacy?
   a. It didn't seem to be a problem.
   b. It wasn't considered an important right.
   c. They really didn't care about it.
   d. They wanted to be left alone.

4. According to the passage, what was there *less* of at that time?
   a. danger
   b. space
   c. concern for law and order
   d. access to information

QUESTION 5

While those changes substantially improved the quality of life for most
Americans, they also put in jeopardy their ability to keep their affairs
private.

5. Which of the following best describes the results of the changes
   mentioned in the sentence?
   a. They were both good and bad.
   b. They made life better for Americans.
   c. They made life worse for Americans.
   d. They took away privacy.

CHAPTER six

Money Matters

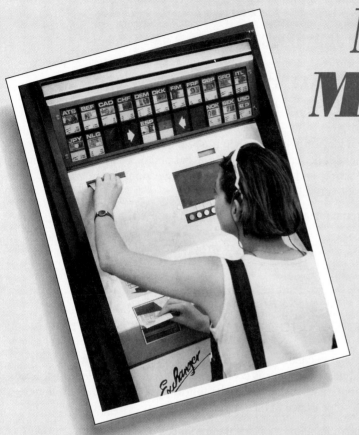

in this chapter

The first selection describes the success story of a business that is making money and creating jobs across many national borders. The second selection, about a recent trend in American companies, gives you an opportunity to practice reading faster. The third selection, written by one of the great short-story writers of the English language, focuses on a more personal aspect of the financial question: the embarrassment and difficulties that a lack of money can cause in a social situation.

Executive Takes Chance on Pizza, Transforms Spain

Before You Read

Anticipating the Contents

exercise 1

Try to get a general idea of what an article is about before beginning it. This will help you comprehend it better. Look at the title and photo. Then take one minute to skim the whole article and answer the following question. Compare your answer with those of your classmates.

What are some factors that helped this man succeed?

_____

_____

_____

Scanning for Members of Word Families

exercise 2

A good way to expand vocabulary is through word families—groups of words related in form and meaning, such as *combine, combined,* and *combination.* Scan the reading selection for words related to the following. (Clues are given in the order of the words' appearance in the article.)

1. *pizza*   A noun meaning "a place that produces or sells pizza"

_____

2. *modern*   A verb meaning "becoming modern"

_____

3. *manage*   A noun meaning "the act or manner of managing"

_____

4. *prosperous*   A verb meaning "to do well or become prosperous (wealthy)"

_____

5. *convenient*   A noun meaning "quality of being convenient, easy, or suitable"

_____

6. *afford*   An adjective meaning "able to be afforded by a person's financial means, not too expensive"

---

7. *mental*   A noun meaning "mental outlook, way of thinking"

Executive Takes Chance on Pizza, Transforms Spain

MADRID, Spain—Leopoldo Fernandez was earning $150,000 a year as an executive in Spain with Johnson & Johnson when he decided to open a pizzeria on the side.

5 "Keep in mind, I knew nothing about pizza. My job was about selling heart valves, heart monitors, surgical instruments," said the 47-year-old Cuban-American, a former marketing director for the U.S. medical sup-10 ply company.

Six years later, Fernandez is the president of TelePizza, a multinational with projected sales of $120 million this year. By year's end, the Madrid-based pizza busi-15 nessman's name will adorn more than 200 outlets in 10 countries. The company, one of the first to answer a need for convenience goods in modernizing Spain, may even be the world's fastest growing pizza chain, ac-20 cording to a recent issue of the trade magazine *Pizza Today* and research by TelePizza.

"I though I'd just open five little stores and keep my job at Johnson & Johnson," recalled Fernandez in an interview as he 25 puffed a $5 Cuban cigar. Two small Cuban flags are placed on his desk top.

Success came "so quickly my biggest problem has been keeping on top of the growth—money management, people man-30 agement, training. Most new businesses grow at 10–20 percent yearly. We've grown at 10 percent a month since we opened," Fernandez said.

After his first shop prospered in Madrid, 35 Fernandez left his job, sold his house and stocks, and cobbled together $300,000 to put into the business. From then on, new pizzerias opened rapidly, first in Spain and then abroad.

At the time TelePizza began in the late 1980s, pizzas were available in Spain only in Italian restaurants, and home delivery of any food was rare. But with more women in the workplace and Spain still modernizing, there was a growing need for convenience foods. TelePizza's success is widely credited with setting off a boom in home-delivered fast food in Spain.

Hundreds of motorbikes now ply Madrid's streets delivering everything from pizza to traditional specialities like Spanish tortillas (egg and potato omelettes) and paella.

Like the Domino's chain of U.S. fame, TelePizza's pies come fast—the company guarantees that pizzas will arrive in under 30 minutes, depending on where customers live. They are fairly affordable, with a pie for up to four people costing $13, compared with $6 for a McDonald's quarter-pounder, fries and Coke, undelivered.

Some say Spain's growing appetite for fast food is undermining the country's healthy Mediterranean diet. "There's a saying, when we were poor we made better eating choices than we do now," said Consuelo Lopez Nomdedeu, a nutritionist with the government-run National College of Health. But Fernandez dismissed such complaints. "The key is variety in the diet," he said. "I wouldn't eat pizza daily or hamburgers—(nor would I eat) Spanish dishes like lentils or garbanzos."

Along with crediting the untapped Spanish market for his success, Fernandez noted that growing up as an immigrant in the United States probably also helped. Like many other refugees fleeing the Castro revolution, Fernandez moved to Florida from Cuba in 1960 with his parents.

"An immigrant has to find ways to succeed because he's on the bottom," said Fernandez, who also has worked for Procter & Gamble Co., the leading U.S. consumer products company.

"Here, my advantage is that I understand Spanish mentality better than Americans do —and I understand Americans better than Spaniards do," Fernandez said.

So far, his recipe for success is working.

Fernandez said TelePizza outsells its three biggest rivals in Spain—Domino's, Pizza Hut and Pizza World—combined. The company has a fleet of more than 2,000 motorbikes in Spain and sells 25,000 pizzas daily in the Spanish market.

About two-thirds of TelePizza outlets in Spain are franchises while 90 percent of the 40 stores abroad are company-owned. In addition to Spain, there are TelePizza outlets in Mexico, Colombia, Chile, Portugal, Belgium, Greece and Poland—with stores in France and Brazil set to open before year's end.

"We plan to go into the U.S. in due time," Fernandez said. "For now we are maturing and learning from growth markets."

Stephen Wade

After You Read
Using the Context to Explain Business Terms

Use the context and the clues in parentheses to explain the following business terms.

1. *multinational* (line 12. Break the word apart to find its meaning.)

2. *projected sales* (lines 12 to 13. Think about what a project is and the time frame it refers to.)

3. *chain* (line 19. Imagine a picture of a chain, made up of separate parts called links.)

4. *boom* (line 47. The meaning can be inferred partly from the sound of this word.)

5. *untapped market* (lines 73 to 74. To tap something means to "open or start it," as in *tapping an oil well.* Do you know the meaning of the prefix *un-*?)

6. *franchises* (line 97. Notice these stores are contrasted with others that are "company-owned.")

7. *growth markets* (line 105. Take a guess from the words themselves.)

Talking It Over

In small groups, discuss the following questions.

1. What problems did Mr. Fernandez have at first?

2. Why do you think that TelePizza is doing so well?

3. What does the Spanish nutritionist think of the recent changes in Spanish eating habits? Do you agree with her opinion or with that of Mr. Fernandez?

4. What kinds of "fast food" are popular where you live? What do you think of them?

5. How does Mr. Fernandez's nationality as a Cuban-American help him?

6. Nobody knows the future, but sometimes it's fun to speculate (make guesses about future results). In your opinion, should TelePizza expand into the United States as Mr. Fernandez suggests? Will it succeed in the United States? Why or why not?

Finding Out More Through Magazines

activity 2

The article mentions a trade magazine called *Pizza Today*. What kind of articles do you think are in this magazine? Go to the library and find the section that has trade magazines. Find a magazine that focuses on a field that interests you—perhaps the hotel business, engineering, health products, or some other trade or business. Make a photocopy of one of the articles, skim it, and bring it to class. Write the source (the name of the magazine, the issue number or date, and the page numbers) on the photocopy. Work in small groups and take turns telling what you have learned from the article.

focus on testing

Reading Between the Lines

In many reading-comprehension tests, you are asked to read a passage and choose the best answer to one or more questions about it. Often these questions ask you to make an inference about the reading passage. Remember that an inference is a true idea that is not stated directly but can be inferred (concluded or deduced) from what is stated. In English, this is often called "reading between the lines."

Look at the first question of the following exercise. In order to choose the correct inference, you must decide why three of the ideas are *not* correct inferences. The test is trying to fool you, so be careful! First, one of the choices is false (or probably false). Which one is that? Another one is only possibly true, but we don't have enough information to decide. It may be true, or it may be false. Which one is that? Another of the choices is true, but it is already directly stated in the passage in different words. So it is not really an inference. Which answer is that? Now, through the process of elimination, we have eliminated three choices and are left with the one correct answer. Which letter is it?

exercise Following are three passages from the article "Executive Takes Chance on Pizza, Transforms Spain." Each passage is followed by a question about it. Circle the *one* best answer, a, b, c, or d, to each question.

QUESTION 1

Leopoldo Fernandez was earning $150,000 a year as an executive in Spain with Johnson & Johnson when he decided to open a pizzeria on the side. "Keep in mind, I knew nothing about pizza. My job was about selling heart valves, heart monitors, surgical instruments," said the 47-year-old

Cuban-American, a former marketing director for the U.S. medical supply company.

1. What can be inferred from the passage about Leopoldo Fernandez?
   a. He is middle-aged.
   b. He was born in Cuba.
   c. He is a risk taker.
   d. He was poor before starting a business.

QUESTION 2

At the time TelePizza began in the late 1980s, pizzas were available in Spain only in Italian restaurants, and home delivery of any food was rare. But with more women in the workplace and Spain still modernizing, there was a growing need for convenience foods. TelePizza's success is widely credited with setting off a boom in home-delivered fast food in Spain.

2. What can be inferred from the passage about TelePizza's customers?
   a. They like to buy on credit.
   b. They do not like Italian restaurants.
   c. Many are very traditional.
   d. Many are working women.

QUESTION 3

Along with crediting the untapped Spanish market for his success, Fernandez noted that growing up as an immigrant in the United States probably also helped. Like many other refugees fleeing the Castro revolution, Fernandez moved to Florida from Cuba in 1960 with his parents.

"An immigrant has to find ways to succeed because he's on the bottom," said Fernandez, who also has worked for Procter & Gamble Co., the leading U.S. consumer products company.

3. What can be inferred from the passage about Fernandez' opinion of immigrants?
   a. Immigrants usually don't work as hard as others.
   b. Immigrants usually work harder than others.
   c. Immigrants are employed by big companies.
   d. Immigrants receive support from their families.

SELECTION **two**

Who Owns What in America?

Before You Read
Reading for Speed

exercise

Take a moment to look at the title and illustration of the next reading selection. Then read the questions at the end. Look at a clock or watch and mark down the time. Then start reading as fast as you can, using your skimming technique (or clustering if you prefer) to find out the answers to the questions. (See Chapter Two, pages 23 to 26, "How to Read Faster," to review skimming or clustering.) As soon as you finish, write out the answers. Then write down the time.

Time started: _____   Time finished: _____

How many minutes did it take you? Check your answers with your teacher or classmates. Did you comprehend the reading? Are you faster or slower than most of the class?

Do not be discouraged if you are slow. Some people are better at speed and some at comprehension. By reading quickly to answer questions, you can learn to move your eyes faster and improve your speed. Practice each day with newspaper or magazine articles of approximately the same length, answering the question: *What is the main idea of this article?* Record your times, and you will soon see an improvement.

Ready? Write down the time. Begin.

There are many ways to improve your reading. One way is to try to read faster. There is so little time and so much to read! The following selection is by the famous American writer Andy Rooney. He is well known for his tongue-in-cheek (light and humorous) writing on many subjects. This magazine article has a tongue-in-cheek tone, but it makes a serious point about modern business.

Who Owns What in America?

We used to toast Pepperidge Farm bread for breakfast in my house; then the little company that made it was taken over by Campbell Soup, a big company, and I don't
5 think the bread's as good as it used to be.

Whenever a big company takes over a small company, the product almost always gets worse. Sue me, but it's true. The takeover is so popular with big business it's
10 hard to know who owns what in America.

Take, for example, the International Telephone and Telegraph Company. They do some telephone business, I guess, but they also own Sheraton Hotels, the Hartford Fire

Insurance Company, the company that publishes Who's Who in America, and the bakeries that make Hostess Twinkies.

Most of the tobacco companies have taken over so many other companies that they've dropped "tobacco" from their names. Philip Morris bought that fine old German beer Löwenbräu, which they now make in such fine old German cities as Fort Worth, Texas. Liggett, known for its Chesterfield cigarettes, owns J & B Scotch and the company that makes Champion barbells. The former Reynolds Tobacco Company owns Chun King foods, Hawaiian Punch, and Vermont Maid syrup, which is 2 percent maple and not made in Vermont.

Who would you think owns Montgomery Ward? Sears Roebuck? Wrong. Mobil Oil owns Montgomery Ward.

Pepsi-Cola owns Wilson, which makes tennis balls. And don't try to find a Coca-Cola in a Pizza Hut because Pepsi-Cola owns them, too.

General Mills, which bought Bruce Jenner, the champion of breakfasts, owns Lacoste, the company that makes the tennis shirt with the little alligator on it. General Mills also owns the game of Monopoly.

Hershey makes chocolate bars, but also owns the San Giorgio Macaroni Company.

Consolidated Foods makes Sara Lee cheesecake, which seems fitting, and Electrolux vacuum cleaners, which doesn't.

ABC, Number 1 in television, owns *Prairie Farmer* magazine, but CBS isn't worried. It owns *Field & Stream* and *Woman's Day*.

Recently the Kellogg Company paid $56 million for a company called Mrs. Smith's Pies.

Big companies love homey-sounding little names like Mrs. Smith's Pies. We decided to go to Pottstown, Pennsylvania, where the pies are made, to see if we could find out what Mrs. Smith is going to do with the $56 million.

ROONEY: Pardon me, do you know where Mrs. Smith is?

MAN: Mrs. Smith?

ROONEY: Yeah.

MAN: What Mrs. Smith is that?

WOMAN: Right. No, look, go here to the end of the alley and make a right.

ROONEY: Where's the main office, do you know? Will Mrs. Smith be there?

MAN: A Mr. Smith?

ROONEY: No, *Mrs.* Smith. Is it *Mr.* Smith's Pies?

ROONEY: Hi. You're Mrs. Smith, are you?

WOMAN: No, I'm not.

ROONEY: *(in factory parking lot)* Is there a Mrs. Smith? Smith isn't around at all?

MAN: No, there's a . . . there's no Smiths connected with the company at this time. It's owned by Kellogg's.

Who owns what in America? Not Mrs. Smith.

Andy Rooney

After You Read
Scanning for Details

exercise **1** Use your scanning technique to quickly find the following facts.

1. According to the article, what happens to a product when a big company takes over a small company?

_____

2. Is this kind of takeover common or uncommon?

_____

3. Why have most tobacco companies dropped the word *tobacco* from their names?

_____

4. Give an example from the article of a company that owns another company in the same line of business.

_____

5. Give an example of a company that owns another company in a completely different line of business.

_____

6. In the information given by the author, which of these two cases is more common?

_____

7. Who is Mrs. Smith? Why does the author mention her?

_____

Examining the Point of View

exercise **2** Now that you have finished the timing and evaluating of your comprehension, take a moment to think about the author's point of view. In your opinion, how does he feel about the practice of business takeovers in the United States? Why do you think he feels this way? Do you agree or disagree with this point of view? Explain.

_____

_____

_____

_____

_____

The Luncheon

Before You Read
Predicting the Action

It is helpful when you read a narrative (a story or description) to try to think a bit ahead of what you are reading. Just as in cooking or chemistry, certain ingredients in a story should bring about particular results. However, William Somerset Maugham, the author of the next reading selection, like most master storytellers, tries to surprise us, especially through the use of irony. Look for clues in the context and predict what is going to happen next. The following story will be interrupted at a few points and you will be asked some questions to guide you. Do not worry about understanding every word. Maugham has a very rich vocabulary, and there will be many unfamiliar words. Just try to follow the main thread of the story.

William Somerset Maugham (1874–1965) is one of the most popular novelists and short-story writers in the English language. Born in Paris and educated in England, he worked as a secret agent for the British government in World War I and then spent the rest of his life writing and traveling throughout many parts of the world. He is famous for this clear style and penetrating understanding of human nature. Many of his stories are based on personal experience and use flashbacks and irony. The following story is a good example of these techniques. A flashback is a scene representing an earlier event that is inserted into a story. By scanning the first part of the following reading, can you find the point at which the flashback begins?

Irony is the use of words, characters, or actions that express the opposite of what is true or expected. This is a device employed by authors to create humor, but there is also a lot of irony in serious situations in everyday life. If the house of the fire chief burns down, we can say it is *ironic.* When someone looks out at a rainstorm and says, "What a lovely day for a picnic!", he or she is using irony. Keeping this in mind as you read the short story, try to notice which parts are ironic. Pay special attention to the ending, since it is very common for Maugham to try to surprise his readers with an ironic ending.

The Luncheon

I caught sight of her at the play and in answer to her beckoning I went over during the interval and sat down beside her. It was long since I had last seen her and if someone had not mentioned her name I hardly think I would have recognized her. She addressed me brightly.

"Well, it's many years since we first met. How time does fly! We're none of us getting any younger. Do you remember the first time I saw you? You asked me to luncheon."

Did I remember?

It was twenty years ago and I was living in Paris. I had a tiny apartment in the Latin Quarter overlooking a cemetery and I was earning barely enough money to keep body and soul together. She had read a book of mine and had written to me about it. I answered, thanking her, and presently I received from her another letter saying that she was passing through Paris and would like to have a chat with me; but her time was limited and the only free moment she had was on the following Thursday: she was spending the morning at the Luxembourg and would I give her a little luncheon at Foyot's afterwards? Foyot's is a restaurant at which the French senators eat and it was so far beyond my means that I had never even thought of going there. But I was flattered and I was too young to have learned to say no to a woman. (Few men, I may add, learn this until they are too old to make it of any consequence to a woman what they say.) I had eighty francs (gold francs) to last me the rest of the month and a modest luncheon should not cost more than fifteen. If I cut out coffee for the next two weeks I could manage well enough.

Prediction *What do you think of the request that the woman has made of the main character? Why do you think that he accepted it? Do you think he is going to get into trouble? Why or why not?*

French society people in the early part of the twentieth century.

30 I answered that I would meet my friend—by correspondence—at Foyot's on Thursday at half past twelve. She was not so young as I expected and in appearance imposing rather than attractive. She was in fact a woman of forty (a charming age, but not one that excites a sudden and devastating passion at first sight), and she gave me the impression of having more teeth, white and large and even, than were necessary for any practical purpose. She was talkative, but since she seemed inclined to talk

35 about me I was prepared to be an attentive listener.

I was startled when the bill of fare was brought, for the prices were a great deal higher than I had anticipated. But she reassured me.

"I never eat anything for luncheon," she said.

"Oh, don't say that!" I answered generously.

40 "I never eat more than one thing. I think people eat far too much nowadays. A little fish, perhaps. I wonder if they have any salmon."

Well, it was early in the year for salmon and it was not on the bill of fare, but I asked the waiter if there was any. Yes, a beautiful salmon had just come in—it was the first they had had. I ordered it for my guest. The

45 waiter asked her if she would have something while it was being cooked.

Prediction   *What did the man notice about the woman's appearance? Does it perhaps give a clue to her character? From what she has said so far, do you expect her to order any more food? Why?*

"No," she answered, "I never eat more than one thing. Unless you had

50 a little caviar. I never mind caviar."

My heart sank a little. I knew I could not afford caviar, but I could not very well tell her that. I told the waiter by all means to bring caviar. For myself I chose the cheapest dish on the menu and that was a mutton chop.

"I think you're unwise to eat meat," she said. "I don't know how you

55 can expect to work after eating heavy things like chops. I don't believe in overloading my stomach."

Then came the question of drink.

Prediction   *What do you think the woman is going to say about the question of drink? What do you think she is going to do? And the man?*

60 *Why?*

"I never drink anything for luncheon," she said.

"Neither do I," I answered promptly.

"Except white wine," she proceeded as though I had not spoken.

"These French white wines are so light. They're wonderful for the di-

65 gestion."

"What would you like?" I asked, hospitable still, but not exactly effusive.

She gave me a bright and amicable flash of her white teeth.

"My doctor won't let me drink anything but champagne."

I fancy I turned a trifle pale. I ordered half a bottle. I mentioned casually that my doctor had absolutely forbidden me to drink champagne.

"What are you going to drink, then?"

"Water."

She ate the caviar and she ate the salmon. She talked gaily of art and literature and music. But I wondered what the bill would come to. When my mutton chop arrived she took me quite seriously to task.

"I see that you're in the habit of eating a heavy luncheon. I'm sure it's a mistake. Why don't you follow my example and eat just one thing? I'm sure you'd feel ever so much better for it."

"I *am* only going to eat one thing," I said, as the waiter came again with the bill of fare.

Prediction   *The waiter has come once again. What will happen next?*

She waved him aside with an airy gesture.

"No, no, I never eat anything for luncheon. Just a bite, I never want more than that, and I eat that more as an excuse for conversation than anything else. I couldn't possibly eat anything more—unless they had some of those giant asparagus. I should be sorry to leave Paris without having some of them."

"Madame wants to know if you have any of those giant asparagus," I asked the waiter.

I tried with all my might to will him to say no. A happy smile spread over his broad, priestlike face, and he assured me that they had some so large, so splendid, so tender, that it was a marvel.

"I'm not in the least hungry," my guest sighed, "but if you insist, I don't mind having some asparagus."

I ordered them.

"Aren't you going to have any?"

"No, I never eat asparagus."

"I know there are people who don't like them. The fact is, you ruin your palate by all the meat you eat."

Prediction   *What is ironic about the story up to now? Do you think the man or the woman will order more food?*

We waited for the asparagus to be cooked. Panic seized me. It was not a question now of how much money I should have left over for the rest of the month, but whether I had enough to pay the bill. It would be mortifying to find myself ten francs short and be obliged to borrow from my guest. I could not bring myself to do that. I knew exactly how much I had and if the bill came to more I had made up my mind that I would put my hand in my pocket and with a dramatic cry start up and say it had been picked. Of couse it would be awkward if she had not money enough either to pay the bill. Then the only thing would be to leave my watch and say I would come back and pay later.

The asparagus appeared. They were enormous, succulent, and appetizing. The smell of the melted butter tickled my nostrils as the nostrils of Jehovah were tickled by the burned offerings of the virtuous Semites. I watched the abandoned woman thrust them down her throat in large voluptuous mouthfuls and in my polite way I discoursed on the condition of the drama in the Balkans. At last, she finished.

"Coffee?" I asked.

"Yes, just an ice cream and coffee," she answered.

I was past caring now, so I ordered coffee for myself and an ice cream and coffee for her.

"You know, there's one thing I thoroughly believe in," she said, as she ate the ice cream. "One should always get up from a meal feeling one could eat a little more."

"Are you still hungry?" I asked faintly.

"Oh, no. I'm not hungry; you see, I don't eat luncheon. I have a cup of coffee in the morning and then dinner, but I never eat more than one thing for luncheon. I was speaking for you."

"Oh, I see!"

Then a terrible thing happened. While we were waiting for the coffee, the head waiter, with an ingratiating smile on his false face, came up to us bearing a large basket full of peaches. They had the blush of an innocent girl; they had the rich tone of an Italian landscape. But surely peaches were not in season then? Lord knew what they cost. I knew too—a little later, for my guest, going on with her conversation, absentmindedly took one.

"You see, you've filled your stomach with a lot of meat"—my one miserable little chop—"and you can't eat any more. But I've just had a snack and I shall enjoy a peach."

The bill came and when I paid it I found that I had only enough for a quite inadequate tip. Her eyes rested for an instant on the three francs I left for the waiter and I knew that she thought me mean. But when I walked out of the restaurant I had the whole month before me and not a penny in my pocket.

Prediction   *So far the luncheon has gone badly for the man. Since you know that Somerset Maugham likes irony and surprise endings, can you think of some way he might turn the situation around? Will the man somehow get his revenge?*

"Follow my example," she said as we shook hands, "and never eat more than one thing for luncheon."

150   "I'll do better than that," I retorted. "I'll eat nothing for dinner tonight."

"Humorist!" she cried gaily, jumping into a cab. "You're quite a humorist!"

But I have had my revenge at last. I do not believe that I am a vindictive man, but when the immortal gods take a hand in the matter it is pardon-
155   able to observe the result with complacency. Today she weighs twenty-one stone.*

W. Somerset Maugham

_____

* The stone is a British unit of measurement. One stone equals fourteen pounds.

After You Read

Recalling Idioms and Expressions

 Fill in the following summary of the story with idioms or expressions used in the selection. To help you, either the meaning is given in parentheses or the first or last word is given in italics.

SWEET REVENGE

He (saw) _____ _____ _____ her at a
play. She said to him, "How *time* _____ _____ ," and
he remembered twenty years earlier when he was so poor that he could hardly
keep (himself alive) _____ _____ _____
together. She had asked him to take her to a restaurant that was far (too
expensive for him) *beyond* _____ _____ . He agreed, but
his *heart* _____ when she ordered a very expensive meal. Ironically,
she (scolded him) *took* _____ _____ _____
for ordering one small chop. Afterward, he ordered coffee because he was *past*
_____ . Twenty years later, he saw that the immortal gods had
(participated) _____ _____ _____ in his
revenge: She was enormous!

Talking It Over

In small groups, discuss the following questions.

1. Why do you think the woman behaved as she did? Do you think she wanted to take advantage of the young man or was she simply ignorant of his money problems?

2. What should the young man have done to get out of this difficult situation?

3. How has the author used irony in this story?

4. Have you ever been in an embarrassing situation because of money? If so, how did you get out of it?

5. Why do you think some people continually have money problems? Is it the fault of credit cards? Of lack of experience or training?

Thoughts About Money

In small groups, talk about the following quotations about money. Do you know any others?

"Money buys everything except love, personality, freedom, immortality, silence, peace." —*Carl Sandburg*

"One can accumulate enough wealth to buy a golden bed, but one cannot buy sound sleep with money." —*Daniel Arap Moi*

"I am not against wealth. I am against wealth that enslaves." —*Gandhi*

"I've been with money and without; I prefer to be with." —*Pat Roggensack*

WHAT DO YOU THINK?

Using Credit Cards

 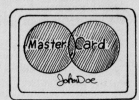 

One of the fastest-growing ways in the world to buy and sell things is through credit cards. People are offered opportunities through banks and large companies to sign up for a credit card. Buy now, pay later. You can pay for clothes, hotels, rental cars, airline tickets, and even cars and groceries. But credit card companies charge 12 to 20 percent interest on the money you borrow on their cards. Many people go into debt because they overuse their credit cards. What do you think? Are credit cards a good idea? Do you like the idea of paying with cash or check better? Is it better to pay off your credit card purchases on a monthly or yearly basis? Should you take money from your savings account to pay off your credit card purchases?

CHAPTER seven

Leisure Time

in this chapter

One of the great advances in modern society is an increase in the number of leisure hours for a large percentage of the population. People are no longer forced to work all day long simply to provide for their basic necessities. With this change comes the new problem of filling these free hours with recreational activities. This chapter focuses on three of today's most popular forms of recreation in North America: TV, gambling, and sports.

SELECTION one

Living with Television

Before You Read

Skimming to Identify the "Voices" in a Reading Selection

 *exercise* **1**

An author sometimes presents different voices in a reading by quoting (repeating) the exact words of other people. Skim the following article to answer these questions.

1. How many members of the Delmar family are quoted in the article?
   a. 1
   b. 2
   c. 3
   d. 4

2. On what subject does the *voice of the author* express an opinion in the middle of the article?
   a. The high cost of TV sets
   b. The different types of TV programs popular in various cultures
   c. The relationship between an American family and their TV
   d. The negative influence of TV commercials on some children

3. Whose voice appears at the end of the article, giving some statistics?
   a. Amy Blank's
   b. Bonnie Delmar's
   c. Connie Chung's
   d. Steve Nielsen's

Guessing the Meaning of Colloquial Expressions

 *exercise* **2**

Most of the different voices in the article use *colloquial expressions*, expressions that are common in conversation but not in formal speech or writing. Read the following excerpts from the article and decide from context which meaning corresponds to the expression in italics. (Scan for the expressions if you need more of the context.)

1. Bonnie was watching the David Letterman show when she *drifted off* the night before.
   a. began to read
   b. fell asleep
   c. turned off the light

2. She watches "This Morning" for a few minutes, *catching up on* what has happened.
   a. reading the news of
   b. taking a rest from
   c. finding out about

3. She *threw a fit* when the TV broke.
   a. played a game
   b. felt happy
   c. became upset

4. I said, "*You've got to be kidding.*"
   a. It's nice to make jokes.
   b. Your attitude is unbelievable.
   c. You have to laugh more.

5. I just don't *buy it* that too much TV is bad for you.
   a. agree
   b. understand
   c. purchase

6. Nobody wants to admit they watch TV—it's got the connotation: the *boob tube*—but all these people, what are they doing?
   a. difficult apparatus
   b. intellectual pastime
   c. idiot machine

7. "Let's face it, their kids *can be real pains in the neck.*"
   a. often cause problems
   b. have poor health
   c. obey the rules

Television, popularly known as TV or "the tube," has been around in the United States and Canada for half a century, and it is still a controversial topic—that is, a topic that arouses strong and contradictory opinions. What do you think about the effect of TV on life in North America? Is it harmful or beneficial? The following newspaper article from *The Washington Post* talks mainly about the use of TV by one American family, the Delmars of Maryland.

Living with Television

Gaithersburg, Maryland

The first TV to come on is the one in the master bedroom, a 13-inch Hitachi. The time is 8:20 A.M. The alarm clock goes off, and Bonnie Delmar opens her eyes and im-
5 mediately reaches for the remote.* Her husband, Steve, has already left for work. The children are still asleep. The house is quiet. On comes CBS because Bonnie was watching the David Letterman show when she
10 drifted off the night before. She watches "This Morning" for a few minutes, catching up on what has happened in the last seven hours in the world beyond her Gaithersburg home.
15   The second TV to come on is the 19-inch Zenith in the bedroom of Bonnie's daughter, Ashley, age 7 years and 10 months. The time is now 8:45, and Ashley and her younger brother, Steven, get dressed while watching
20 "The Bozo Show." The Zenith is the newest TV in the house, purchased a few weeks before to replace the 26-inch Sony that had been in Ashley's room until the color picture tube went bad. "She threw a fit when the
25 Sony broke," Bonnie says of Ashley's reaction. "So Steve and Steven went out and got her a new TV, and she wasn't happy about it. I mean, she cried. She wanted a big screen. I actually laughed at her. I said, 'You've got to
30 be kidding,' and that made her more furious. She was saying, 'How can you give me such a small TV?' But, anyway, that's over. She's fine now."
  The third TV to come on is the 27-inch
35 Hitachi by the kitchen table. It's now a few

---

*The *remote* is a common way of referring to the remote control, a small electronic gadget used to change TV channels, volume, etc., from a distance.

minutes after 9. The Hitachi has an especially complex remote, but Steven has mastered it, despite being only 6. He picks it up and changes the channel to "Barney and
40 Friends." "I love you, you love me," the Barney theme song begins, but Steven sings his own variation, learned from Ashley, who learned it at school. "I hate you, you hate me," he sings, "let's kill Barney one two
45 three . . ." "Steven!" Bonnie says, laughing, "how's it really go?" "I don't know," Steven says. He picks up the remote again and switches to cartoons, while Bonnie goes over to the counter by the sink and turns on
50 the 5-inch, black-and-white, battery-powered Panasonic.
  It is now 9:10 A.M. in the Delmar house. Fifty minutes have gone by since the alarm. Four TVs have been turned on. It will be an-
55 other 16 hours before all the TVs have been turned off and the house is once again quiet.
  By the sink, Bonnie continues to watch "Regis and Kathie Lee."
  At the table, Ashley and Steven watch
60 Speedy Gonzalez in "Here Today, Gone Tamale." Looking at them, it's hard to imagine three happier people.
  "Mom," Ashley says later, after she has gone to school and come home and resumed
65 watching TV, "I'm going to watch TV in Heaven."
  "You're going to watch TV in Heaven?" Bonnie says.
  "Yeah," Ashley says.
70   "Well," Bonnie says, "let's hope they have it on up there."
  Of all the relationships of modern civilization, none is more hypocritical than the relationship between an American family
75 and its television set.

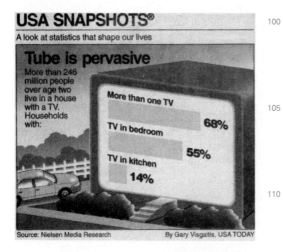

USA SNAPSHOTS®

A look at statistics that shape our lives

Tube is pervasive

More than 246 million people over age two live in a house with a TV. Households with:

More than one TV **68%**

TV in bedroom **55%**

TV in kitchen **14%**

Source: Nielsen Media Research   By Gary Visgaitis, USA TODAY

We worry that TV causes violent behavior, and yet we keep watching violent shows. We complain that TV is getting too graphic, and yet we are buying sets with sharper pictures and larger screens. TV is our angst. TV is our guilt. We worry about it. We blame it. We feel bad about how much we really watch it. We lie.

Except for the Delmars.

"I just don't buy it that too much TV is bad for you," says Steve, 37, the chief financial officer of a company that makes automated telephone answering systems, who gets home from work around 7. He eats dinner while watching Dan Rather. . . ,* settles down in the den by the 19-inch Sony, watches a few hours of sports, goes back to the bedroom, turns on the Hitachi and falls asleep with it. "Nobody wants to admit they watch television—it's got the connotation: 'the boob tube'—but all these people, what are *they* doing? I'm not sure if they have any more intellect. It's not like they're all going to the Smithsonian† or anything."

---

*Newscaster on the evening news programs
†The Smithsonian Institute is a famous museum in Washington, DC.

"Let's see," says Bonnie, 35, a housewife and former restaurant hostess with a bachelor's degree in elementary education, totaling up how much TV she watches a day. "It just depends on if I'm home or not. If I'm home, I'm watching. Probably 9 hours a day is average. There are some days I might actually watch 16, 17 hours, but there are some days I'm out and about, and I don't get to watch as much."

At the Delmars', there are six TVs, and plans are to refinish the basement and add two more. At the Delmars', not only is TV always on, it is like a member of the family, part of nearly every significant moment in their lives.

"I love it. I love it. I can't help it. I love it," Bonnie says. "Why should I be ashamed of saying that?"

Not that TV is the only thing Bonnie does. "I don't just sit and watch TV," she says. "I'll clean while I watch. I'll read the paper. I'll work on crafts. I like making dollhouse furniture with Ashley. I'll fold laundry." She also reads books, volunteers at the school several times a week and works on the yard.

If TV is so bad, Bonnie says, why are her kids doing so well? If it's so bad, why is Steven so happy, and why is Ashley excelling in school? Just the other day, at a parent-teacher conference, Ashley's teacher called her a terrific student and concluded by saying to Bonnie, "You will be seeing great things from Ashley"—and to Bonnie's way of thinking, TV is one of the reasons why. As she says after the conference, "I have friends who think it's terrible that I let my kids eat candy, that I let my kids watch TV, that I don't have a lot of rules, but I'll tell you what: Set my kids and their kids in the same room and see who's better behaved. They're really, really sweet kids. And a lot of these parents who try to do everything right—no TV, lots of reading, lots of rules—let's face it, their kids can be real pains in the neck."

Ninety-eight percent of American households have TV according to Nielsen Media Research; 77 percent have at least one VCR; 62 percent get cable. TV is under scrutiny by everyone, from politicians who propose ratings for TV shows and video games, to academicians and sociologists who produce study after study about its dulling effects on developing brains.

Also concerned are a group of twenty worried mothers who come together one evening at an elementary school in Silver Spring, Maryland, not far from the neighborhood where Bonnie grew up. This evening, they are listening to Amy Blank, who is with the Maryland Campaign for Kids' TV, an organization that monitors children's programming on area TV stations. She turns to a chart that says, "Most children will see 8,000 murders and 10,000 acts of violence before they finish elementary school."

"They won't do any other thing, other than eat or sleep, that many times," she says. "That's what we're teaching them. It's okay to kill 8,000 people. It's okay to hurt or maim 10,000 people. It's okay. TV does it, so it's okay."

Hours and Minutes Spent Watching TV, Per Week, 1990

Country	TV Watching
United States	29:05
Japan	28:28
United Kingdom	25:35
France	20:54
Belgium	20:08
Austria	19:24
Germany	19:15
Denmark	17:33
Ireland	16:55
Netherlands	16:48
Switzerland	15:25
Sweden	15:01
Norway	14:22
Finland	12:28

Source: A. C. Nielsen Co., Northbrook, IL

She shows another chart of what parents should do, a list that includes limiting the amount of time children watch TV.

"I think we're seeing tremendous effects on our kids and on our society," she says. "I mean, we're a broken society. We really are. We're struggling. There's so much incredible pain out there. And many of us just don't know where to hide, and don't know what to do."

Meanwhile, back in Gaithersburg, where the Delmars are watching TV, life is untroubled as usual.

David Finkel

After You Read
Word Detective

Play detective and find the following words in the article, using your scanning skills and the *clues* given below. (The words are asked for in order of their appearance in the article.)

1. A way of referring to the main bedroom (usually the largest in the house):

   the _____ bedroom.

2. A word to describe someone who is "very angry":

   _____.

3. A long adjective beginning with *h* that means "pretending to have good

   attitudes without really having them": _____.

4. An adjective ending with *ic* and meaning "pictorial, vivid":

   _____.

5. A German word that begins the same way as the English word *anguish* and

   has a similar (but stronger) meaning:_____.

6. A noun meaning "careful observation," as in the phrase: *under*

   _____ .

7. The opposite of "sharpening" or "making brighter," as in the phrase

   _____ *effects.*

Talking It Over

In small groups, discuss the following questions.

1. What do you think of the Delmars and their TV habits?
2. What evidence do you find in the article for the good influence of TV?
3. What evidence do you find for the bad influence of TV?
4. Do you think that TV is too graphic in the way it shows violence? What is your opinion of TV in general? Should parents limit the number of hours their children watch TV or not?
5. Why does the author feel that most Americans are hypocritical about TV? Are you hypocritical about TV?
6. In your opinion, why does the author use different voices in the article? Do you like this technique?

Analyzing the Use of Anecdotal Evidence

exercise **2**

What do you think of the way the author uses the Delmars to represent American families? Is it fair? This kind of evidence is called *anecdotal evidence,* the use of anecdotes (short amusing stories or examples) to make a point. In your own words, what is the point that the author wants to make about American families?

_____

_____

_____

Analyzing the Evidence in Graphs or Charts

exercise **3**

Another type of evidence is the statistical evidence (presented in numbers and percentages) in graphs and charts. Look at the graph on page 137 and the chart on page 138 and answer these questions.

1. Are the Delmars a typical American family with regard to their TV habits? Why or why not?

2. What other countries probably have families with TV habits similar to those of the Delmars?

3. Do you think that affluence (high income, wealth) is a determining factor in TV watching, or not? Explain.

Taking Part in an Informal Debate

activity **2**

Half the class should try to defend the statement below, and the other half should try to show that it is wrong. Support your arguments by taking evidence (examples, quotes, statistics) from the article, the charts, or other sources and by giving opinions based on your own observation.

Television basically has a good influence on society because it does more good than harm.

For Casinos, "Six-Hour Visitors" Make a Full House

Before You Read

Identifying the Point of View

exercise

Authors do not always state their opinions directly. Often we must infer their point of view by reading "between the lines." In an article such as the following—about senior citizens who go to gambling casinos—an author could write in favor of this practice, against it, or from an *objective point of view* (one that is neutral, neither *for* nor *against*). Vocabulary can be a clue to point of view. Skim the article, paying attention to the words used to describe the seniors and the casinos. Are the words negative or positive? Then choose the best way to complete this sentence by placing a check (✓) in the correct box.

In the following article, the point of view of the author toward casino gambling by seniors is

1. positive (in favor of this) ☐
2. negative (against this) ☐
3. objective (neither in favor nor against) ☐

Are you a gambler? Gambling is a controversial subject, a subject that leads to debate and discussion. It used to be illegal in most parts of the United States and Canada, and some forms of gambling are still illegal in certain places. Some people view it as a harmless form of fun that makes life more interesting—especially for those with time on their hands. Others think of it as an evil enterprise that takes money from the poor and gives it to the rich. What do you think of gambling? Do you have a definite opinion about it? The following article examines a very popular type of gambling in North America. Read the article to learn more and form your own point of view about this controversial subject.

For Casinos, "Six-Hour Visitors" Make a Full House

She's a 77-year-old slightly overweight white-haired widowed grandmother from northeastern Pennsylvania who has worked the past fifteen years for the state at a mini-
5 mum wage "Green Thumb" job. But five or

10 six times a year, she and two of her closest friends pay $22 to a bus company that hauls passengers the four hours to Atlantic City, New Jersey.

"I can't afford not to go," Gloria Adams

---

says with a twinkle. Depending upon which casino the bus goes to, and which day of the week it is, each bus rider receives $10 to $15 in tokens from the casino, usually another $3 to $5 good for the next trip, and a $3 to $5 meal credit. She can choose from any of 92 restaurants or 30 cocktail lounges; if she eats at one of the lower-priced buffets, her meal is almost free. To lure 31 million "visitor trips" a year, one-third of whom come by bus, casinos spend about $800 million a year, one-fourth of their revenue, on promotion.

For most senior citizens, the $15 to $25 worth of "comps" is sufficient. But for the late evening "high rollers," the ones who think nothing of dropping a few hundred every blackjack hand or roll of the craps dice, the casinos will provide free limousine or helicopter service, luxury suites, food, beverages, show tickets, myriad trinkets from key chains to suits, and just about anything a loser could want.

Every day, about 800 buses, each carrying 40 to 50 passengers, most of them women over 55 years of age, pull into the casinos, stay six hours, then leave. With travel time, combined with limited bus parking, the casinos have figured that six hours is the "right" time for the "low-rollers."

On the casino floors, the senior citizens scramble to their favorite slots—they have 23,000 to choose from—and most won't leave for three or four hours, just shoving coin after coin into the machines, watching the dials spin and hoping for a jackpot. They'll crowd the nickel slots first; few ever try one of the 46 $100 slots. They'll put in five quarters, get a cherry and win two quarters which hit the metal coin tray and boldly announce yet another "winner." Sometimes,

they'll get minijackpots of 5, 10, even 20 times what they shoved into the slot. But they'll recycle the change, hoping for the Slotbusters payoff that'll give them and their grandchildren an income for life.

Sometimes, even if there are people waiting, they'll play two slots at once; if one doesn't pay, maybe its neighbor will.

And most go home with less money than they came with.

It's not unusual for bus travelers to drop $100 or $200 in their allotted six hours at the casino. A few have dropped most of their entire month's Social Security checks.

For their part, the casinos tell their players—in TV commercials, on all the printed literature, even in random announcements beamed from concealed loudspeakers—to "bet with your head, not over it." But then they put an acre of machines, tables, dealers, and provocatively dressed hostesses into an air-conditioned room that has no windows or clocks and entice their victims to sign up for plastic card memberships that, when inserted into slots, record the number of times a coin was dropped and lead to even more trinkets to lure them back into the casino.

The casino also sends employees around to convert currency into coins, provides free drinks for parched throats that yell encouragement to the machines, and [gives] "wipes" for fingers that become dirty handling all those winning coins. For those who have arthritis or don't have the energy to pull a lever, the slots even have push buttons. The casinos want their victims to sit there, in one spot, and lose. If they could figure out a way to catheterize* the players so they don't even have to go to the bathroom, they would.

Gloria Adams often comes back with more than she began with. "I know my limits, and I don't go over them," she says, emphasizing that unlike some players, she never resorts to using a MAC card to get "just a little more" playing cash.

It doesn't upset the casinos. They like it when people win. Nothing entices other people to lose money like the ching-chang of coins dropping into slot trays and the excited boasts of winners back home. But most of the gamblers are supposed to spend the freebies, then gamble some more. It has worked very well for more than 15 years.

Walter Brasch

*A medical term meaning to drain bodily fluids with a tube, as is often done for patients in hospitals.

After You Read

Guessing the Meaning of Slang from Context

 The word *comps* in line 25 is an example of the slang or jargon connected with gambling. If you know that the word *complimentary* means something given for free (such as a "complimentary drink"), then you can guess that *d* is the definition for *comps*. However, there is another word in the list that also corresponds to *d*. Can you guess which one it is? Scan the article to see the other slang terms in context and match them to their definitions.

1. _____ comps

2. _____ token

3. _____ high rollers

4. _____ low rollers

5. _____ jackpot

6. _____ MAC card

7. _____ freebies

a. people who gamble small amounts

b. people who gamble big money

c. a large amount of money won

d. items you get for free

e. document that gets you instant credit

f. plastic or metal coin used in exchange for goods or services

Identifying the Use of Onomatopoeia

Onomatopoeia is a long, hard word for an easy concept: words that imitate their meaning in their sound. For example, in English the sound of dynamite exploding is *boom!* At the end of the article, there is a reference to the *ching-chang* of coins dropping into trays. Pronounce each word on the left and use your ear to match it to what it describes.

1. _____ ding dong	**a.**	air going out of a tire
2. _____ bang bang	**b.**	vegetables frying in a pan
	c.	ringing a doorbell
3. _____ pop	**d.**	shooting a gun
4. _____ crash	**e.**	a chair falling down
	f.	breaking a balloon
5. _____ sizzle		
6. _____ hiss		

Paraphrasing the Main Idea

The author of this article uses both statistics and anecdotal evidence (colorful stories or examples) to develop a main idea. In your own words, write that idea. Do you agree with it or not? Why?

_____

_____

_____

_____

Building a Word Description

activity **1**

Look at the first sentence of the article. It describes the typical gambler at some casinos this way: (1) age (adjective), (2) and (3) appearance (adjectives), (4) marital status (adjective), (5) family relationship (noun), (6) origin (phrase beginning with *from*), (7) reference to work or accomplishment (clause beginning with *who*). Use this formula to make up original sentences that describe some famous people. See if your classmates can guess who they are.

example: She's a beautiful, young, tiny-footed, unmarried, orphan girl from a fairy tale who marries a handsome rich prince and lives happily ever after. (Cinderella)

Would You Like to Take a Gamble?

Prepare a short talk about some form of gambling—perhaps one that is popular in your culture or with your friends. In small groups, take turns giving your talks. Describe how the gambling works and how much money people usually win or lose. If possible, tell what kinds of lures are used to get people to participate. Then give your point of view about this form of gambling and ask if others would like to try it or not. Here are a few possibilities to talk about: horse racing, dog racing, mah jong, bingo, poker, cockfights, roulette, lotteries, football bets.

Talking It Over

In small groups, discuss the following questions.

1. Who is Gloria Adams? Why does the author talk about her?

2. Can you explain Gloria's words: "I can't afford not to go"?

3. How much do the casinos in Atlantic City spend each year to lure (attract) customers? In your opinion, why are they so "generous"?

4. What is the difference in the treatment between the high rollers and the low rollers?

---

focus on testing

Previewing the Questions

Use the timed-reading exercise in the next selection, "Soccer and American Football," to practice reading under the stress of test conditions. Imagine that you are taking an exam and must keep an eye on the clock. The exam questions that you will have to answer follow the reading.

What is the first thing you should do before beginning? Preview. Go immediately to the questions at the end of the reading to see what kind of information is asked for. Is it small details or large ideas? Skim the reading selection. Where is the information you need for these questions? Is it in one section, or will you have to read two or more sections to answer some questions?

After previewing, read the selection for the answers.

Soccer and American Football

Before You Read

Timed Reading

Use the following selection to practice reading fast for a special purpose. Read to find out what differences and similarities there are between soccer and American football. Then take the quiz at the end. Try to finish both in 12 minutes.

Soccer is probably the most popular team sport in the world, but in the United States, American football is king—even though soccer is now gaining favor among some fans. In what ways are they alike? In what ways are they different? To find out, read the following two-part selection about the two sports, taken from the book *Rules of the Game.*

Soccer and American Football

Soccer is a ball game played by two teams, each made up of 11 players. The object of the game is to put the ball into the opponents' goal, and the winning team is the one that scores the greater number of goals.

The field. The field is rectangular and must be 50 to 130 yards long. At
5   either end there is a goal and a goal area enclosed in the larger penalty area. The posts and crossbar of the goals must be of equal width and of the same width as the goal line. The touchlines and the goal lines are part of the playing area.

The ball. The ball is made of leather or other approved material. At the
10   start of a game it must weigh 14 to 16 ounces and should be inflated to a pressure of 15 pounds per square inch. The ball may not be changed during a game without the referee's permission.

Officials. A referee controls the game and is assisted by two linespeople.

Dress. The goalkeeper must wear different colors to distinguish him or
15   her from the other players and the referee. All other players on the team must wear uniform jerseys or shirts, shorts, and socks. Shin pads are an optional protection. Boots may be studded or have bars of leather and rubber across the soles. Studs must be of solid leather, rubber, plastic, aluminum, or similar material, but they must be rounded and not less than $1/2$
20   inch in diameter or more than $1/2$ inch long from the mounting. Gloves are frequently worn by goalkeepers. Numbers are usually worn on the back of the jersey.

Teams. Each team has 11 players, one of whom is the goalkeeper.

25 *Substitutes.* One or two substitutes are usually permitted, depending on the competition, but must be named before the game. Once substituted, a player may not return to the game.

Duration. The game is played in two halves of 45 minutes each; the teams change ends at halftime. The halftime interval may not exceed 5 minutes, except by consent of the referee.

A soccer game in Mexico City's Estadio Azteca (Aztec Stadium)

30 *Playing the ball.* Except at throw-ins, the goalkeeper is the only player allowed to play the ball with his or her hands or arms, and that may be done only within the team's own penalty area. 35 Players may, however, use any other part of the body in order to stop, control, or pass the ball, move with it, or score. They may use their (1) feet, (2) head, (3) thigh, (4) chest.

40 *Scoring.* A goal is scored when the whole of the ball has crossed the goal line under the crossbar and between the goal posts, provided that the attacking team has not infringed the laws.

45 *Result.* The team scoring the greater number of goals wins. If the number of goals scored is equal, the result is a draw, though in some competitions draws are resolved by: replays, a period of extra time (usually two halves of 15 minutes each) immediately after the 90 minutes; a series of penalty kicks; or the toss of a coin.

50 ## American Football

In American football two teams with 11 players on the field attempt to score points by kicking goals or putting the ball behind their opponents' goal line in an approved manner. The winning team is the one that scores the greater number of points.

55 *The field.* The area between the end lines and sidelines is the field of play. The field is divided between the goal lines by parallel yard lines, 5 yards apart. These are intersected by short inbound lines 70 feet 9 inches from each sideline. Between the inbound lines there are marks at 1-yard intervals. All measurements are made from the inside edges of the lines. 60 Sidelines and end lines are out of bounds; goal lines are in the end zones.

The ball. The ball is an inflated rubber bladder enclosed in a leather case—length: 11 to $11\frac{3}{4}$ inches; long circumference: 28 to $28\frac{1}{2}$ inches; short circumference: $21\frac{1}{4}$ to $21\frac{1}{2}$ inches; weight: 14 to 15 ounces.

The officials. Officials have individual functions, but they are equally responsible for signaling and recording fouls. They all wear uniforms, including a white cap with a visor, and carry a whistle and a flag. The officials are the: (1) referee, (2) umpire, (3) linesman, (4) field judge, (5) back judge, and (6) line judge.

Dress. Each player wears: (1) a helmet made of plastic or leather; (2) a face mask made of nonbreakable molded plastic with the edges either rounded or edged with rubber coated wire; (3) a jersey in the team color, which must not be similar to the color of the ball; (4) numbers at least 8 inches high on the chest and 10 inches high on the back (ends are numbered 80 to 89, tackles 70 to 79, guards 60 to 69, centers 50 to 59, backs 10 to 49); (5) chest and shoulder padding; (6) rib and kidney padding; (7) pants; (8) below-the-belt padding; (9) thigh padding; (10) shin padding; (11) light-weight shoes.

Football game between the 49ers and the Rams

Teams. Each team has 11 players, one of whom is the captain. No team is allowed more than 40 players in uniform.

Substitution. Unlimited substitution is allowed, but substitutes are allowed on the field only when the ball is dead (not in play).

Duration. There are 60 minutes actual playing time, divided into four quarters, of which two comprise a half. Playing time excludes stoppages and other interruptions. There is a 2-minute interval between the periods of each half; only an incoming substitute may enter the field. There is a 15-minute interval at halftime.

Playing the ball. Players may kick, carry, and throw the ball subject to certain restrictions, such as the number of forward passes allowed. They may not bat or punch: (1) a loose ball toward the opponents' goal lines; (2) a loose ball in an end zone; (3) the ball when a player has possession.

A pass in flight may be batted in any direction by the defending side, but the offensive side may only bat such a ball to prevent the other team from intercepting the ball.

If the player with the ball touches the ground with any body part except hands or feet, the ball is dead. A team in possession is allowed 30 seconds to put the ball into play.

Scoring. (1) A touchdown (6 points) occurs when a player carries the ball across the opponents' goal line or recovers a loose ball on or behind the opponents' goal line. (2) After a touchdown, the scoring team is allowed an attempt to score an additional point from a scrimmage taken between the inbound line and at least 2 yards from the opponents' goal line. The point may be scored from a kick, another touchdown, or a safety. As soon as the opposition touches the kicked ball, it is dead. (3) A field goal (3 points) occurs when a player kicks the whole of the ball through the opponents' goal, without it touching the ground or any of his own players, from a place kick or drop kick after a scrimmage or from a free kick after a fair catch. After a missed field-goal attempt, the ball is returned to the line of scrimmage or the 20-yard line, whichever is farther from the goal line. (4) A safety (2 points) occurs when a team sends the ball into its own end zone and it becomes dead in its possession or out of play behind its goal line. It is also awarded if a team in possession commits a foul behind its goal line.

Overtime period. If the game ends in a tie, a 15-minute sudden-death period is played. The kickoff is determined by the toss of a coin, and the game is won by the first team to score in the extra period. If there is no score, the tie stands.

Rules of the Game

After You Read

Comprehension Quiz

Tell whether each of the statements below and on the next page applies to soccer (S), American football (F), or both (B).

1. __B__ The game is played by two teams of 11 players each.

2. __B__ A substitute may be sent in to replace a player taken out of the game.

3. __S__ Once a player leaves, he or she is not permitted to play again in that game.

4. __F__ Many substitutes can be sent in during the game.

5. __S__ The goalkeeper is an important player.

6. __F__ The officials include a referee, a linesman, and a field judge.

7. __F__ The numbers on the back of the players' uniforms tell spectators what position they are playing.

8. __S__ The players wear shirts, shorts, and boots that are usually studded. *cleats*

9. __F__ The players must wear helmets and a lot of padding.

10. _B_   There are goal lines at both ends of the field.

11. _S_   Most of the players are not allowed to carry the ball in their hands.

12. _S_   A player is allowed to hit a loose ball toward the opponents' goal with his or her head, feet, or chest.

13. _F_   After a touchdown, the scoring team is permitted to attempt to score an extra point.

14. _B_   The ball may weigh 15 ounces.

15. _B_   The game may end in a draw or tie.

Talking It Over

activity

In small groups, discuss the following questions.

1. Why do you think that so many people like to watch soccer and football?

2. On the basis of what you have read, which of the two games do you think is more complicated? Why? *Football*

3. What sports are important in your life? *None*

4. Some people feel that the salaries of the top players in many sports are too high. Do you agree or not? Why? *yes specially y football and basketball*

WHAT DO YOU THINK?

Exercising

Do you think exercise is good for you? Why or why not? Look at the list of sports and other activities and the calories burned per hour by doing the activities. What activities from the list do you prefer? Why?

Activity	Calories Burned	Activity	Calories Burned
Badminton	300–660	Housework	180–360
Basketball	480–720	Judo/karate	480–720
Bowling	300–360	Lying in bed	78
Cycling	300–720	Sailing	180–420
Carpentry	180–540	Sitting	90
Decorating	240–300	Soccer	480–720
Dancing	420–540	Table tennis	300–540
Golf	180–360	Volleyball	240–480
Handball	480–720	Walking	170–300

CHAPTER eight

Creativity

in this chapter

Exactly what makes a person creative? A precise answer to this question will always remain a mystery, but this chapter presents readings about three people who have become famous in the twentieth century for their creative work in very different fields: science, architecture, and filmmaking. Another selection, written by one of the world's best-known anthropologists, discusses the controversial question: Are men more creative than women?

New York Botanist Wins Nobel Medical Prize

Before You Read

Scanning and Inventing Definitions for Technical Terms

 *exercise*

Scan the first half of the article for the important technical terms that belong in the blanks below. The first letter of each term is provided to help you. Fill in the rest of the word. Then, using clues from the context and the hints given, write a definition in your own words for each term.

1. In the first paragraph, we see that McClintock's discovery involves

g_____. The third paragraph tells us what these are.

Definition: _____

_____

2. Before McClintock made her discovery, these elements were thought to be

stationary—that is, without movement. The first paragraph tells us that she

found that they in fact move from one part of the c_____ to

another. What does this term mean?

Definition: _____

_____

3. The title tells us that McClintock is a b_____ . In the fourth

paragraph, we learn what she worked with. Usually a branch of science is

defined by what is worked with or studied. For example, a linguist is a

person who studies languages because *lingua* means language.

Definition: _____

4. The fourth paragraph states that McClintock's discovery aids the under-

standing of how b_____ can become resistant to antibiotic drugs.

We know that these drugs are used to fight certain diseases and infections.

So, we can give a working definition of this term by telling what it causes.

Definition: _____

_____

The title of this article tells what it is about: a scientist who won the famous Nobel Prize in the field of medicine. Even now, after her death in 1992, this scientist, Barbara McClintock, continues to attract special attention for two reasons: (1) she was a woman in a field in which few women have excelled, and (2) she was known as a *maverick* whose work was so original that it was disregarded for many years. This ability to see ahead of her times is described in a biography of McClintock: "Later, in her mid-forties, her research in the cytogenetics of maize (corn), brought her to concepts so new and so radical that her colleagues had difficulty 'hearing them.'"*

In any article about a person winning an award, three questions immediately come to mind: *Who? What?* and *Why?* Who is this person? What did she or he do? Why is it important? You should focus on these three questions as you read the article.

New York Botanist Wins Nobel Medical Prize

Barbara McClintock, Ph.D., an eighty-one-year-old American botanist won the 1983 Nobel Prize for Medicine. Dr. McClintock won the prize alone because she
5 worked and published by herself. She was honored for her discovery that genes unexpectedly can wander from one position on a chromosome to another, causing sudden evolutionary changes.
10 Her discovery of these wandering genetic elements known as "jumping genes" was made some thirty years ago and originally was regarded with doubt and disbelief by other scientists because it went against
15 the accepted view that genes were stationary. Only recently, with the development of molecular biology into a major scientific discipline, has the importance of her work been recognized.
20 Officials of the Nobel committee in Stockholm, Sweden, called her work "the second great discovery of our time" in ge-

Barbara McClintock, Ph.D. Nobel officials called her discovery of jumping genes "the second great discovery of our time" in genetics.

*From *A Feeling for the Organism*, by Evelyn Fox Keller, Preface.

netics—second to the discovery that genes are strands of chemicals arranged in a dou-
25 ble helix* that can separate and transmit hereditary traits.

Dr. McClintock's pioneering studies involved changes in the color of corn kernels. She grew crop after crop of purplish maize
30 and observed its changes over long years. Her work has led other scientists to an understanding of how jumping genes can allow bacteria to become resistant to antibiotic drugs, how viruses work, how normal cells
35 may be transformed into cancer cells, and, by laboratory methods based on her work, how inherited genes can be mechanically transferred from one living organism to another.

40 Dr. McClintock was the first woman to win the Nobel Prize for Medicine alone and the third woman to win that award. She was the third woman to win any unshared Nobel science prize. Marie Curie was first in 1911

45 for discovering radium and polonium, and Dorothy Crowfoot-Hodgkin was second in 1964 for determining the molecular structure of penicillin and other substances. Both won for chemistry.

50 After learning that she had won the award, the shy and retiring scientist said that she was overwhelmed by "such an extraordinary honor." She added, "It might seem unfair, however, to reward a person for hav-
55 ing so much pleasure over the years, asking the maize plant to solve specific problems and then watching its responses."

Dr. McClintock once said, "You don't need the public recognition; you just need the
60 respect of your colleagues." She commented that she knew when she was conducting the research that it was not "acceptable," but she said, "That was all right. . . . When you know you're right, you don't care. You know
65 sooner or later it will come out in the wash."

American Medical News

---

*Two spiral chains of complementary nucleic acid

After You Read
Summarizing Written Information

activity **1**

The following outline for a summary of the article is based on the key questions that should be answered in this type of article: *Who? What? Why?* Working in small groups, fill in the outline in your own words as fully as possible.

1. Barbara McClintock: *Who* was she? (Personal data about age, education, where and how she worked.)

_____

_____

_____

_____

_____

_____

2. *What* did she discover? (Data about her work, its novelty [newness], her methods.)

_____

_____

_____

_____

_____

3. *Why* is it important? (Data on the significance of her discovery and how it might be used.)

_____

_____

_____

_____

_____

4. More about *who* she was. (More about her character and personality; her own thoughts about her work. Do you understand her statements quoted at the end of the article? What can you infer about her from the type of language she uses?)

_____

_____

_____

_____

_____

Stories Behind Words

activity **2**

First read the following paragraph about the Nobel Prize. Then, in small groups, discuss the questions that follow.

The Nobel Prize takes its name from its founder, the Swedish chemist and engineer Alfred Nobel (1833–1896), who was also the inventor of dynamite. Ironically, the reason for his invention was to promote peace. He claimed that he wanted "to produce a substance or a machine of such frightful efficacy for wholesale devastation that wars should thereafter become altogether impossible." Seeing that his invention was being used for totally opposite purposes, he determined at least to produce some good from the vast amounts of money his invention had earned him, and so he established the Nobel Prize.

1. How much do you know about the Nobel Prize? Do you know when and where it is awarded? In what fields?

2. Do you think that the Nobel Prize and other similar awards help or hinder the advancement of the arts and sciences? Why?

3. In your opinion, are these prizes sometimes awarded for reasons other than merit? Do you know of any people who received the Nobel Prize although they didn't deserve it? Do you know of any people who should have received the Nobel Prize but didn't?

Finding Out About Creative People

activity **3**

In what way was Barbara McClintock creative? In small groups, think of some creative people who were not appreciated when they were doing important work. You may choose them from the fields of science, politics, business, the arts, or some other field. Prepare a brief report (oral or written, according to your teacher's instructions) on one of these people, using the basic organization of *who, what,* and *why.* Encyclopedias provide a ready source of information on famous people. Can you think of any other sources?

SELECTION **two**

Guggenheim Museum U.S.A.

Before You Read

Checking Your Knowledge of Shapes and Forms

exercise

When you read the following article, you will notice a number of references to shapes and forms. So here is a brief review of the names of some of them. Study the illustrations on page 157; then complete sentences 1 to 6 appropriately.

1. A square extended into three dimensions is a _____ .

2. A _____ extended into three dimensions is a pyramid.

3. Any two-dimensional figure with four sides and four right angles is a

   _____ .

4. A closed, two-dimensional figure that usually has more than four sides is a

   _____ .

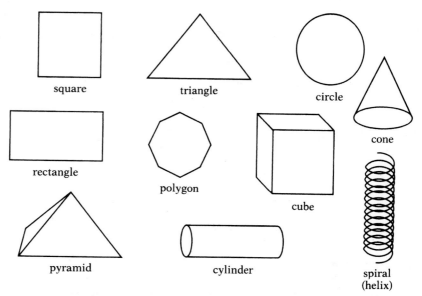

square triangle circle cone rectangle polygon cube pyramid cylinder spiral (helix)

5. The combination of a cylinder and a pyramid is a _____ . (Ice cream is often served in these.)

6. Some seashells (and bed springs and screws) are in the form of a

_____ , which may also be called a _____ .

A common characteristic of many creative works is innovation, the starting of something new. This quality is certainly apparent in the famous Guggenheim Museum, as you can see by looking at the photos that illustrate the following article. Although opened in 1959, the museum still strikes the eye as new and unusual. What other famous examples of innovative or unusual architecture do you know? What kind of person do you think would design a building like this? What reasons do you think he or should would have?

Guggenheim Museum U.S.A.

In 1932, New York's Museum of Modern Art assembled what was clearly meant to be a definitive exhibition of modern architecture. It presented the work of Frank Lloyd Wright along with that of Le Corbusier,* and Ludwig Mies van der Rohe and Walter Gropius, two leaders of Germany's revolutionary design school, the Bauhaus.† On that occasion, Wright commented, "I warn you that having made an excellent start, I fully intend not only to be the greatest architect that has ever been but also the greatest of all future architects."

5

Le Corbusier (1887–1965) was a Swiss architect and city planner who lived in France. His buildings are characterized by daring and original design.
†A school of design founded in Germany in 1919 and continued in Chicago after 1937. The Bauhaus taught the importance of technical mastery and craftsmanship.

Wright's pride in his own work was understandable. When his three co-exhibitors were still in grade school, he was already designing remarkably innovative houses, any one of which could have established him as first among contemporary architects. With the help of devoted assistants, Wright had created dozens of these houses, year after year. By 1932, Wright's work had become highly individualistic—often with hints of expressionism* that would surface in his design for the Guggenheim Museum.

Frank Lloyd Wright's childhood had been shaped by a New England heritage of liberal Protestantism and an acceptance of the "natural philosophy" that was expressed in the writings of Walt Whitman and Henry David Thoreau. These two American writers believed that much of modern human anguish was due to urban environments and loss of contact with nature. The human foot had been made to touch earth, not concrete, and human dwellings were meant to be in harmony with their natural surroundings. In the spirited and energetic atmosphere of the times, it is perhaps not surprising that Wright also developed that insistence upon absolute freedom of mind that marks the true pioneer as well as the renowned artist. This is why he so often seemed more concerned with finding the proper form for an idea than with pleasing his clients. To Wright, the artistic integrity of his work was far more important than its practical function. Once, when the owner of one of his houses called to say that rain was dripping on him from a crack in the ceiling, Wright is said to have suggested that the man move his chair.

Both Wright's genius and obstinacy came to play their roles in his design for the Guggenheim Museum in New York City. In the early 1940s, Solomon R. Guggenheim, who was committed to the development of modern painting, found himself in need of more space to house a growing collection of pictures. He decided that a museum of modern art ought to be the work of a leading modern architect. Ironically, he turned to Wright, a man known to have little liking for twentieth-century painting, and commissioned him to design the new museum. Wright's creation is one of the most original buildings in the world, a museum with its own place in the history of art. Yet as a picture gallery, it is a failure. Ultimately, the only thing it displays well is itself.

Perhaps at the time that the plans for the Guggenheim were being drawn up, the administrators of the museum were unaware of Wright's growing rejection of conventional square and rectangular forms of city buildings and blocks. Wright was continually searching for natural forms

---

*A style of painting developed in the twentieth century, in which the expression of emotion is considered more important than the representation of reality. Colors and forms are often distorted or exaggerated.

Solomon R. Guggenheim Museum, which house a private collection of paintings

appropriate to human needs, forms that he described as "organic architecture, opening onto the world rather than insulating people from it." So
he had begun to explore the possibilities of the triangle, the polygon (recalling the form of mineral crystals), and even the circle. For some time, he
had been ready to take the logical step from the circle to the spiral, the
form of conch shells, "plastic and continuous." This form is more properly
called a helix, and is really a circle carried to the third dimension. Wright
boldly designed the new building in the shape of an inverted conical spiral, and convinced Solomon Guggenheim that this form would make a
magnificent museum.

The museum is essentially a long ramp that starts at ground level and
spirals upward in five concentric turns, continually growing wider so that
it opens out toward the top. Within the spiral is a vast central space, illuminated primarily by a huge skylight. At the first-floor level, the main spiral is joined with a smaller, round building, used for readings, lectures,
and offices. A broad horizontal rectilinear base connects both elements
and also relates the museum as a whole to its rectilinear environment of
city blocks and conventional buildings.

In defense of his stunningly original design, Wright declared that he was not merely playing a game with forms: He believed that the helix was really the best shape for a picture gallery. He claimed that the conventional manner of displaying paintings in one dreary room after another distracts the attention of visitors by making them concerned with the condition of their feet rather than the masterpieces on the walls. According to Wright, this museum fatigue was the result of bad architecture. At the

The interior of the Guggenheim Museum, with its spiral exhibition area

Guggenheim, visitors would enter on the ground floor and be carried by elevator up to the top, where they would begin to slowly wind down along the spiral. Any weariness would be counteracted by the natural form of the shell, which would gently "spiral" visitors down to the first floor. As they descended, they would be able to study the paintings hung along the outward-leaning walls. In this way, each work of art would be viewed at an angle—as Wright believed the artist himself had seen it on the easel. But in reality, the museum is a challenge. Visitors must make their way down a ramp at an angle, studying paintings hung on a wall that both curves and slopes.

As a building, however, the Guggenheim Museum defines a magnificent space and has become a compulsory stop on even the most basic tour of New York. The startling effect of the Guggenheim lies in its unusual form and stark simplicity. While it was under construction—and remaining upright in apparent defiance of gravity—Wright would smirk happily and say of his colleagues, "They'll spend years trying to work it out."

Flavio Conti

After You Read
Making Inferences and Drawing Conclusions

exercise **1**

What inferences can you make or conclusions can you draw about Wright and his relationships with people from the following statements taken from the article?

1. "Wright commented, 'I warn you that having made an excellent start, I fully intend not only to be the greatest architect that has ever been but also the greatest of all future architects.'" (lines 6 to 8)

_____

_____

_____

2. "With the help of devoted assistants, Wright had created dozens of these [innovative] houses, year after year." (lines 12 to 13)

_____

_____

_____

3. "Once, when the owner of one of his houses called to say that rain was dripping on him from a crack in the ceiling, Wright is said to have suggested that the man move his chair." (lines 30 to 32)

_____

_____

_____

Word Detective

exercise **2**

Play detective and find the following words in the article, using the clues given below and the number of blanks as aids.

1. An adjective beginning with *c* that means "present-day"

_ _ _ _ _ _ _ _ _ _ _ _ (paragraph 2)

2. A noun beginning with *p* that means "a person who goes before, preparing the way for others in a new region or field of work." This word is often used to refer to the early settlers of the American West.

_ _ _ _ _ _ _ _ (paragraph 3)

3. A synonym for *stubbornness* that begins with *o*

_ _ _ _ _ _ _ _ _ (paragraph 4)

4. The opposite of *original* or *unusual,* beginning with *c*

_ _ _ _ _ _ _ _ _ _ _ _ (paragraph 5)

5. Two synonyms for *tiredness,* one beginning with *f* and the other with *w*

_ _ _ _ _ _ _   _ _ _ _ _ _ _ _ _ (paragraph 7)

6. A smile is *not* always nice: a noun that begins the same way as the word *smile* but means a smile that is offensive, insulting, or irritating

_ _ _ _ _ (paragraph 8)

Talking It Over

In small groups, discuss the following questions.

1. Exactly what is innovative about Wright's design for the Guggenheim? Why did he choose to build it this way?

2. Referring to the Guggenheim Museum, the article states: "Yet as a picture gallery, it is a failure. Ultimately, the only thing it displays well is itself." Is this a fact or an opinion? Explain.

3. When you travel to new cities, do you pay attention to their architecture? Does it have an influence on you? In which city or region has the architecture impressed you the most? Why?

4. If you have seen the Guggenheim Museum, describe your reaction to it. If you have not seen it, tell what you think of it based on the article and photos.

5. For you, what is most important about a building?

focus on testing

Thinking Twice About Tricky Questions

The multiple-choice exercise is a common test format for reading comprehension. Usually it requires that you look back and scan for information. The items generally follow the order of appearance, so when you do the following exercise, look for the answer to question 1 at the very beginning of the selection—"Guggenheim Museum U.S.A."—in the first two paragraphs.

You will see that question 1 is "tricky" because the answer is not given directly. You must make inferences. Look at each of the possibilities. Two of them relate to age, but the other is different. Check that one first. Is there evidence that Wright was "unknown" at that time? If not, how can you infer his age, compared to the other participants in the exhibit?

Look at the rest of the items in the exercise. Which ones are straight memory questions with answers given directly in the reading? Which ones are "tricky" and require inferences?

exercise   Circle the letter of the best response, according to the reading selection "Guggenheim Museum U.S.A."

1. When the exhibition of modern architecture was presented in New York in 1932, Frank Lloyd Wright was
   a. the oldest of the participants
   b. the youngest of the participants
   c. unknown

2. In his architectural work Wright was most concerned with
   a. expressing his heritage of liberal Protestantism
   b. finding the correct form for an idea
   c. making his clients happy

3. It is ironic that Solomon Guggenheim chose Wright to design his museum of modern art because
   a. it is one of the most original buildings in the world
   b. he found himself in need of more space for his collection
   c. Wright did not like modern art very much

4. Wright was searching for an "organic architecture" that would use forms found in nature, such as the
   a. square
   b. cube
   c. polygon

5. One of the strikingly original aspects of the Guggenheim Museum is that it follows the form of an upside-down cone in a
   a. spiral
   b. pyramid
   c. rectangle

6. Another unusual characteristic of the Guggenheim is that
   a. it is illuminated only by five huge skylights
   b. visitors view paintings while they walk down a ramp
   c. paintings are displayed in one dreary room after another

SELECTION three

We Can't Just Sit Back and Hope

Before You Read

Inferring the Intended Image of an Interview

An interview gives the reader a double point of view: that of the interviewer and that of the person being interviewed. We can make judgments about the person from that person's own words (enclosed in quotation marks) and also from the interviewer's comments. Of course, the interviewer cannot tell us everything, so she or he selects topics and quotes to project a particular image of the person inter-

Mosaic I • Reading

viewed. Look at the title and skim the interview. Then decide which of the following descriptions fits the image of Steven Spielberg that the author Dotson Rader intends to show.

1. A hard-working, ambitious man intent on gaining fame and money
2. A sensitive man influenced by family and traditional values
3. A temperamental genius with a deep desire to create beauty

Steven Spielberg is one of today's most successful Hollywood movie directors. A mark of his creativity is the great diversity of his films. Look at the list at the end of the article. How many different types of movies are on it? The following interview with Spielberg presents a personal view of the man and his motivation for making films.

We Can't Just Sit Back and Hope

Very early on, when he was eight, Steven Spielberg was drawn to filmmaking, although he had seen few movies, mostly Disney features. He recalls being fascinated by
5 visual images—comic books, art and TV, even though his parents let him watch very little, instead keeping a blanket over the set. He was a slow reader. He didn't read as a boy, he says, he *gazed*. Out of his obsession
10 with the visual came a gift for storytelling. I asked what compelled him to tell stories.

"I was always drawn to stories because my need was I wanted to be the center of attention," he replied, smiling. "It's as simple
15 as that. I'd be in a new school, and needed to stand out. What I discovered was I love telling stories. I come from a family of three younger sisters, and we were all fighting for our position in the family, and we were all
20 trying hard to be recognized by our parents. My sisters did things that were unique, but I did something that was more unique than all of them put together. I had a movie camera, and I could make movies."

25 His first movie camera was an 8-mm Kodak borrowed from his father.

"I could use my sisters as actors in my films, I could trash them in any way I felt like," he explained with boyish delight. "Kill
30 them over and over and it was all in the interest of telling a good story. And then I could show my little 8 mm films to my parents and get them to react. It was how I originally found my position in the family. I discovered
35 something I could do, and people would be interested in it and me. I knew after my third or fourth little 8 mm epic that this was going

to be a career, not just a hobby. I had learned that film was power."

When Spielberg was a teenager, his parents divorced, and the hurtful impact of that event would become a recurring theme in his movies — children uprooted by divorce, young lives suddenly rendered incomplete. He has said that his film, *E.T.—The Extraterrestrial* was born of his longing for an older brother and a father who slipped away.

In his late teens, Spielberg moved with his family from Arizona to northern California, where he attended high school and continued making his movies. He neglected his academic studies, and his grades reflected it. After graduation, he wasn't accepted by any major film school, so he attended Cal State at Long Beach. During this period, he made a 22-minute short, *Amblin',* a road picture about a girl and boy hitching from the Mojave Desert to the ocean. This small movie changed his life.

Amblin' won awards at the Venice and Atlanta film festivals, and it caught the eye of Sidney Sheinberg, then head of TV production at Universal. Sheinberg signed Spielberg to a seven-year contract.

What makes so many of his films so successful? What makes them different?

"I don't know what makes them different," he replied. "Ninety percent of my movies are old-fashioned in the way a Frank Capra or a Preston Sturges movie is. A lot of the films I've made probably could have worked just as well 50 years ago, and that's just because I have a lot of old-fashioned values.

"I'm a fuddy-duddy. I'm a real stick-in-the-mud fuddy-duddy. I'm very 'retro,' as my son calls me. I don't let my kids watch a lot of television, as my parents didn't let me.

But I do think it's a mistake to censor from my children the news. I don't want them coming of age and suddenly realizing that there's a whole world out there that they missed and they're ill-prepared to accept."

Spielberg is a doting and . . . protective father. Given that, I said, how can he defend the sex and violence in American entertainment?

"I don't," he answered, "but neither do I want government censorship. We [in show business] have to be responsible for the content of what we put on the airwaves, in theaters, or sell in video and record stores. But there's a fine line between censorship and good taste and moral responsibility."

Given the suffering of this century and given the violence in our own American towns, I asked if he saw much hope.

Scene from the Universal City Studios and Amblin Entertainment movie *Jurassic Park*

"I've always been very hopeful," Spielberg replied. "But we can't sit back and be inactive. We all have to be more active in 100 our groups, communities, religions, in affecting world opinion. We can't just sit by and hope the guns and drugs will go away. We have a responsibility. We have a duty to voice our opinion and to work to fix the 105 world."

Dotson Rader

After You Read
Finding Synonymous Vocabulary

 Find the words in the article that are close in meaning to the italicized words or phrases.

1. As a boy, Spielberg didn't read very much; he *watched intently.*

_____

_____

2. Out of his *great preoccupation* with the visual came his gift for storytelling.

_____

_____

3. He wanted to do something more *special and different* than the things his sisters did.

_____

_____

4. Many of his movies have certain *repetitive* themes.

_____

_____

5. Spielberg didn't do very well at *scholarly* studies.

_____

_____

6. He has a lot of *traditional* values that are reflected in his films.

_____

_____

7. As a father, he is concerned about violence but does not want to *remove the opportunity of viewing* the news from his children.

_____

_____

Paraphrasing Main Ideas

 In your own words, explain the following ideas presented in the interview.

1. The relationship between Spielberg's position in the family and his career

_____

_____

2. The divorce of his parents and the influence it had on him

_____

_____

3. Spielberg's views on censorship

_____

_____

4. His feelings about hope and responsibility

_____

_____

Talking It Over

 In small groups, discuss the following questions.

1. In your opinion is the position of a child in the family (as oldest, youngest, etc.) important for the child's character? Explain.

2. Did luck play a role in Spielberg's becoming a director?

3. What are "old-fashioned values"? Are they necessary for good films?

4. Do you think there should be more censorship of films to eliminate a lot of the sex and violence? Why or why not?

5. What movie do you consider a creative work of art? Why?

WHAT DO YOU THINK?

Creativity in Men and Women

Margaret Mead, one of the most famous and widely read anthropologists of the twentieth century, expressed her ideas on creativity in men and women. Why do you think that men have achieved more than women in almost every field throughout history? Read the following selection by Mead. Do you agree with her views on marriage and public achievement? Do you think that men are more creative than women? Why or why not? Do you believe that given equal opportunities in all fields—science, business, art, politics—women and men can create equally? Which of Mead's three positions on male and female creativity do you agree/disagree with?

Are Men More Creative Than Women?

Throughout history it has been men, for the most part, who have engaged in public life. Men have sought public achievement and recognition, while women have obtained their main satisfactions by bearing and rearing children. In women's eyes,
5   public achievement makes a man more attractive as a marriage

partner. But for men the situation is reversed. The more a woman achieves publicly, the less desirable she seems as a wife.

There are three possible positions one can take about male and female creativity. The first is that males are inherently more creative in all fields. The second is that if it were not for the greater appeal of creating and cherishing young human beings, females would be as creative as males. If this were the case, then if men were permitted the enjoyment women have always had in rearing young children, male creativity might be reduced also. (There is some indication in the United States today that this is so.) The third possible position is that certain forms of creativity are more congenial to one sex than to the other and that the great creative acts will therefore come from only one sex in a given field.

Margaret Mead
Selections from *Some Personal Views,* 1979

Human Behavior

The way people behave can be viewed in many ways. Human behavior is studied in a disciplined and sometimes scientific way by anthropologists, psychologists, and sociologists. It has also been observed and recorded for centuries in literature. Here we start with a selection from an anthropology textbook that examines the way people evaluate their own culture and other cultures. Next are a short story and a poem that focus on people's attitudes toward their environment.

SELECTION **one**
Ethnocentrism

Before You Read
Scanning for a Key Definition

The title of the selection is a term commonly used by anthropologists, but the average English-speaking reader would not be familiar with it. In fact, the purpose of the whole selection is to give you an idea of what this term means and why it is important. Scan the first two paragraphs to find the author's explanation and write your own working definition of the term here.

ethnocentrism: _____

_____

_____

Is *eskimo* or *inuit* the correct term for the people who inhabit the Arctic? Should we feel repelled if we are asked to eat snake or dog? The following selection, taken from a textbook on anthropology, discusses these and other questions related to human behavior. Anthropology is defined in the dictionary as "the science that deals with the origins, physical and cultural development, racial characteristics, and social customs and beliefs of humankind." What do you imagine when you think of anthropologists? Do you think they are more concerned with the present or the past?

Ethnocentrism

Culture shock can be an excellent lesson in relative values and in understanding human differences. The reason culture shock occurs is that we are not prepared for these differences. Because of the way we are taught our culture, we are all *ethnocentric.* This term comes from the Greek root *ethnos,* meaning a people or group. Thus, it refers to the fact that our outlook or world view is centered on our own way of life. Ethnocentrism is the belief that one's own patterns of behavior are the best: the most natural, beautiful, right, or important. Therefore, other people, to the extent that they live differently, live by standards that are inhuman, irrational, unnatural, or wrong.

Ethnocentrism is the view that one's own culture is better than all others; it is the way all people feel about themselves as compared to outsiders. There is no one in our society who is not ethnocentric to some degree, no matter how liberal and open-minded he or she might claim to be. People will always find some aspect of another culture distasteful, be it

5

10

15

172   Mosaic I • Reading sexual practices, a way of treating friends or relatives, or simply a food that they cannot manage to get down with a smile. This is not something we should be ashamed of, because it is a natural outcome of growing up in any society. However, as anthropologists who study other cultures, it is something we should constantly be aware of, so that when we are tempted to make value judgments about another way of life, we can look at the situation objectively and take our bias into account.

Ethnocentrism can be seen in many aspects of culture—myths, folktales, proverbs, and even language. For example, in many languages, especially those of non-Western societies, the word used to refer to one's own tribe or ethnic group literally means "mankind" or "human." This implies that members of other groups are less than human. For example, the term *eskimo,* used to refer to groups that inhabit the arctic and subarctic regions, is an Indian word used by neighbors of the Eskimos who observed their strange way of life but did not share it. The term means "eaters of raw flesh," and as such is an ethnocentric observation about cultural practices that were normal to one group and repulsive to another. On the other hand, if we look at one subgroup among the Alaskan natives, we find them calling themselves *inuit,* which means "real people" (they obviously did not think eating raw flesh was anything out of the ordinary). Here, then, is a contrast between one's own group, which is real, and the rest of the world, which is not so "real." Both terms, *eskimo* and *inuit,* are equally ethnocentric—one as an observation about differences, the other as a self-evaluation. However, *inuit* is now seen as a more appropriate term because of its origin.

Another example of ethnocentrism in language can be found in the origin of the English term *barbarian.* Originally a Greek word, the term was used to refer to tribes that lived around the edge of ancient Greek society. The Greeks referred to these people as *barbars* because they could not understand their speech. *Bar-bar* was the Greek word for the sound a dog makes, like our word *bow-wow.* The Greeks, in a classic example of ethnocentrism, considered those whose speech they could not understand to be on the same level as dogs, which also could not be understood. They did not grant such people the status of human being, much as the word *eskimo* gives those people subhuman status.

Shifting from language to myths and folktales, we find a good example of ethnocentrism in the creation myth of the Cherokee Indians. According to this story, the Creator made three clay images of a man and baked them in an oven. In his haste to admire his handiwork, he took the first image out of the oven before it was fully baked and found that it was too pale. He waited a while and then removed the second image; it was just right, a full reddish-brown hue. He was so pleased with his work that he sat there and admired it, completely forgetting about the third image. Finally he smelled it burning, but by the time he could rescue if from the oven it had already been burnt, and it came out completely black!

Food preferences are perhaps the most familiar aspect of ethnocentrism. Every culture has developed preferences for certain kinds of food and drink, and equally strong negative attitudes toward others. It is interesting to note that much of this ethnocentrism is in our heads and not in our tongues, for something can taste delicious until we are told what it is. We have all heard stories about people being fed a meal of snake or horse meat or something equally repugnant in American culture and commenting on how tasty it was—until they were told what they had just eaten, upon which they turned green and hurriedly asked to be excused from the table.

Certain food preferences seem natural to us. We usually do not recognize that they are natural only because we have grown up with them; they are quite likely to be unnatural to someone from a different culture. In southeast Asia, for example, the majority of adults do not drink milk. To many Americans it is inconceivable that people in other parts of the world do not drink milk, since to us it is a "natural" food. In China, dog meat is a delicacy; but the thought of eating a dog is enough to make most Americans feel sick. Yet we can see how this is a part of a cultural pattern. Americans keep dogs as pets and tend to think of dogs as almost human. Therefore, we would not dream of eating dog meat. Horses, too, sometimes become pets, and horse meat is also rejected by most Americans, although not because of its taste. You may have eaten it without knowing it, and you probably would not recognize it if someone didn't tell you what you were eating. On the other hand, we generally do not feel affection for cows or pigs, and we eat their meat without any feeling of regret. In India a cow receives the kind of care that a horse or even a dog receives in our country, and the attitude of Indians toward eating beef is similar to our feeling about eating dog meat. On the other hand, in China dogs are not treated as kindly as they are in the United States. Since they are not pets, the attitude of Chinese people toward dogs is similar to our attitude toward cows.

John Friedl

Whereas in America cows are viewed as a favorite food (top), in India they are sacred; treatment of animals from culture to culture shows strong ethnocentrism.

After You Read

Word Detective

exercise 1   Scan the reading selection for the words that correspond to the following clues.

1. Two synonyms that mean "the way one looks at the world" (paragraph 1)

   _____ , _____ _____

2. Two antonyms for "narrow-minded" (paragraph 2) _____

   _____

3. A hyphenated term that means "an estimate about the worth or goodness of oneself" (paragraph 3) _____ - _____

4. Two adjectives beginning with *r* and meaning the opposite of "pleasing" (paragraphs 3 and 6) _____ _____

5. A noun that means "a crude, ignorant person" and has its origin in the sound made by a dog (paragraph 4) _____

6. Another word for "shade" in reference to colors (paragraph 5)

   _____

7. An adjective meaning "impossible to believe" (paragraph 7)

   _____

Finding Support for Main Ideas

exercise 2   Either orally or in writing, according to your teacher's instructions, give examples from the selection to support the following main ideas.

1. Ethnocentrism is present in language.

2. Ethnocentrism is present in myths.

3. Ethnocentrism is present in food preferences.

Talking It Over

In small groups, discuss the following questions.

1. What is the meaning of the term *culture shock,* which is used in the first paragraph of the selection? When does culture shock occur? Is it a good or a bad experience for the person to go through?

2. Can you think of any examples of ethnocentrism, besides the ones given in the article?

3. What do you think is the main purpose of the article?

4. If you were visiting a foreign country and were asked to eat dog or snake meat, what would you do?

5. What has been your most difficult experience involving unusual food or other customs?

focus on testing

Finding Statements and Implied Ideas in Passages

Reading-comprehension tests often ask you to choose answers to questions about a selection, or passage, on the basis of what is stated or implied. The correct answer is stated directly in the passage (sometimes in different words), or it is suggested (implied) as a logical result of what is stated. In the second case—when the answer is implied—it is more difficult to choose.

exercise 1   For questions 1–4, choose the letter of the correct answer on the basis of what is stated in the passage "Ethnocentrism." Then look back at the paragraphs referred to. In what lines did you find the answers?

1. (paragraph 1) The Greek root of the word *ethnocentric* means
   a. lesson
   b. difference
   c. group
   d. outlook
   Answer found: _____

2. (paragraph 1) An ethnocentric person believes that his or her culture is
   a. as good as other cultures
   b. better than some cultures
   c. worse than many cultures
   d. the best of all cultures
   Answer found: _____

3. (paragraph 2) Who is ethnocentric?
  a. evil people with no education
  b. liberal anthropologists
  c. members of societies far away
  d. everyone to some degree

  Answer found: _____

4. (paragraph 3) What does *inuit* mean?
  a. eaters of raw flesh
  b. real people
  c. subarctic
  d. strangers

  Answer found: _____

exercise 2   Choose the letter of the correct answer on the basis of what is implied in the passage "Ethnocentrism." Then look back at the paragraphs referred to. Where and how is each answer implied?

5. (paragraph 5) What makes the Cherokee Creator myth ethnocentric?
  a. It shows the Creator as a Cherokee.
  b. It shows reddish skin as the ideal.
  c. It presents God as a person who makes mistakes.
  d. It presents the white, the red, and the black.

  Answer implied: _____

6. (paragraphs 6 and 7) What is the cause of the differing food preferences among different cultures?
  a. Some foods are naturally pleasing and others distasteful to the human tongue.
  b. Each group has a different body type and mental makeup that needs certain foods.
  c. People tend to like what is familiar to them and to dislike what is unfamiliar.
  d. Human beings have delicate constitutions and reject meat unless forced to eat it.

  Answer implied: _____

SELECTION two

A Clean, Well-Lighted Place

Before You Read
Guessing the Meaning of New Words from Context

Read the following excerpts from the story and decide from context which meaning corresponds best to each italicized word. Even though some of the words are Spanish, the meaning should still be clear from the context.

1. "'Last week he tried to commit suicide,' one waiter said.
   'Why?'
   'He was in *despair*.'
   'What about?'
   'Nothing.'
   'How do you know that it was nothing?'
   'He has plenty of money.'"
   a. poor health
   b. a sad state of mind
   c. financial trouble

2. "The waiter took the bottle back inside the café. He sat down at the table with his *colleague* again."
   a. client
   b. boss
   c. co-worker

3. "'Finished,' he said, speaking with that *omission of syntax* stupid people employ when talking to drunken people or foreigners. 'No more tonight. Close now.'"
   a. shortening of phrases
   b. strange accent
   c. blurred speech

4. "'Are you trying to insult me?' [younger waiter speaking]
   'No, *hombre*, only to make a joke.' . . .
   'Each night I am reluctant to close up because there may be someone who needs the café.' [older waiter speaking]
   '*Hombre*, there are bodegas open all night long.'"
   a. a funny insult
   b. a word you say to a friend
   c. the name of one of the waiters

5. "'A little cup,' said the waiter.
    The barman poured it for him. . . .
    'You want another *copita*?' the barman asked."
    a. a small alcoholic drink
    b. a tiny saucer
    c. a spicy Spanish food

6. "Now, without thinking further, he would go home to his room. He would lie in the bed and finally, with daylight, he would go to sleep. After all, he said to himself, it is probably only *insomnia*. Many must have it."
    a. a serious illness
    b. severe nervous depression
    c. the inability to sleep

Ernest Hemingway (1899–1961) is one of the most widely read of all modern American authors. His books have been translated into many languages. He is not the sort of writer who describes his characters in great detail. Therefore, the reader must infer a lot about the characters from what they say and do. Scan the story quickly for the speech and action of the people in it. Which predominates: dialogue or action? How many characters are there? As you read, try to understand what is going on in the mind of each one.

Ernest Hemingway at his typewriter

A Clean, Well-Lighted Place

It was late and everyone had left the café except an old man who sat in the shadow the leaves of the tree made against the electric light. In the daytime the street was dusty, but at night the dew settled the dust and the old man liked to sit late because he was deaf and now at night it was quiet and he felt the difference. The two waiters inside the café knew that the old man was a little drunk, and while he was a good client they knew that if he became too drunk he would leave without paying, so they kept watch on him.

"Last week he tried to commit suicide," one waiter said.

10 "Why?"

"He was in despair."

"What about?"

"Nothing."

"How do you know it was nothing?"

15 "He has plenty of money."

They sat together at a table that was close against the wall near the door of the café and looked at the terrace where the tables were all empty except where the old man sat in the shadow of the leaves of the tree that moved slightly in the wind. A girl and a soldier went by in the street. The

20 street light shone on the brass number on his collar. The girl wore no head covering and hurried beside him.

"The guard will pick him up," one waiter said.

"What does it matter if he gets what he's after?"

"He had better get off the street now. The guard will get him. They

25 went by five minutes ago."

The old man sitting in the shadow rapped on his saucer with his glass. The younger waiter went over to him.

"What do you want?"

The old man looked at him. "Another brandy," he said.

30 "You'll be drunk," the waiter said. The old man looked at him. The waiter went away.

"He'll stay all night," he said to his colleague. "I'm sleepy now. I never get into bed before three o'clock. He should have killed himself last week."

The waiter took the brandy bottle and another saucer from the counter

35 inside the café and marched out to the old man's table. He put down the saucer and poured the glass full of brandy.

"You should have killed yourself last week," he said to the deaf man. The old man motioned with his finger. "A little more," he said. The waiter poured on into the glass so that the brandy slopped over and ran down

40 the stem into the top saucer of the pile. "Thank you," the old man said. The waiter took the bottle back inside the café. He sat down at the table with his colleague again.

"He's drunk now," he said.

"He's drunk every night."

45 "What did he want to kill himself for?"

"How should I know."

"How did he do it?"

"He hung himself with a rope."

"Who cut him down?"

"His niece."

"Why did they do it?"

"Fear for his soul."

"How much money has he got?"

"He's got plenty."

"He must be eighty years old."

"Anyway I should say he was eighty."

"I wish he would go home. I never get to bed before three o'clock. What kind of hour is that to go to bed?"

"He stays up because he likes it."

"He's lonely. I'm not lonely. I have a wife waiting in bed for me."

"He had a wife once too."

"A wife would be no good to him now."

"You can't tell. He might be better with a wife."

"His niece looks after him."

"I know. You said she cut him down."

"I wouldn't want to be that old. An old man is a nasty thing."

"Not always. This old man is clean. He drinks without spilling. Even now, drunk. Look at him."

"I don't want to look at him. I wish he would go home. He has no regard for those who must work."

The old man looked from his glass across the square, then over at the waiters.

"Another brandy," he said, pointing to his glass. The waiter who was in a hurry came over.

"Finished," he said, speaking with that omission of syntax stupid people employ when talking to drunken people or foreigners. "No more tonight. Close now."

"Another," said the old man.

"No. Finished." The waiter wiped the edge of the table with a towel and shook his head.

The old man stood up, slowly counted the saucers, took a leather coin purse from his pocket and paid for the drinks, leaving half a peseta tip.

The waiter watched him go down the street, a very old man walking unsteadily but with dignity.

"Why didn't you let him stay and drink?" the unhurried waiter asked. They were putting up the shutters. "It's not half-past two."

"I want to go home to bed."

"What is an hour?"

"More to me than to him."

90 "An hour is the same."

"You talk like an old man yourself. He can buy a bottle and drink at home."

"It's not the same."

"No, it's not," agreed the waiter with a wife. He did not wish to be un-

95 just. He was only in a hurry.

"And you? You have no fear of going home before your usual hour?"

"Are you trying to insult me?"

"No, *hombre,* only to make a joke."

"No," the waiter who was in a hurry said, rising from pulling down the

100 metal shutters. "I have confidence. I am all confidence."

"You have health, confidence, and a job," the old waiter said. "You have everything."

"And what do you lack?"

"Everything but work."

105 "You have everything I have."

"No. I have never had confidence and I am not young."

"Come on. Stop talking nonsense and lock up."

"I am of those who like to stay late at the café," the older waiter said. "With all those who do not want to go to bed. With all those who need a

110 light for the night."

"I want to go home and into bed."

"We are of two different kinds," the older waiter said. He was now dressed to go home. "It is not only a question of youth and confidence although those things are very beautiful. Each night I am reluctant to close

115 up because there may be someone who needs the café."

"*Hombre,* there are *bodegas* open all night long."

"You do not understand. This is a clean and pleasant café. It is well lighted. The light is very good and also, now, there are shadows of the leaves."

120 "Good night," said the younger waiter.

"Good night," the other said. Turning off the electric light he continued the conversation with himself. It is the light of course but it is necessary that the place be clean and pleasant. You do not want music. Certainly you do not want music. Nor can you stand before a bar with dignity although

125 that is all that is provided for these hours. What did he fear? It was not fear or dread. It was nothing that he knew too well. It was all a nothing and a man was nothing too. It was only that and light was all it needed and a certain cleanness and order. Some lived in it and never felt it but he knew it

all was *nada y pues nada y nada y pues nada*.* Our *nada* who are in *nada*,
130 *nada* be thy name thy kingdom *nada* thy will be *nada* in *nada* as it is in
nada. Give us this *nada* our daily *nada* and *nada* us our *nada* as we *nada*
our *nada* and *nada* us not into *nada* but deliver us from *nada*; *pues nada*.
Hail nothing full of nothing, nothing is with thee. He smiled and stood before a bar with a shining steam pressure coffee machine.
135 "What's yours?" asked the barman.

"*Nada*."

"*Otro loco más*,"† said the barman and turned away.

"A little cup," said the waiter.

The barman poured it for him.
140 "The light is very bright and pleasant but the bar is unpolished," the
waiter said.

The barman looked at him but did not answer. It was too late at night
for conversation.

"You want another *copita*?" the barman asked.
145 "No, thank you," said the waiter and went out. He disliked bars and
bodegas. A clean, well-lighted café was a very different thing. Now, without thinking further, he would go home to his room. He would lie in the
bed and finally, with daylight, he would go to sleep. After all, he said to
himself, it is probably only insomnia. Many must have it.

Ernest Hemingway

Nada is the Spanish word for "nothing." *Y pues nada* means "and then nothing." The older waiter then
recites the most famous of all Christian prayers, the "Lord's Prayer," which begins "Our Father which art in
Heaven, hallowed be Thy name. . . ." However, instead of saying the correct words, he replaces many of
them with the word *nada*. Afterward, he does the same with a small part of another prayer.
†Another crazy one

After You Read

Making Inferences About Character from Speech and Actions

 Make inferences about the characters in the story from the following words and
actions.

1. We are told that the old man who is drinking tried to commit suicide the
week before. (line 9)

The old man: _____

_____

_____

2. When asked what the old man was in despair about, one of the waiters says,

" 'Nothing.'

'How do you know it was nothing?'

'He has plenty of money.' " (lines 13 to 15)

The waiter who spoke last: _____

_____

_____

3. The younger waiter says, " 'He'll stay all night. . . . I'm sleepy now. I never get into bed before three o'clock. He should have killed himself last week.' " (lines 32 to 33)

The younger waiter: _____

_____

_____

4. After the younger waiter has told the old man that the café is closed, the older waiter says, " 'Why didn't you let him stay and drink? . . . It's not half-past two.' " (lines 85 to 86)

The older waiter: _____

_____

_____

5. After the man and the younger waiter leave, the older waiter stays for a while and thinks. He recites a prayer in his mind but substitutes the word *nada* for many of the important words. (lines 129 to 132)

The older waiter: _____

_____

_____

Expressing the Theme

exercise **2**

A story presents specific characters with their problems, interactions, and feelings. From these specific events, you can usually make a generalization about human behavior or human nature; this is the *theme* or main idea of the story. In one sentence, write what you think is the theme of "A Clean, Well-Lighted Place."

_____

_____

_____

Talking It Over

activity

In small groups, discuss the following questions.

1. At one point, the older waiter says to the younger one, "'We are of two different kinds.'" What does he mean by this? Do you believe there are two different kinds of people?

2. Why do you think that Hemingway used some Spanish words in the story?

3. What element of the story do you think is the most important: the characters, the plot, or the setting? Why?

SELECTION **three**

The Spell of the Yukon

Before You Read
Hearing Rhyme and Rhythm in Poetry

exercise

Like many poems, "The Spell of the Yukon" should be recited aloud and not just read silently. Only then will you get its full flavor. That way you can hear its rhyme and rhythm. *Rhyme* means that some lines end with the same sounds. *Rhythm* means that the lines have a steady number of beats. Read the poem aloud several times or listen to your teacher or a friend read it. Try to hear the patterns of the rhyme and rhythm. Then answer these questions.

1. Which lines rhyme? Is there a regular pattern?

2. Can you hear the strong beats in each line? Although the rhythm in this poem is somewhat irregular, most lines have the same number of strong beats. How many do you hear in each line?

3. Because Service wrote in the rough and colorful style of the gold rush men, he often used slang words, words used by country people or even strong words that are inappropriate in polite conversation (except for expressing very strong feelings). What words like these can you find in the poem? Why are these words appropriate here?

Now read the poem silently for its meaning. Try to understand what kind of man is speaking in the poem and what he is feeling.

Have you ever wanted something very badly, worked and suffered for it, and then, after getting it, found out that it didn't make you happy? This is the experience described in the following poem by Canadian poet Robert Service (1874–1958). In 1896, gold was discovered in the Klondike area of the Yukon, a remote part of northern Canada, and the great "gold rush" was on. Thousands of people came from all walks of life with one dream: to get rich quick. Some did. Some became millionaires overnight only to lose everything in a card game the next day. Others died from the cold in a land where temperatures often drop to –50 C°, or else were murdered or killed in accidents or fighting. The style of life was rough and hard. Robert Service lived in the Yukon during this period, working in a bank. He wrote his impressions of the Klondike gold rush in poems that became immensely popular and have remained so to this day. His style is rough and direct like the men he describes, but his poems are full of charm and humor and a deep love for the untamed wilderness of the Yukon.

The Spell of the Yukon

I wanted the gold, and I sought it;
    I scrabbled and mucked like a slave.
Was it famine or scurvy*—I fought it;
    I hurled my youth into a grave.
5   I wanted gold, and I got it—
    Came out with a fortune last fall—
Yet somehow life's not what I thought it,
    And somehow the gold isn't all.
No! There's the land. (Have you seen it?)
10   It's the cussedest† land that I know,
From the big, dizzy mountains that screen it
    To the deep, deathlike valleys below.
Some say God was tired when He made it:
    Some say it's a fine land to shun;‡
15   Maybe; but there's some as would trade it
    For no land on earth—and I'm one.

You come to get rich (damned good reason);
    You feel like an exile at first;
You hate it like hell for a season,
20   And then you are worse than the worst.
It grips you like some kinds of sinning;
    It twists you from foe to a friend;
It seems it's been since the beginning;
    It seems it will be to the end.

       . . .

---

*Disease due to lack of vitamin C
†From the verb *to cuss* or *to swear*
‡Avoid

25   The summer—no sweeter was ever;
      The sunshiny woods all athrill;
  The grayling* aleap in the river,
      The bighorn† asleep on the hill.
  The strong life that never knows harness;
30   The wilds where the caribou‡ call;
  The freshness, the freedom, the farness—
      O God! how I'm stuck on it all.§

  The winter! the brightness that blinds you,
      The white land locked tight as a drum,
35   The cold fear that follows and finds you,
      The silence that bludgeons¶ you dumb.
  The snows that are older than history,
      The woods where the weird shadows slant;
  The stillness, the moonlight, the mystery,
40   I've bade them good-bye—but I can't.

  There's a land where the mountains are nameless,
      And the rivers all run God knows where;
  There are lives that are erring and aimless,
      And deaths that just hang by a hair;
45   There are hardships that nobody reckons;
      There are valleys unpeopled and still;
  There's a land—oh it beckons and beckons,
      And I want to go back—and I will.

  They're making my money diminish;
50   I'm sick of the taste of champagne.
  Thank God! when I'm skinned to a finish
      I'll pike to the Yukon again.
  I'll fight—and you bet it's no sham-fight*;
      It's hell!—but I've been there before;
55   And it's better than this by a damnsite—
      So me for the Yukon once more.

----

*A type of fish
†A type of mountain sheep
‡A type of large deer
§(Slang) Caught by it
¶To hit with a heavy weapon
ªFake fight

There's gold, and it's haunting and haunting;
        It's luring me on as of old;
Yet it isn't the gold that I'm wanting
        So much as the finding the gold.
It's the great, big, broad land 'way up yonder,
        It's the forests where silence has lease;
It's the beauty that thrills me with wonder,
        It's the stillness that fills me with peace.

60

Robert Service

The Yukon Territory in northern
Canada is one of the great wilderness
regions left in the world.

Prospectors looking for gold

After You Read
Comprehension Quiz

exercise

Answer the following questions about the poem.

1. What kind of man is supposed to be speaking in the poem? What can we infer about his education by the way he talks?

2. What happened to change his life "last fall"? What can we tell about the man's character from the line "They're making my money diminish"? Whom do you think the pronoun *they* refers to in this case?

3. How does this man describe the Yukon? What does he like about it? Do you think you would like it?

4. How did he expect to feel about his good fortune? How does he really feel now that he has it? What explanation can there be for this change?

5. What plans does the man have for his future? What do you think will happen to him?

Paraphrasing Figurative Language

exercise

Poetry often uses indirect language with figures and images that stand for certain ideas. Read the excerpts from the poem and then paraphrase (express the meaning in direct, simple words) what the poet is saying.

example: "I'm sick of the taste of champagne."

I'm tired of the kind of life that goes with being rich.

1. "I hurled my youth into a grave." (line 4)

_____

_____

2. "It [the land] grips you like some kinds of sinning; it twists you from foe to a friend;" (lines 21 to 22)

_____

_____

3. "There's a land where the mountains are nameless, and the rivers all run God knows where;" (lines 41 to 42)

_____

_____

4. "[There are] deaths that just hang by a hair;" (line 44)

_____

_____

5. "Yet it isn't the gold that I'm wanting so much as the finding the gold." (lines 59 to 60)

_____

_____

Talking It Over

In small groups, discuss the following questions.

1. Do you think the miner's reaction to his new-found wealth is typical for people who strive to reach a goal and accomplish it?

2. Have you ever been in a place that is real wilderness? Why do you think some people feel at home in a place like that? Do you prefer the wilderness to the city? Why?

3. Robert Service is the "Poet of the Yukon." If you go there, you will hear his words quoted everywhere. Have you heard of any other regions of the world that are associated with a particular poet? Or a writer? Or an artist?

4. In your opinion, what place in the world is the most beautiful? What is it like?

WHAT DO YOU THINK?

Blaming Others

This billboard appeared in Tampa, Florida. The billboard is mocking what many people in the United States feel is a growing trend: blaming others. A "crybaby" is a person who cries or complains a lot, usually for no good reason. Does your native language have a word or expression such as crybaby?

Evidence of this trend is the fact that lawsuits in the United States are at an all-time high. When an accident happens, the people involved often try to sue someone else rather than consider how their own behavior might have caused or contributed to the accident. For example, a woman in the United States recently sued a fast-food chain for $1.2 million because she received second-degree burns after spilling a cup of coffee she had placed between her knees. She complained that the coffee was too hot. Do you think she was right or wrong to sue the company? Would a person in your home country probably do the same thing? Why or why not?

CHAPTER ten

Crime and Punishment

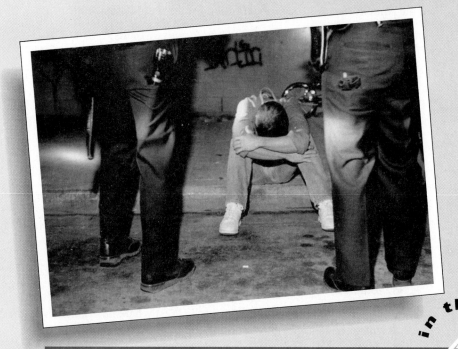

in this chapter

What is the difference between a folk hero and a criminal? We begin with the biography of a legendary outlaw from the American frontier of the 1800s, and we let you make your own judgment. Next is a fictional selection about a man who was tortured and imprisoned during the time of the Red Guard in China, when the definition of crime changed weekly. The third selection is nonfiction: an essay examining the age-old question of Nature versus Nurture with regard to crime.

Soapy Smith

Before You Read

Guessing the Meaning of New Words from Context

exercise **1** Use the context to guess the best definition for the words in italics.

1. Soapy Smith was the town's most *notorious* swindler.
   a. famous
   b. famous in a positive way
   c. evil
   d. famous in a negative way

2. Smith was born in Georgia but spent most of his *formative* years in Texas.
   a. early
   b. later
   c. difficult
   d. happy

3. Young Jeff earned a living as a runner for the hotel, a job in which he *rustled up* customers and thus discovered his natural gift for speech.
   a. attracted with persuasion
   b. scared away with insults
   c. entertained
   d. fought with

4. Smith spent several years drifting in the West where he *eventually* learned sleight-of-hand tricks and made a living in the mining camps.
   a. never
   b. always
   c. after a while
   d. with no problem

5. He married Anna Nielsen, whom few people knew because he kept her *insulated* from his "public" life.
   a. informed
   b. inspired
   c. connected
   d. separated

Skimming for Organization in Biography

> Biography is the life story of a real person, and therefore it is classified as *nonfiction* in libraries and bookstores. Here are the two common ways to organize a biography.
>
> **ORGANIZATION 1**
>
> A. Begin with the person's birth.
> B. Tell the events of the person's life.
> C. Describe the person's death.
>
> **ORGANIZATION 2**
>
> A. Begin with interesting facts about the person.
> B. Tell the events of the person's life from birth to death.
> C. Give a final comment or interesting detail about the person.

**exercise 2**   Skim the brief biography of Soapy Smith and tell which of the two organizations is used. In your opinion, why did the author do it that way?

Today many people complain about the prevalence of gangs and criminals, but in the 1800s in many parts of the United States this was a much bigger problem, and there were often no police to provide protection. Those were the days when the American frontier was moving more and more westward. Outlaws were common, but a few of them became famous, and some have been celebrated in song and legend. What do you think these outlaws were like? Heartless murderers? Brave heroes who helped the poor? Or simply *con men* (slang for swindlers), trying to get rich by tricking others? Read the biography of one of them in this selection. Since, as they say, "truth is stranger than fiction," you might be surprised by what you read.

Soapy Smith

Jefferson Randolph "Soapy" Smith probably ranks as Skagway's* best-known character from the gold-rush days. Certainly, he was its most notorious con man. It is said
5 that at the height of the gold rush, Smith and his gang virtually controlled the town, a reign that ended in a shoot-out with one of Skagway's leading citizens, Frank Reid.

Smith was born in Georgia in 1860 to

*A town in southeastern Alaska near the famous passes that led to the Klondike gold fields

parents who were both members of prominent Southern families. Smith spent most of his formative years in Texas, where his family moved in the 1870s. After his father, a lawyer, fell on hard times, young Jeff was forced to earn a living as a delivery boy and as a runner for a hotel, a job in which he rustled up customers and thus discovered his natural gift for speech.

When still in his teens, Smith hired on as a trail hand on cattle drives, and spent several years drifting about the West. He eventually learned sleight-of-hand tricks and made a living in the mining camps with gambling games such as the peas-under-the-shell* game. He acquired his nickname "Soapy" from a game which involved hiding large bills in bars of soap.

Smith, who was generally opposed to violent methods, graduated to larger operations and set up in Denver where he formed a gang. In Denver, he acquired a wide reputation for his con games, as well as for his generosity to charities, churches, and those in desperate need. Also in Denver, he married a singer by the name of Anna Nielsen, whom he kept insulated from his "public" life and who eventually bore his children.

About 1890, Smith set up operations, including a gambling hall, in Creede, Colorado, a wide-open mining town, but eventually returned to Denver. After numerous run-ins with the law and local politicians, Soapy Smith quit Colorado and, in October 1897,

arrived with his gang in Skagway, apparently with intentions of "taking over" the town.

Working out of an establishment called Jeff Smith's Parlor, an oyster parlor that also offered liquor and gambling, Smith and his gang soon were operating their con games, as well as taking part in some outright robbery, running a protection racket, and overseeing businesses like Smith's "Telegraph Office." This last business, which charged $5 to send a message anywhere in the world, might have been legitimate but for the fact that Skagway had no telegraph lines.

Despite his lawless ways, Smith was liked and respected by many for his charity, which included organizing a program to adopt stray dogs. The townspeople, however, had no use whatsoever for his gang. Eventually, several of Skagway's leading citizens formed a vigilante-style† "Committee of 101" to rid the town of its criminal element. Among the committee's founders was 54-year-old Frank Reid, a former Indian fighter and surveyor who helped lay out the original town.

The showdown between Soapy Smith and Frank Reid began when a young miner, J. D. Stewart, arrived in Skagway from the Klondike carrying $2,700 in gold. Somehow, and apparently with the help of someone, Stewart and his gold parted ways. The Committee of 101, hearing Stewart's loud complaints, suspected Soapy Smith and his gang, and on July 8, 1898, called a meeting on the Skagway wharf to take action.

Soapy Smith tried to force his way into the meeting, but found his path along the

---

*In this popular game, a small dry pea was placed under one of three walnut shells. The person running the game then moved the shells around quickly several times and invited the onlookers to bet money on which shell contained the pea. Since "the hand is quicker than the eye," the person running the game usually won the money. If tricks were used instead of just skill, the game became a "con game."

---

†A vigilante committee is a group formed by citizens to punish criminals when they feel the legal system is not doing enough.

wharf blocked by Frank Reid. After a brief struggle, the two exchanged gunfire and both fell to the deck. Smith died immediately of a bullet through the heart; Reid lingered 12 days longer.

With the death of Soapy Smith, the law-abiding citizens of Skagway got rid of other members of the gang. Most of them were shipped south, and many served time in prison. Smith and Reid were buried near each other in Skagway cemetery, with Reid's tombstone bearing the words, "He gave his life for the Honor of Skagway." Soapy Smith's tombstone became a favorite among souvenir seekers, who believed a piece of the stone would bring them good luck.

Stan B. Cohen

After You Read

Finding Examples to Support Main Ideas

 Like many well-known people, Soapy Smith seems to have been a mixture of good and bad. Fill in the chart with specific examples to show both sides of his character. Include traits, actions, and the opinions of others. An item for each side is given as an example. Then compare your charts in small groups.

The Character of Soapy Smith

good side	bad side
1. Was a good talker (had a natural gift for speech)	1. Earned money by tricking people with con games
2.	2.
3.	3.
4.	4.
5.	5.
6.	6.

Scanning for Compound-Word Synonyms

Many English words are compound, made from combinations of two smaller words. Some have hyphens, such as *would-be,* and others, like *overlook,* do not. Scan the reading to find the compound-word synonyms for the words or phrases in italics.

1. Soapy Smith probably ranks as Skagway's *most famous* character from the gold-rush days.

2. He controlled the town until his reign ended in a(n) *exchange of gunfire* with Frank Reid.

3. About 1890 Soapy set up operations in Creede, Colorado, a *lawless and uncontrolled* mining town.

4. The *inhabitants of the town* had no use for his gang.

5. After numerous *encounters* with the law, Soapy quit Colorado.

6. He and his gang soon were running a protection racket and *supervising* businesses like Smith's "Telegraph Office."

7. The *deciding confrontation* between Soapy and Frank began when a young miner arrived.

8. With the death of Soapy, the _____ citizens (*who generally obeyed the law*) of Skagway got rid of the gang.

Talking It Over

In small groups, discuss the following questions.

1. What was wrong with Smith's Telegraph Office? Do you think there are businesses like this nowadays?

2. What is a *con game*? A *protection racket*? What films have you seen about these activities? How do they portray the people involved?

3. Who was Frank Reid, and how did he die?

4. As long as someone does nothing illegal, he or she is a good person: true or false? Explain.

5. Who is famous in your culture for having broken the law or defied authority? Do you consider this person an outlaw or a folk hero? Why?

Going Beyond the Text: Learning from Biography

Read a biography of a well-known person and prepare a report in oral or written form to share with the class. Look especially to see if this person, like Soapy Smith, has a positive and a negative side, or if he or she seems to be almost completely good or completely bad. Explain your opinion with examples.

SELECTION two

Anecdotes of Minister Maimaiti: A Uygur Man's Black Humor

Before You Read
Surveying an Extended Reading

exercise **1**

The following reading selection is much longer than any other in this book. Use it to practice your skill at reading extended material. First, survey the selection by skimming it quickly to see the overall organization and main ideas. Surveying takes a couple of minutes, but it saves time in the long run by improving both reading speed and comprehension.

After you have skimmed the selection, look at the six sections and tell which one deals with each of the following main ideas. Write the correct number and subhead by each main idea. The first one is done as an example.

MAIN IDEA	SECTION (NUMBER & SUBHEAD)
A. A severe beating that makes the victim happy	_____ _____
B. A comparison and contrast of two brothers	1. Why Was Minister Maimaiti as Young as an Evergreen?
C. How pretending to be crazy fools a guard	_____ _____
D. The transformation of ugliness into beauty by the power of the imagination	_____ _____ _____
E. The important question of what makes a book worthy to be published	_____ _____
F. A comparison and contrast of two weddings	_____ _____

Understanding Humor

exercise 2 Look at the *epigraphs* (quotations placed at the beginning of a reading). Write down what you think they tell us about the author's attitude to humor.

_____

_____

What makes something funny, or humorous, depends partly on culture. On the other hand, humor is often universal like music. Watch for the humorous parts in the following selection and make a note of what words or incidents make you laugh.

What makes something a crime? Is it the evil nature of the action? Or does it depend on the way the action is viewed by society? Can the same action be considered good one day and a crime the next because of a change in politics?

This was certainly the case during the Cultural Revolution in China. During this period the word of Chairman Mao was law, and Mao ruled the Communist Party and all of China with an iron hand. Mao encouraged the young to break with the old traditions and express their loyalty to him alone. Slogans and rules changed from one month to the next with no logic or reason. Many people, especially the educated or intelligent, became targets for roving gangs of young people called Red Guards to beat up or torture. Labeled "Blacks," or "counterrevolutionaries," the innocent victims were declared criminals and sent to prison. On the surface, the reason for this was to do away with the evil old society and create a new society that was truly *proletarian* (of workers). But the real reason was to eliminate any possible rival to Mao, so that he alone would be supreme.

China is a vast country and contains many minority groups who speak their own language and follow ancient traditions. The Uygur people are one such group, and it is an Uygur man by the name of Maimaiti who is the main character in the following story about crime and punishment during the Cultural Revolution. Although the story is fiction, it is obviously based on true experiences or *anecdotes* (short tales about interesting or amusing events) from that turbulent time in history.

Anecdotes of Minister Maimaiti: A Uygur Man's Black Humor

Translated from the Chinese by Qingyun Wu

Six essential elements for sustaining life (in order of their importance): first, air; first, sunshine; first, water; first, food; first, friendship; first, humor.

Happiness comes when tears dry.

The sense of humor is the superiority complex of intelligence.

—from Ancient Philosophical Aphorisms (not yet published)

1. Why Was Minister Maimaiti as Young as an Evergreen?

May 6, 1979. The wind was gentle, the sun was warm, the willows showing the first hint of green. In the Dashizi Muslim Restaurant, I ran into Minister Maimaiti and his twin brother, Saimaiti, neither of whom I had seen for more than ten years. I looked first at Maimaiti:

> Although merciless time had carved mountains and rivers on his face
> His vitality radiated from a thick crown of glossy black hair,
> His ruddy face was as warm and cheering as bread hot from the oven
> and in his laughter hope and cynicism tussled like romping children.

I turned to his brother Saimaiti:

> His bony back quivered like a tightened bow.
> In his dull eyes shadows of death flickered.
> He always sighed before speaking as if his stomach ached.
> In his hand he ever clutched a little bottle of heart pills.

I was so shocked by the contrast, of course, that as soon as I had said "Salamu"* and finished greeting them, I asked, "What has happened to you two these last years?"

"I suffered from the Catastrophe . . ." Saimaiti replied.

Maimaiti added, "I also suffered from the Catastrophe . . ."

SAIMAITI: "I was called one of the 'Black Gang' and locked up . . ."

MAIMAITI: "I was also seized and locked up . . ."

SAIMAITI: "I was beaten . . ."

MAIMAITI: "I was whipped . . ."

SAIMAITI: "I climbed the mountains to carry stone . . ."

MAIMAITI: "I went down into the earth to dig coal . . ."

SAIMAITI: "When I was officially labeled an Active Counterrevolutionary Element, my wife divorced me . . ."

MAIMAITI: "When I was publicly labeled a Three Antis Element (Anti-Party, Anti-people, Anti-socialism) my children's mother married another man . . ."

Ailaibailia!† Six of one, half a dozen of the other. Like peas, the twins' experiences seemed indistinguishable. Confused by this counterpoint of woes, I couldn't help asking, "Since you both suffered the same fates, why does brother Maimaiti look so young and Saimaiti so ancient?"

---

*(Uygur greeting meaning "May you have a long life.")
†Xinjiang slang for "What nonsense!"

With tears quivering in his eyes, Saimaiti moaned, sighed, and beat his sides with his fists.

Pointing at his smiling face, Maimaiti said. "He lacks *this,* you see? He still broods and suffers. But me, I never let a day pass without making a joke."

2. The Crime of Minister Maimaiti (Which Lays Bare the True Nature of the New-Style Wedding That Breaks Away from "The Four Olds")

In 1966 the tide of the Cultural Revolution was surging high. Yet the Uygur people of the remote countryside of Xinjiang Province could make no sense of it. The villagers didn't know who were their targets, or indeed why anyone should be attacked at all. They just did not know how to "make revolution." In fact, they did not even know *why* they should make revolution. They could only shrug their shoulders and say to each other in Uygur expression, "Haven't got any message yet."

Yet by this time the Uygur villagers were so accustomed to the Party's movements, that they felt they were obliged to make some attempt, any attempt, however muddled it might be. Therefore they recited Chairman Mao's Quotations, killed pigeons, and burned the Koran. The teenagers were very excited by all of this because they got to do all those things that had previously been forbidden, while their more conservative elders mostly remained silent.

"Change through class struggle!" That was the motto of the day. Maimaiti's uncle, Mu Ming, Party Secretary of the Fourth Brigade (which changed its name to the Struggle Brigade when the Cultural Revolution began), took the lead by shaving off his beautiful mustache and beard, throwing away his embroidered cap, and putting aside his long tunic in favor of an imitation army uniform. With an imitation soldier's cap on his head, a red band bearing the words "Red Guard" on his arm, and red satchel containing Mao's Red Book slung over one shoulder, Mu Ming, a brand-new man, appeared on the horizon.

At that time Mu Ming's eldest daughter, Tilakizi, was going to be married to Mulajidi, who not only was the most intelligent young man in the village but was also the newly elected Political Commissar. When the news got out, however, the commune Secretary and the Work Team Leader from the central provincial office sent for Mu Ming, Mulajidi, and Tilakizi and sternly warned the young couple that they must firmly break with the "Four Olds" (old ideas, old culture, old customs, old traditions). Included among these "Olds" was the traditional Uygur wedding ceremony: there was to be no slaughtering of sheep, no drinking, no dancing, no wedding presents—and certainly no prayers or blessings. No, their own marriage would have to begin with a new-style proletarian wedding.

"What exactly is this new-style proletarian wedding?" Mu Ming asked, trying to look and sound as much like a Red Guard as possible.

"The ceremony will be as follows. First, all will recite from the Quotations of Mao. Second, you will invite the leaders of the province, county, and commune to give speeches. Finally, the young couple will bow three times to the portrait of chairman Mao, once to the assembled leaders, and once to each other. That's it. Of course, there will be no dowry from either family. However, both sides may exchange copies of the Red Book, portraits of our esteemed Chairman, sickles, and manure forks. No entertainment is allowed. After the wedding, the groom will spend the wedding night watering crops, and the bride will make forty posters of the Chairman's quotations, done in red and yellow paint on wooden boards . . ."

Mu Ming was more than a little surprised to hear this. He had thought that shaving off his mustache and wearing his Red Guard uniform would make him sufficiently revolutionary.

Mulajidi scowled and rolled his eyes. He had assumed that by being a political commissar he could just go through the motions of being a revolutionary. Now he would be forced to act out a senseless charade on his own wedding night, one that no one but a sexless idiot could possibly consent to.

Tilakizi was all tears. As a girl grows older her desire becomes stronger, and Tilakizi had been thinking for months about those first sweet, shy, tender moments when she and Mulajidi could be alone together. But never had she imagined that her wedding would be like one of those political-education classes.

Furious at their reaction, the Commune Secretary and the Team Leaders lambasted the father, daughter, and future son-in-law. After the trio had departed, the Commune Secretary called the League Secretary, the Chairman of the Poor and Middle Peasants Association, the Chairwoman of the Women's Federation into their office. Their job, he explained to them, would be to monitor the trio to discover the true thoughts and feelings of each and then badger them into changing their minds.

By all appearances, this method seemed to be working. The new-style proletarian wedding was duly held. Leaders gave speeches, officials posed with the couple for photos, revolutionary songs were sung, and solemn passages were read. This model wedding was then reported in bulletins, local newspapers, and county broadcasts. And to top it all off, Xinhua News Agency carried the word to the country at large.

Ten days later, Mu Ming's family held the real wedding. Sheep were slaughtered, silks were exchanged, and the bride and groom paid all the customary visits to relatives—it was a true Uygur wedding. Luckily, this underground wedding was not all that risky. In the first place, since the new-style proletarian wedding had already been publicized, it had served its purpose. In the second place, the Party officials were all too busy accusing one another or else defending themselves from such attacks. After the ceremony, the bride and groom were as inseparable as paint and wood.

Of course, Minister Maimaiti knew all about his cousin's wedding. He made an anecdote of it to tell his friends, concluding, "the advantage of the new-style proletarian wedding is that it postponed the real wedding long enough for my uncle to let his beard grow out. The disadvantage is that they had to spend fifty *yuan* more than their real budget, since besides butchering sheep and buying wine for the real wedding, they had to buy watermelon seeds, candy, and cigarettes for the new-style wedding.

These were not times in which to make such mistakes, however. Everyone was accusing everyone else of all sorts of things, and Maimaiti himself was soon under examination for taking "The Black Line" in literature. When his remarks concerning the wedding were denounced as a rightist's attack on the Great Proletarian Cultural Revolution, Maimaiti was seized for questioning.

To protect his uncle and cousin, Maimaiti insisted that he had made up the entire story of the underground wedding. As a result, he had yet one more charge against him, that of "spreading rumors for sabotage and encouraging a return to capitalism." After being convicted, he was tightly sealed in a cowshed.

3. At Last Minister Maimaiti Becomes a Writer Recognized by the People

Now let us turn back the clock a bit. Maimaiti had always been a lover of books, even as a child. In 1958, because of his scholarship and sensitivity, he was selected to be the Provincial Minister of Literature and Arts. This gave him the opportunity to meet many famous writers and poets, which increased his love for literature still more and made him determined to become a writer himself. Therefore he wrote and wrote and wrote. And although his manuscripts were rejected time and again, he kept on writing. Finally a few of his short poems and prose pieces were published in literary magazines and in the popular press. Unfortunately, no one paid the slightest attention to any of them. Readers and critics alike were unanimous in ignoring him. Established writers yawned, while emerging writers left him unread. Every time he petitioned to join the writers union, he was turned down. Eventually he became bitter.

It was only when he was denounced as a member of the Black Gang and sent off to a prison farm that his fortunes changed, because he now was in the company of all the famous writers and poets he had previously admired and envied. At last, he was one of them.

On an April day in 1967, Maimaiti and his colleagues were working in a vineyard when they heard a terrible racket: drums thundering, bugles blowing, and Quotations being chanted in unison. Realizing that a band of "revolutionary warriors" was approaching, the intelligentsia scattered like startled animals in the jungle. Some dived into ditches; some hid behind bushes; others just lay flat among the ants, hoping to avoid another confrontation with the Army of the Revolution.

Unfortunately, Maimaiti had a bad ear infection, and so he heard neither the Red Guards approaching nor his colleagues' shouts of warning. Besides, he had come to enjoy his work in the vineyards and was so absorbed in his digging that he did not even notice that anything unusual was happening. As a result, he alone was left to serve as a target. Before he knew it, the Red Guards had surrounded him. They glared at him. Here stood a dangerous enemy of the people.

"Who are you?" the Red Guards snarled.

"One of the Black Gang, A Three Antis Element," Maimaiti replied meekly. He dropped his hands to his sides and tried to look as ashamed and repentant as possible.

"What were you before?"

"Minister of Literature and Arts."

"Aha! A capitalist roader. A man of the Black Line. What are your crimes, monster?"

"I attacked the breaking away from the 'Four Olds,' worthy comrades, and wrote some reactionary articles."

"Which articles? How many?"

"Well, let me see . . ." Excited to talk about his writing, Maimaiti forgot about his penitent pose. "The first one was about . . ." With extraordinary seriousness, he reported the exact content of all his published articles, including a news report of less than a hundred words.

"What else have you written?"

Maimaiti promptly reported all the manuscripts that had been killed by editors.

"Do you know Zhou Yang?"

"Yes, of course." Actually, Maimaiti only knew the name. In Uygur, the same word is used for "know personally" and "know by name." Naturally his answer was misinterpreted.

The young warriors were startled.

Thinking that this man must be a famous writer, a really dangerous enemy, they began shouting revolutionary slogans. "Crush the enemy under your feet! Knock him from his high seat! Revolution is guiltless; rebellion is reasonable!" and so on.

Soon they grew tired of mere words and began to transpose their ideas into action, of which Maimaiti was the recipient. He did his best to huddle up into a ball, for two reasons: one, to show his submissiveness and, two, to protect his intestines. At the same time, he kept saying "Oh" and "Ouch" in a voice that was neither too loud nor too faint. This moderate moaning was a deliberate ploy, learned from experience. If a victim clenched his teeth and made no noise, the young warriors, thinking he was defying them, would only become more antagonized. If he yelled too much, however, they would interpret this as a protest against their actions and would also become more antagonized. Therefore, the wisest course was to moan piteously but in a carefully modulated tone. By the time they had finished with him, Maimaiti had been beaten black and blue. His gums and nostrils were bleeding. His eyes were swollen like walnuts. It would have taken a nutcracker to open them. His back, sides, legs, and belly were all covered with cuts and bruises. Nevertheless, his heart, liver, spleen, stomach, kidneys, and bladder had all escaped injury. His tactic had worked.

220　　But although the young warriors had broken Maimaiti's body, they still felt that they had not yet touched his soul. So they wrote six big characters on his back with a big brush and smelly black ink, "Black Writer Maimaiti!" Then, in high spirits, the young revolutionary warriors marched off, singing a revolutionary song.

225　　Some twenty minutes later, the other writers crawled out of their hiding places one by one. Some tried to help Maimaiti to his feet. Others tried to console him. Some sighed for him. Others blamed him for not heeding their warnings. But they all agreed that the trouble with Maimaiti was that he worked too hard and was too honest.

230　　Pushing away all helping hands, Maimaiti stood up. Shivering, he spat the blood out of his mouth. Then, disregarding all his other injuries, he pointed to his back and asked what the young warriors had written there.

　　"Black Writer Mai-mai-ti!" they read in unison.

　　"Aha!" Maimaiti shouted. Because of all the blood in his mouth and
235　the loosened teeth, his words weren't clear. Yet his excitement was beyond words.

　　"You don't recognize me as a writer. You never have. But see, the people, they've recognized me at last!"

　　The crowd burst out laughing. They laughed till tears of joy came to
240　their eyes.

After You Read

Vocabulary Check: Separating the Good from the Bad

 *exercise*　Now that you have finished over half of this long reading, check your comprehension. Tell which of the following are considered bad by the officials of the Cultural Revolution, and explain why.

1. proletarian　　　　　**5.** capitalist

2. black　　　　　　　 **6.** revolutionary

3. red　　　　　　　　 **7.** old

4. traditional　　　　　**8.** change

Judging Something True or False

Many reading-comprehension tests include a true/false section. The best strategy is to do all the obvious items first. Then look at the ones remaining. Are they difficult because they seem to be partly true and partly false? Remember that a statement is false if it has even one small part that is false.

exercise 1 Look quickly at the following true/false exercise. Write down the numbers of the items that are not immediately obvious. _____
What makes them tricky or difficult?_____
Compare answers with your classmates.

exercise 2 Write true or false in front of each statement. Correct the false statements to make them true.

1. _____ Maimaiti suffered much more than his twin during the "Catastrophe" (Cultural Revolution).

2. _____ The main difference in their appearance was that Saimaiti had a long mustache and Maimaiti didn't.

3. _____ The Uygur people did not understand what the Cultural Revolution was.

4. _____ The only group who seemed to enjoy those times were the elderly.

5. _____ The new-style wedding ceremony included no singing or dancing.

6. _____ Maimaiti's uncle gave a traditional wedding for his daughter, with a big dinner and gifts.

7. _____ Maimaiti had to go to jail to protect his cousin and her family.

8. _____ Maimaiti was a poor student when he was young.

9. _____ The gang of Red Guard "warriors" recognized Maimaiti because they had read his books.

10. _____ Maimaiti's plan to protect himself during the beating was a failure.

11. _____ The famous writers and poets laughed when they saw Maimaiti after the beating because they did not like him.

Talking It Over

In small groups, discuss the following questions.

1. What is unusual about the character of Maimaiti?

2. Give examples from the reading of the government jargon used during the Cultural Revolution. Have you heard jargon like this?

3. What do you think of the two kinds of wedding? What type of wedding do you like?

4. What parts of the story seemed humorous? Why?

4. Romance in the Cowshed

The Black Gang at the prison farm had to fetch drinking water from a motor-driven pump two kilometers away. This task was so difficult that they arranged to take turns at it. But in that April of 1968, Maimaiti amazed everyone by volunteering to take over this task completely. The shoulder-pole and pails became his own property. At first they thought he was doing extra work in order to secure an earlier release, so they let him alone. But when this continued, someone finally got suspicious and asked him about it.

5

"Why do you go out of your way to do extra work? What are you up to?"

Maimaiti didn't try to hide his secret. In fact, it was with pride that Maimaiti declared, "Near the well lives a very pretty girl."

"A pretty girl?" The men of the Black Gang could hardly believe their ears.

"A pretty girl. More than a pretty girl." He began to declaim a poem he had written in her honor.

Her beauty is both sun and moon but
Shines with a lovelier light;
Her shimmering hair reflects a halo of love.
When I see her,
My heart bursts into flame,
My body turns to charcoal,
And tears of love spill from my eyes.
She is my love,
My light, and all my joy.

When the men heard this, they were dumbfounded. Then they made up their minds to follow him. And although Maimaiti knew their intentions, he didn't seem to mind.

He didn't even seem to mind when his "pretty girl" was discovered to be a fifty-year-old woman with a baggy goiter, a cataract, and a bent back. The men of the Black Gang laughed uproariously, calling him a liar, an idiot, and so on. But to their surprise, Maimaiti just smiled to himself and waited for the commotion to die down.

Then, with patient irony, he said, "You fine writers and poets—how can you write? Where is your imagination? We've been here for twenty dry months, I would think that anyone in a flowered blouse and red scarf would be beautiful to any of us."

This time no one laughed, except Maimaiti, who simply went on smiling and laughing to himself.

5. Why Didn't Minister Maimaiti Shut the Door When He Slept at Night?

In the barracks where the Black Gang slept, Maimaiti's bed was nearest the door, and this was how all the trouble began. At bedtime, whenever someone closed the door, Maimaiti would open it again. This led his colleagues to attempt to explain to him the complexities of class struggle. Society wasn't yet perfect, and so there might be thieves around. Even though all the prisoners were members of the Black Gang, most were nevertheless wearing wristwatches. Many had money and grain coupons in their pockets.

"You fail to understand logic," Maimaiti told them with his usual indifference. "Thieves, robbers, and all other sorts of bad men are, after all, human beings. Is this not true? We, on the other hand, have been told that we are not human beings but incarnations of Satan. If men do not fear Satan, should Satan be afraid of men?"

Unfortunately, this was overheard by a guard. He at once called Maimaiti in for questioning.

THE GUARD: "You've been spreading poisonous dissension among the prisoners, haven't you?"

MAIMAITI: "I wouldn't dare."

THE GUARD: "You're angry because you've been classified as monsters. You're full of resentment."

MAIMAITI: "Oh, no. I'm absolutely content."

THE GUARD: "You're a reactionary."

MAIMAITI: "I certainly am an incarnation of Satan."

THE GUARD: "You've always been a reactionary."

MAIMAITI: "Yes indeed. I've always been an incarnation of Satan."

THE GUARD: "Why are you such a reactionary?"

MAIMAITI: (lowering his head) "I was influenced by Liu Shaoqi."

The guard (upon hearing the name Liu Shaoqi) relaxes somewhat, thinking that Maimaiti's political consciousness has been raised at least a little. Adopting a softer tone, he continues: "Confess honestly. The Party is always lenient with those who confess their crimes. If you confess your crimes, you can be remolded, and the sooner you are remolded, the sooner you can return to the ranks of the people!"

Maimaiti: "I am determined to turn myself from an incarnation of Satan into a man, and as quickly as I can."

The guard: "Then think carefully about what you have done. Don't think that you can hide any of your crimes from us. And don't try confessing the minor ones to cover up the serious ones. Confess the grave ones now, and we'll be much easier on you."

Maimaiti (lowering his head and wringing his hands as if he were undergoing a convulsive inner struggle): "There is a crime . . . but no, it's too horrible to talk about."

The guard (his eyes lighting up): "Out with it! Out with it! Whatever it is, if you confess now, I can assure you that we won't parade you in a high paper hat, and won't club you like a dog."

Maimaiti (meekly): It was I who started the First World War. And I'm ashamed to say that's not all. I started the Second World War as well. And now—oh—it's too horrible—I'm feeling the impulse to start a third."

The guard (hopelessly confused): "Er???"

6. The Return of Minister Maimaiti

Nothing that Maimaiti said or did caused him to be set free. But after the downfall of the Gang of Four, it was determined that Maimaiti had been persecuted unjustly, so he was not only released from the cowshed but also restored to his former position as Minister of Literature and Arts for Xinjiang Province.

Time passed, and Maimaiti, as Minister of Literature and Arts, was required to read all the new literature about the suffering of intellectuals during the Cultural Revolution. "So many comic possibilities have turned sour under their pens," he complained and then set about writing a novel of his own about the Cultural Revolution. When he had finished, he asked a friend to translate it into Chinese for him. Then he requested a leave of absence from his post and, using his own money, traveled all the way to Beijing to hand the manuscript personally to the editor-in-chief at the Chinese People's Literature Press.

Out of special concern for a minority writer, the editor-in-chief quickly got to work on it. When he was through, however, he had to point out to Maimaiti that the structure was too loose and that the tone and depiction of character were too playful. Moreover, he added, the book was superficial. For all these reasons, the book could not be published.

Minister Maimaiti argued with him about this.

"The book has to be published, even if what you've said is true, because if people read this book, they won't commit suicide during future political movements—if there are any."

The editor was deeply moved by this because he himself had more than once considered suicide during those troubled years. Finally he said that he would keep the manuscript and reconsider it.

But he murmured to himself, "For the prevention of suicide . . . can I really give this as a reason for publishing the book? What will the other editors say?"

It was at the Dashizi Muslim Restaurant, where I mentioned meeting Maimaiti at the beginning of this story, that he told me about his problems with his manuscript. In fact, he asked me to talk to the editor-in-chief about it on his behalf.

"If you need to give the editor a few gifts, I have plenty of raisins and butter here," he added.

"I think the problem is your manuscript," I replied, trying to look stern. "If it's good, all presses will compete to publish it. Giving gifts to our editors, what nonsense. It's a question of quality."

"Quality indeed," he replied. "But who is to judge exactly what quality is?"

Just then, the waiter came with our delicious food—fried meat, steamed meat, spiced meatballs, and sweet and sour ribs. Minister Maimaiti opened a bottle of Ancient City wine, filled his cup, and, holding his glass high, gave the following toast to me and to all his readers.

Ah, life! You may not be always sweet,
But you are never only bitter.
You may seem to drown a man,
Yet you flow forward, wider and wider.
Sometimes you seem stagnant and waveless,
Yet you are constantly changing in a profusion of colors.
In your ice is always fire.
In your sorrow always joy.
Prisons, knives, whips—
How can they hold life back?
Threats, slanders, lies—
Can they pull joy up by its root?
Do not weep, for tears disgust a man.
What is tragedy? A game, too affected.
Let's burst out laughing,
The power of laughter is the power of life!

Able to laugh, able to live.
Dare to laugh, dare to live.
Love laughter, love life.

At this, Minister Maimaiti drained his cup to the bottom.

Wang Meng

After You Read
Word Detective

Play detective and scan for the following words in the story, using the clues given below.

1. A long word starting with *d* that means "surprised to the point of being speechless" _____ (part 4)

2. An adverb meaning "in a loud manner" _____ (part 4)

3. A synonym for *devil,* beginning with *s* _____ (part 5)

4. An antonym for *strict* that also ends in *t* _____ (part 5)

5. A compound word meaning *defeat* and starting with the same letter _____ (part 6)

6. A three-syllable synonym for *portrayal,* starting with the letter *d* _____ (part 6)

Finding the Basis for Inference

Choose the correct inference about Maimaiti's character from each pair. Then give at least one example of an incident or detail from parts 4, 5, and 6 of the reading selection to support that inference.

1. **a.** Maimaiti had lots of energy.　　**b.** Maimaiti was lazy.

2. **a.** Maimaiti was dependent for his self-esteem on the opinion of others. 　　**b.** Maimaiti had his own ideas and did not care too much what others thought.

3. **a.** Maimaiti was simple-minded.　　**b.** Maimaiti was clever and a good actor.

4. **a.** Maimaiti was brave.　　**b.** Maimaiti was a coward.

5. **a.** Maimaiti followed a strict code of honesty.　　**b.** Maimaiti did not mind breaking rules.

Talking It Over

In small groups, discuss the following questions.

1. In your opinion, what did Maimaiti want to teach his fellow prisoners by talking about his "pretty girl"?

2. What do you think the guard interviewing Maimaiti thought of him? What did Maimaiti think of the guard?

3. What's your opinion of the reason Maimaiti gave for publishing his book? If you were an editor, would you publish it or not? Explain.

4. What is the main message of Maimaiti? Do you agree with it?

Minister Maimaiti in the World of Today

Work with a partner. One of you should play the role of Minister Maimaiti and the other the role of an interviewer, using the questions that follow. As an alternative, answer the questions in writing as if you were Minister Maimaiti.

1. Minister, many people say that today's society is in bad shape, with so much war and poverty. What do you think about the world situation?

2. What is your favorite TV program?

3. In your opinion, who is the most interesting person alive? Why?

4. Minister, what is your secret ambition?

5. What is your opinion of the writing done by the students in this class?

SELECTION **three**

Born Bad?

Before You Read
Surveying an Extended Nonfiction Reading

A nonfiction piece discussing a controversial question with two distinct sides generally has one of the following three kinds of organization:

1. It first presents one side of the question, then the other, each in a complete fashion. It then discusses what is right and wrong with each side and comes to some sort of conclusion.
2. It presents various different aspects of both sides of the question, a little at a time. It concludes that there is about an equal amount of truth on both sides.
3. It introduces the question and then presents evidence mostly in favor of one side, usually the side that is not popular. It mentions the other viewpoint briefly.

Before beginning the piece, survey it by skimming to decide which of the three types of organization it uses. The article is not divided into parts, so it is more difficult to get a general view. First, look at the title, photos, and chart for visual clues. Second, read the first paragraph and the first sentence of all the other paragraphs.

Which type of organization is used in this article: 1, 2, or 3?

Finding the Main Point in Long, Complex Sentences

"You can't see the forest for the trees." This is a common saying about the difficulty of finding the main point among many details. This is the problem with long sentences that have many clauses. Write down the connector words and then the main idea in each of the following sentences from the selection.

To find the main idea:

1. Cross out the connector words that introduce secondary clauses, along with the ideas following them.
2. See what is left and write it down.
3. If the idea seems incomplete, add a part—but not too much—in simple words to fill out the idea so it will make sense.

The first sentence is done as an example.

1. ~~Much as it may contradict the science of the past, which blamed crime on social influences such as poverty and bad parenting,~~ the outlaw may be onto something.

   connectors: Much as_____ , which_____

   *main idea:*_The outlaw may have the right idea, different from____

   _____the popular idea._____

2. But many researchers now believe that the reason one individual commits a crime and another person doesn't may have as much to do with neurological differences as it does with differences in upbringing or environment. (*Hint:* Remember that the word *but* can sometimes introduce the main idea of a sentence.)

   connectors: _____

   *main idea:*_____

3. After evaluating recent research on violence, a special panel gathered by the National Research Council (NRC) in Washington published a lengthy report last fall noting that "even if two individuals could be exposed to identical experiences, their potentials for violent behavior would differ because their nervous systems process information differently." (*Hint:* This sentence has a main idea within a main idea. Can you find both?)

connectors: _____

main idea: _____

main idea within main idea: _____

4. This fact suggests that certain hormones, particularly androgens, which characterize maleness, may help tip the balance from obeying to breaking the law.

   connectors: _____

   main idea: _____

5. While there's no such thing as a "crime gene," or indeed any single determinant that leads a person to break the law, each child is born with a particular temperament, or characteristic pattern of psychological response.

   connectors: _____

   main idea: _____

6. She found that lead poisoning, which is known to impair aspects of brain functioning, is the single best predictor of boys' disciplinary problems in school: such problems in turn are strongly associated with later adult crime.

   connectors: _____

   main idea: _____

7. After collaborating with Dr. Tomas Bouchard, Jr., on famous studies of more than 55 pairs of identical twins adopted separately at birth and reared apart, Dr. David Lykken, a psychologist at the University of Minnesota's Twin Research Center, says that "these traits correlate as strongly in twins who have been raised apart as in twins who were raised together."

   connectors: _____

   main idea: _____

WANTED

JOHN HERBERT DILLENGER

$10,000.00

WANTED

KATE "MA" BARKER

$5,000.00

What are the roots of crime? Does a criminal learn how to be evil because of stress and harsh treatment and the bad example of others? Or is a person born with evil inside, like a time bomb ready to explode? This is the question of Nature (the traits we inherit from our family) versus Nurture (the influence of our environment): Which is the main motor of crime? The following article explores this age-old problem that is still relevant in our times.

Born Bad?

New research points to a biological role in criminality

The tattoo on the ex-con's beefy arm reads: BORN TO RAISE HELL. Much as it may defy the science of the past, which blamed crime on social influences such as poverty and bad parenting, the outlaw may be onto something. Though no one would deny that upbringing and environment play important parts in the making of a criminal, scientists increasingly suspect that biology also plays a significant role.

Poverty and family problems, sex-role expectations, community standards—all may predispose individuals toward crime. But many researchers now believe that the reason one individual commits a crime and another person doesn't may have as much to do with neurological differences as it does with differences in upbringing or environment. After all, says Dr. James Q. Wilson, a professor of management and public policy at UCLA, "it's hard to find any form of behavior that doesn't have some biological component."

After evaluating recent research on violence, a special panel gathered by the National Research Council (NRC) in Washington published a lengthy report last fall noting that "even if two individuals could be exposed to identical experiences, their potentials for violent behavior would differ because their nervous systems process information differently."

First and most obvious among the clues that biology plays a role in criminal behavior is the simple fact that throughout history, crime has occurred in all cultures. One element in the universality of crime is the human capacity for aggression. Nobel prize-winning ethologist Konrad Lorenz, author of *On Aggression,* argued that just as people have an instinct for eating and drinking, nature evolved in them the impulse for aggression. Though Lorenz thought it was peculiar to people and rats, aggression has now been observed in every vertebrate species studied. In people, only a fine line separates aggression from violence—defined by researchers as behavior intended to inflict harm on others. "Criminals are, on the whole, angry people," says Harvard psychologist Richard Hernstein. "That's well substantiated."

Another simple fact pointing to a biological basis for criminality is that in all societies, about 90% of violent criminals are men—many of them young. The great majority of other crimes are also committed by men. Among animals too, the male is almost always more aggressive. This fact suggests that certain hormones, particularly androgens, which characterize maleness, may help tip the balance from obeying to breaking the law.

While there's no such thing as a "crime gene," or indeed any single determinant that leads a person to break the law, each child is born with a particular temperament, or characteristic pattern of psychological response. As Wilson notes, "One is shy, the other bold; one sleeps through the night, the other is always awake; one is curious and exploratory, the other passive. These observations are about differences that cannot be explained wholly or even largely by environment."

Linking an individual's temperament to criminality is, of course, a much more con-

$5000 REWARD
FRANK JAMES
DEAD or ALIVE

$10,000.00
DEAD or ALIVE
WILLIAM H. BONNEY
BILLY THE KID
Pat Garrett, Sheriff

tentious matter. To search for the roots of violence, the members of the NRC panel asked several key questions. Why do some children show patterns of unusually aggressive behavior—hitting, kicking, biting peers or parents, or being cruel to animals—at an early age? Why do only a small percentage of those children commit violent crimes as adults? The panel concluded: "Research strongly suggests that violence arises from *interactions among* individuals' psychosocial development, their neurological and hormonal differences, and social processes." There is no basis, the researchers added, for giving one of these elements more weight than another.

Nonetheless, two camps have emerged to debate whether criminality is influenced more by nature (biology) or nurture (environment). And this is no mere ivory tower* question. Public interest mounts with the statistics: Some 35 million offenses against people or households, 20% of them violent, are reported in the U.S. every year.

Research that may help resolve this nature–nurture question focuses mostly on three areas: biochemical imbalances, genetic

*Place or situation removed from worldly or practical affairs

factors and physical damage such as head injury around the time of birth. Some studies suggest a link between criminal behavior—particularly the violent sort—and birth-related trauma, premature birth or low birth weight. Similarly, a woman's use of alcohol, cocaine, tobacco or other drugs during pregnancy also appears, in some instances, to damage fetal development in a way that is related to later criminality. On a more positive note, however, one recent study concluded that when children who'd had a traumatic birth grew up in a stable family environment, they were no likelier than anyone else to develop into criminals.

Childhood injury to brain tissue may also figure in later criminal behavior. Law professor Deborah Denno of Fordham University in New York City, studied a group of nearly 500 boys from birth to age 23. She found that lead poisoning, which is known to impair aspects of brain functioning, is the single best predictor of boys' disciplinary problems in school; such problems in turn are strongly associated with later adult crime. Denno had expected to find family factors most strongly implicated in delinquency and criminal behavior and was astonished by her results.

Both animal experiments and cases of human head injury and brain damage have pinpointed areas of the brain where impairment or seizure can trigger aggression. In monkeys, researchers can elicit "sham rage" by using electrodes to stimulate the limbic system, a group of structures deep within the brain that influence emotions. A rare condition called intermittent explosive disorder is linked to periodic seizures in the same brain area.

Convincing evidence from the field of behavioral genetics implies that certain biological predispositions to criminal behavior are inherited. Like test pilots and mountain climbers, delinquents and criminals tend to be born with relatively calm nervous systems that allow them to face risky situations with minimal stress. Other personality traits, including aggressiveness and impulsivity, partly depend on genes.

After collaborating with Dr. Tomas Bouchard, Jr., on famous studies of more than 55 pairs of identical twins adopted separately at birth and reared apart, Dr. David Lykken, a psychologist at the University of Minnesota's Twin Research Center, says that "these traits correlate as strongly in twins who have been raised apart as in twins who were raised together." Moreover, the largest twin study of criminality ever conducted, published in Denmark in 1987, found that when a male identical twin* committed a crime, his twin was five times likelier than the average Danish man to commit a crime as well; when a fraternal twin† committed a crime, his twin was three times likelier than other Danish men to break the law.

One way or another, says Harvard psychologist Jerome Kagan, there's no question that people inherit different neurochemistries. He has categorized babies by their patterns of excitability and identified four basic types. "Think of them as different breeds of puppies," he says, "just as Pekingnese, for example, are naturally more irritable than beagles."

Dr. Kagan's research suggest that 35% to 40% of babies are born with a very relaxed approach to the world around them. Many of the babies he studied react to stress with a low degree of excitability, as gauged by physical indicators such as heartbeat, blood pressure and adrenaline secretion. By the time these children are between 20 and 30 months old, they can frequently be described as extroverted and relatively fearless. (Of the fraction who warrant the description *extremely* fearless, 80% are boys.)

According to Kagan, this personality type results from the unique combination of a baby's basic pattern of excitability with his physical response to his environment. But the baby's family also influences the type of adult he becomes. For example, if a relaxed baby who's not very excitable is raised by loving, attentive parents, he might grow up to be an intellectual risk taker—an artist, a scientist or a politician. But in an unfavorable family environment, the same child might become, say, a bank robber.

Yet another area of research concerns biochemical imbalances. Even hypoglycemia (low blood sugar) has been linked to antisocial behavior. Mr. Matti Virkkunen, a psychiatrist at the University of Helsinki in Finland, has found that the condition is more common among alcoholic, impulsive, violent offenders than among ordinary people.

The fact is that no single influence turns an individual into a criminal. Human traits —impulsivity or fearlessness—are by themselves neutral; they're as characteristic of leaders and artists as they are of criminals.

---

*Twin developed from one fertilized ovum; twins look very much alike
†Twin who developed from two fertilized ova; twins can look quite different from one another

Fyodor Dostoyevsky recognized this paradox in *Crime and Punishment,* as did Robert Louis Stevenson in *The Strange Case of Dr. Jekyll and Mr. Hyde.** The French sociologist Emile Durkheim even declared that he would not want to live in a society without crime.

Ominous statistics indicate that Durkheim's fears about life in an utterly safe so-ciety are unlikely to be realized in the near future. The huge number of murders and muggings, rapes and robberies taking place in our society today ensure that scientists will expand their research on criminality and violence. "There's no magic bullet, no single approach that will end crime," says Harvard's Hernstein. "But each new advance in research raises the possibility of a constructive remedy."

Glenn Garelik

*Two nineteenth-century novels that present famous studies of people who have a good side to their character and an evil, criminal side at the same time

After You Read
Analyzing a Line of Argument

Look back through the article and fill in the following chart with different points mentioned to support each side of the Nature-Nurture argument. Then finish the statement, telling what you infer as the main idea of the article.

nature (genetics, biolology)	nurture (environment, influence)
1. Neurological differences as reason for committing a crime	1. Poverty, bad parenting as social influences of crime
2. _____	2. _____
3. _____	3. _____
4. _____	4. _____

Conclusion: The selection concludes that _____

is probably (as important as/more important than/less important than)

_____ in causing crime.

Drawing Conclusions from a Graph

exercise 2 Look at the graph and answer the questions.

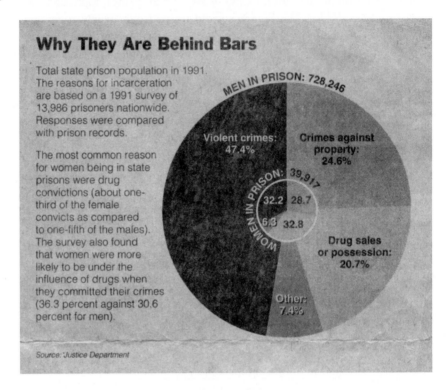

1. What is the difference between the large circle and the small circle? Which one represents men and which women?

2. According to the graph, are men or women more likely to commit violent crimes?

3. Which group is more likely to commit more crimes related to drugs? More crimes related to property?

4. Which of the differences are significant and which seem very small?

5. How do you explain the differences between men and women with regard to crime?

Talking It Over

activity 1 In small groups, discuss the following questions.

1. What people have you heard of who seemed to be "born bad"?

2. In your opinion, what factors in the environment cause crime? Explain.

Mosaic I • Reading

3. A person grows up to be a serial murderer. Therefore, his parents did something very wrong. True or false? Why?

4. Do you think that in times of war or terrible stress, almost anyone becomes a criminal? Explain.

5. What do you think of Emile Durkheim's idea about living in a society without crime (mentioned in the last paragraph)? Do you agree with him? Why or why not?

What Would You Do?

activity **2**

In small groups, read the following situations and decide what you would do in each case.

1. You go to a famous geneticist (doctor specializing in genetics) because you are worried about your family history. There are several ancestors who were criminals and one relative alive today is in prison. What would you do? Why?
   a. I would never marry.
   b. I would marry but not have any children.
   c. I would marry and have children.

2. You are a member of the jury at a murder trial. Malcolm, a young man 20 years old, admits that he killed his stepfather. His stepfather had beaten him many times and continually used abusive language to make him feel evil and worthless. At the time of the killing, Malcolm was completely drunk after consuming a whole bottle of whiskey. The defense lawyer argues that Malcolm was not fully responsible for his actions because his mind was clouded by alcohol. Also, he had been beaten and humiliated so much that he was full of hatred and thought of himself as evil. What would you do? Why?
   a. Sentence Malcolm to life imprisonment for murder with no possibility of parole, as suggested by the prosecution
   b. Sentence Malcolm to a shorter term (5–10 years) of prison for manslaughter
   c. Recommend that Malcolm receive several years of rehabilitation, as suggested by the defense

WHAT DO YOU THINK?

Using the Death Penalty

"An eye for an eye, a tooth for a tooth." This Biblical statement from the Old Testament is indicative of one type of thinking about crime and punishment. If someone takes another person's life, the life of that someone should also be taken. This practice is called "capital punishment" in English. It means that the state has the right to kill the killer.

Do you agree with this type of punishment? Do you think that the threat of capital punishment stops people from committing murder? Do you think killers should be kept in prison for life instead of being executed? Why or why not? What are the various types of punishments for different crimes in your country?

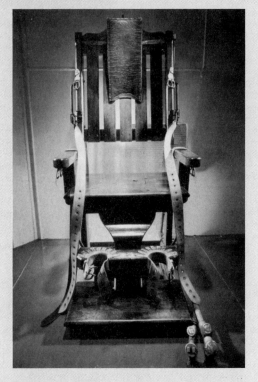

Chair in the gas chamber at Central Prison, Raleigh, North Carolina

CHAPTER eleven

The Physical World

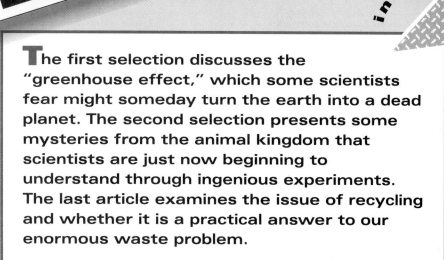

in this chapter

The first selection discusses the "greenhouse effect," which some scientists fear might someday turn the earth into a dead planet. The second selection presents some mysteries from the animal kingdom that scientists are just now beginning to understand through ingenious experiments. The last article examines the issue of recycling and whether it is a practical answer to our enormous waste problem.

Hothouse Earth

Before You Read

Separating Fact from Opinion

*exercise*

As you read, try to separate facts from opinions. Notice that at times statements are qualified by subordinate clauses or by modals such as *may, might, could,* or *would* in such a way as to indicate that they are based on opinion. On the other hand, phrases such as "it is clear" or "it is certain" or the quoting of exact statistics or measurements usually accompany statements based on facts. Scan the article to find one example of a fact and one of an opinion. Write them down here:

Fact: _____

_____

Opinion: _____

_____

Compare your answers with those of your classmates.

Is the earth getting warmer each year? If so, what effects will this have? What is the "greenhouse effect," which some scientists say might destroy our planet? Will the burning of fossil fuels (coal, oil, natural gas) cause the earth to become a dead planet like Venus? The following article from *Discover* magazine discusses these and other questions.

Hothouse Earth

Carbon dioxide from fossil fuels will probably cause a "greenhouse effect" that warms the climate. But how drastically, and how soon?

Headlines warned of rising temperatures and melting polar ice caps. Television newscasters spoke grimly about palm trees sprouting on New York City's Fifth Avenue and floods inundating Charleston, South Carolina, and Galveston, Texas, and other coastal cities.

These warnings appeared because scientists from the Environmental Protection Agency (EPA) and the National Academy of Sciences (NAS) issued reports on the severe climate changes that could result from the "greenhouse effect"—the gradual warming of the atmosphere caused by an increase in carbon dioxide levels from the burning of fossil fuels.

The EPA report concluded that average global temperatures could start to rise within a few decades—some say the rise has already begun—and reach levels nine degrees Fahrenheit higher than today's temperatures by the end of the next century. This, the experts said, could wreak havoc with global weather patterns, change annual amounts of rainfall, swell or dry up rivers, and raise the level of the seas. Farming, building, and the political stability of nations could be profoundly disrupted.

While admitting that this forecast was somewhat uncertain, the scientists warned against treating it as a cry of wolf. "We are deeply concerned about environmental changes of this magnitude," the National Academy of Sciences said.

Although there is considerable debate over how severe the greenhouse effect will be, one thing seems certain: Carbon dioxide levels are on the rise. Measurements at the federal atmospheric observatory on Mauna Loa volcano in Hawaii show that the concentration of the gas in the atmosphere has risen steadily from 315 parts per million in 1958 to 340 parts per million today. Air pockets trapped in glacial ice indicate that in the mid-nineteenth century, the concentration was only about 265 parts per million.

The evident culprit, scientists conclude, is the burning of coal, oil, synthetic fuels, and natural gas. These fossil energy sources release an estimated five and a half billion tons of carbon into the atmosphere each year as colorless, odorless CO_2 gas.

The increased carbon dioxide is probably not a threat to health, since normal indoor levels of the gas can run 1,000 parts per million or higher without apparent harm. However, it could profoundly affect the way the earth is heated by the sun. The sun's energy strikes the earth principally in the form of visible light. As the earth heats up, it radiates this energy back into space, but at the much longer wavelengths of infrared light, or heat. Carbon dioxide lets the visible light pass through, but absorbs energy at infrared wavelengths. Thus, the more carbon dioxide in the atmosphere, the more the earth's heat is blocked from escaping—just as a blanket holds in the heat of a sleeper's body. In the late 1800s, the Swedish scientist Svante Arrhenius gave this phenomenon its name when he compared it to the way glass traps air heated by the sun in a greenhouse.

Some scientists think the greenhouse effect already has begun: Average global temperatures have risen about one degree Fahrenheit in the past ninety years (with a dip from the mid-1940s to 1970). Others argue that the rise could be due to natural temperature fluctuations.

Nevertheless, most scientists agree that the accumulation of carbon dioxide has reached the point where an increase in temperature is imminent. The EPA study said average global temperatures probably would rise nearly four degrees by the twenty-first century—a total warming greater than that since the last ice age.

Rising temperatures would be just the beginning. The heating would shift global rainfall patterns, the EPA warned, bringing drought to some now-fertile areas and irrigating some deserts. Likewise, alpine glaciers and polar ice caps could melt substantially, causing the seas to rise two feet by the end of the century. Many low-lying communities could be flooded. Worst of all, the report said, the effect may be irreversible.

These grim conclusions were seconded, but in more cautious language, by the 496-page report released by the National Academy of Sciences. The NAS echoed some of the EPA's predictions, but saw in them "reason for caution, not panic." True, the study said, a four-degree heating would probably bring a 40 to 76 percent decrease in the amount of water in western rivers. But the NAS saw a silver lining in some of the dark clouds. A summer melting of the arctic ice pack, it pointed out, could open a land passage between the Atlantic and Pacific and encourage oil and gas exploration in the Arctic Ocean. Both agencies noted that increased carbon dioxide would make photosynthesis more efficient, increasing crop yields.

Even some of the good effects could have bad consequences, however. Russia and Canada, for example, could stand to benefit from a warming trend because it would make more of their frigid land farmable. And that fact might make them less likely to cooperate with any worldwide ban on fossil fuels. "Given that these two countries (and Eastern Europe) burn 25 percent of the world coal," the NAS report said, "it is hard to see how a carbon dioxide control strategy can succeed without them."

Most scientists agree with climate modeler James Hansen of the Goddard Institute for Space Studies in New York City that the report's predictions were "within the range of plausibility." That fact showed the faith that scientists now have in the computer models on which such studies are based. The EPA, for example, used separate computer simulations to predict world fuel consumption, the world distribution of carbon, and the temperature of the atmosphere. These models are extremely complex.

Running a climate model is like creating a world, says Jerry Mahlman, a meteorologist at Princeton's Geophysical Fluid Dynamics Laboratory. "First you turn on the sun, then you put in some oceans, add the atmosphere, and start the earth spinning." Climate modelers are not ready to call themselves God, he declares. "Our models don't have that kind of precision."

Even if the math is right, scientists can never be sure that they have included all the variables and modeled them accurately. The biggest source of uncertainty in climate models is the oceans. Other important variables are clouds and gases like nitrous oxide, methane, ozone, and chlorofluorocarbons, which also contribute to the greenhouse effect.

Some critics of this research have maintained that the world faces such great dangers from population growth, diminishing food supply, and the spread of nuclear weapons that the greenhouse threat seems mild by comparison. Others argue that since the earth has endured a long string of ice ages in the last two million to three million years, any warming is likely to be temporary. Even so, those who try to minimize the problem must also explain away the harsh conditions on the planet Venus. There, a runaway greenhouse effect is thought to account for surface temperatures approaching 900 degrees Fahrenheit; Venus's cloud-shrouded atmosphere is about 97 percent carbon dioxide.

Although few scientists think the earth will go the way of Venus, most agree that planning for the greenhouse problem should start soon. The EPA's John Hoffman says, for example, that the estimated $210 million damage that would result from the flooding of Charleston, South Carolina, could be cut in half by such measures as revised city planning and dikes. Similarly, catch basins and reservoirs could be built to supplement water supplies in drying regions. As Hoffman puts it, "We feel carbon dioxide is a very serious thing, but we think there *is* time to do research, and there *is* time to adapt." Meanwhile, scientists will be keeping an eye on the thermometer for the first definite sign that the greenhouse era has arrived.

Kevin McKean

After You Read

Separating Fact from Opinion

 On the basis of your reading of the article, tell which of the statements below and on the next page are facts (F) and which are opinions (O). If you are unsure about certain ones, scan the article for them and examine their context.

1. _____ Palm trees will someday be sprouting on New York City's Fifth Avenue.

2. _____ Average global temperatures have already begun to rise because of the greenhouse effect.

3. _____ Carbon dioxide levels in the atmosphere have risen in the past twenty-five years.

4. _____ Carbon dioxide lets visible light pass through but absorbs energy at infrared wavelengths.

5. _____ The melting of alpine glaciers and polar ice caps will soon cause the seas to rise and flood many coastal areas.

6. _____ An increase of carbon dioxide to even double the amount presently in the air would probably not be damaging to health.

7. _____ In the late 1800s, a Swedish scientist invented the term *greenhouse effect*.

8. _____ Higher temperatures throughout the world would have good as well as bad effects.

9. _____ Since the earth has endured numerous ice ages over the last few million years, any warming will be temporary.

10. _____ The atmosphere of the very hot planet Venus is about 97 percent carbon dioxide.

Comprehending Complex Sentences

exercise **2**

Study the following complex sentences from the article. Find the secondary clause(s) in each sentence and decide how it changes the meaning of the main clause. Then, in small groups, check your understanding by selecting the phrase that best completes the explanation.

1. "Although there is considerable debate over how severe the greenhouse effect will be, one thing seems certain: Carbon dioxide levels are on the rise." The severity of the greenhouse effect is
   a. one thing that seems certain.
   b. definitely on the rise.
   c. not acknowledged as a fact by everyone.
   d. not talked about very much.

2. "Thus, the more carbon dioxide in the atmosphere, the more the earth's heat is blocked from escaping." The earth will get hotter if
   a. carbon dioxide increases.
   b. carbon dioxide decreases.
   c. the block becomes smaller.
   d. some atmosphere escapes.

3. "Even if the math is right [in computer simulations], scientists can never be sure that they have included all variables and modeled them accurately." To make a correct computer simulation, a scientist must
   a. include all variables.
   b. model the variables in the right way.
   c. do the mathematics accurately.
   d. all the above.

4. "Some critics of this research have maintained that the world already faces such great dangers from population growth, diminishing food supply, and the spread of nuclear weapons that the greenhouse threat seems mild by comparison." Some scientists feel that the greenhouse effect is
   a. the greatest danger now facing the world.
   b. less serious than other dangers at present.
   c. the cause of several related dangers.
   d. not really a danger at all for the moment.

Stories Behind Words

exercise
All languages contain words or phrases with a special meaning taken from well-known stories or sayings. The preceding article includes two such phrases.

1. In lines 30 to 31 we are told that scientists warned against treating the forecast of rising temperatures as a "cry of wolf." This phrase is taken from the popular story about a young shepherd boy who liked to play tricks on his neighbors. He used to cry "Wolf! Wolf!" just for fun. At first everyone would come running to help him, but soon they realized that he was only fooling them. One day a wolf really did come, and he cried out: "Wolf! Wolf!" but no one came. So the wolf ate all his sheep. Now that you know the story, write down the meaning of a "cry of wolf."

   _____

   _____

2. According to lines 107 to 108, the NAS basically agreed with the grim predictions of the EPA about the greenhouse effect, but saw "a silver lining in some of the dark clouds." A common English saying often quoted to people with problems is "Every cloud has a silver lining." This refers to the patch of sunlight often seen underneath dark storm clouds. Now that you know the saying, explain what it means to see "a silver lining in some of the dark clouds."

   _____

   _____

   _____

   _____

   _____

   _____

   _____

Understanding Acronyms

exercise 4

An acronym is a word formed from the first letters (or first few letters) of words in a set phrase. Acronyms are often used to refer to international or governmental agencies, such as WHO for the World Health Organization, or NAFTA for the North America Free Trade Agreement. Some technical words that have come into the English language in recent decades are really acronyms, such as RADAR (RAdio Detecting And Ranging). Write down the meanings of the following acronyms. If you do not know some of them, you can look them up in a dictionary. Answers are on page 237.

INTERNATIONAL AGENCIES

NATO_____

OPEC_____

UNESCO_____

Turhan/Istanbul

U.S. AND CANADIAN GOVERNMENT AGENCIES

NASA_____

CIDA_____

TECHNICAL TERMS

LASER_____

SCUBA_____

SNAFU_____

AIDS_____

Talking It Over

In small groups, discuss the following questions.

1. Explain the comparison made between carbon dioxide in the atmosphere and a blanket over a sleeper's body. (paragraph 7)

2. Exactly what is the "greenhouse effect"?

3. How is a computer used to forecast environmental problems? Why is it difficult to be certain of the results?

4. What other uses have you heard of for computer simulations?

SELECTION two

Migration and Homing

Before You Read
Outlining as You Read

Make an informal outline of the selection as you read. First, skim the selection in one or two minutes. As in most textbook writing, the paragraphs are long, so you can use the topic of each paragraph as a heading. Look at the first sentence or two to find the topic. Write the topics in brief phrases, not complete sentences. Put down the three headings here.

1. _____

2. _____

3. _____

Compare them with those of other members of your class to find the shortest yet most complete way of writing the headings. Now write these on a sheet of paper, leaving a good deal of space in between. Then read the selection carefully and fill in examples and explanations under each heading. Notice that the textbook occasionally asks the reader a question and then gives the answer. Do you think it is important to write these down in your notes? Why or why not?

Everyone knows that many animals have special abilities and instincts that we human beings lack. What examples can you think of? The following excerpt from the college biology textbook *Life on Earth* describes two examples of this that have puzzled people since ancient times. How do birds travel thousands of miles across open oceans and find their way to one particular island? How can animals return home after being carried far away? The following selection discusses some of these explanations.

Migration and Homing

The annals of natural history contain many astonishing examples of the ability of animals to find their way home after making distant journeys. Salmon, for example, are born in freshwater streams and soon afterward journey down to sea. Several years later, after they have attained maturity, they swim back upstream to spawn and, in many cases, to die. The particular stream that serves as the journey's end is almost invariably the same one in which they were born. It is chosen out of dozens or hundreds of equally suitable streams. The expression "almost invariably" is used advisedly in this case. In one investigation by Canadian biologists, 469,326 young sockeye salmon were marked in a tributary of the Fraser River. Several years later almost 11,000 were recovered after they had completed a return journey to the very same stream, but not a single one was ever recovered from other streams nearby. What underwater guideposts can these fish possibly follow? It has been discovered by A. D. Hasler and his associates at the University of Wisconsin that the salmon, like many other fish, have an acute sense of smell and are able to remember slight differences in the chemical composition of water. The most reasonable theory to explain salmon homing is that each individual remembers the distinctive "fragrance" of its native stream. As it moves upstream it makes the correct choice each time a new tributary is encountered, until finally it arrives home.

Human beings unaided by maps and compasses could not match the long journeys routinely made by birds.

Long-distance migration is especially common in birds, because many species must make annual journeys between their nesting grounds and prime feeding areas far away. Each year over 100,000 sooty terns, an attractive tropical sea bird, travel from the waters off the west coast of Africa all the way across the Atlantic to Bush Key, a tiny island near the tip of Florida. Here they build their nests and breed. Once the young can fly, all journey back over the Atlantic. Why do the sooty terns migrate at all? Like many other sea birds, they find protection from cats, foxes, and other predators on isolated islands. It is evidently safer for them to make an entire transoceanic voyage to reach one such haven than it would be to try to nest on the nearby African shores. A somewhat different reason lies behind the north-south migration of birds in the temperate zones. Each spring a legion of migratory forms, from robins, thrushes, and warblers to geese and ducks, makes its way north into the greening countryside, where large quantities of food are becoming freshly available. Working rapidly, they are able to rear one or more broods of young. As winter approaches and the food supply declines, all head south again. Some species proceed all the way to Central and South America. The record annual journey in the Western Hemisphere is made by the golden plover, one group of which travels from northern Canada to southern South America. A second group of the same species migrates from Alaska to Hawaii and the Marquesas Islands. Human beings could never make such journeys unaided by maps and navigational instruments. How do the birds do it? A large part of the answer lies in their ability to use celestial clues. At migration time, caged starlings become unusually restless. If permitted to see the sun, they begin to fly toward the side of the cage that lies in the direction of their normal migration route. However, when the sky is overcast and the sun is obscured from view, their movements persist, but they are nondirectional. Other migratory birds fly at night and can evidently use the position of the stars to guide them. This surprising fact has been established by several biologists, including S. T. Emlen of Cornell University, who allowed a type of bird called indigo buntings to attempt flights under the artificial night sky of a planetarium. The birds oriented "correctly" with reference to the planetarium sky even when the positions of its constellations did not correspond with the position of the true constellations outside. Thus other outside influences were eliminated, and it could be concluded that the birds were able to orient to what they believed to be the position of the stars.

Even more impressive than the guidance of migratory movements by celestial clues is the phenomenon of homing. If you were blindfolded,

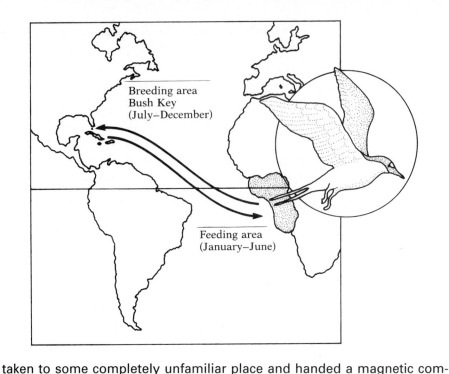

Breeding area
Bush Key
(July–December)

Feeding area
(January–June)

taken to some completely unfamiliar place and handed a magnetic compass, you could head north, south, or in any direction you arbitrarily chose—but you could not head home. Simple compass reading is also the essential ability demonstrated by migrating birds. But it is not enough in itself to explain how homing pigeons are able to return to their own lofts from as far as 600 miles away in a single day. Nor is it enough to account for such feats as that of one particular Manx shearwater (a kind of sea bird), which, after being carried in an airplane from England to Boston, flew back across the Atlantic and arrived at its nest in England twelve days later. For a bird to travel home over unfamiliar terrain requires true navigation—that is, the ability to reckon its position on the surface of the earth with reference to the position of the distant goal. One of the currently most attractive hypotheses is that the birds somehow sense the earth's magnetic field, which varies systematically from point to point over the earth's surface. Evidence supporting this idea has come from experiments by William T. Keeton of Cornell University, who attached tiny magnets to the necks of homing pigeons in order to cancel the effects of the earth's magnetic field. Birds thus encumbered lost their homing ability, but birds burdened with nonmagnetic metal bars placed at the same position on the neck managed to travel home correctly. These birds were used as "controls" in the experiments.

From *Life on Earth*

After You Read

Defining Words from Context

Write short definitions or explanations for the following words from the article. Scan for those you do not know. The meaning can be determined from context. Sometimes the meaning is explained several paragraphs after the word is first mentioned.

1. *spawn* (verb)_____

2. *tributary* (noun)_____

3. *migration* (noun)_____

4. *celestial* (adjective) _____

5. *homing* (noun) _____

Comparing Outlines

In small groups, compare your outlines. Did you write too much or too little under any of the headings? Choose the outline that would be the best aid for study and explain why.

Talking It Over

In small groups, discuss the following questions.

1. What other animals, besides birds and fish, seem to have special abilities and instincts that we human beings lack? What is the most interesting example of this that you have heard?

2. The experiments on homing discussed at the very end of the article used certain birds called "control" birds. Can you explain what they are and why "controls" like these are necessary to make the experiment scientific?

3. What do you think of the use of animals for scientific experiments? Is it justifiable to kill animals or cause them pain in order to gain more knowledge?

Answers to Exercise 4, page 232

International Agencies: North Atlantic Treaty Organization; Organization of Petroleum Exporting Countries; United Nations Educational, Scientific, and Cultural Organization; **U.S. and Canadian Government Agencies:** National Aeronautics and Space Administration; Canadian International Development Agency; **Technical Terms:** Light Amplification by Stimulated Emission of Radiation; Self-Contained Underwater Breathing Apparatus; Situation Normal: All Fouled Up; Acquired ImmunoDeficiency Syndrome

Doing the Easy Ones First

Tests include some items that are designed to be easy, some to be moderately difficult, and others to be hard. Usually students do the items in the order given. Sometimes they get stuck on the hard items and do not finish the test during the time limit. A good strategy is to quickly do the easy items first, skipping the ones that seem hard. Then go back and do the difficult ones.

Skim the following exercise to find the easy items that you can do right away. Which ones are they?_____

Compare the item numbers you wrote with the ones selected by your classmates. Did you all choose the same ones? Now look at the remaining ones. What makes them harder?

Practice picking out hard items quickly and leaving them for later. Use this technique for exercises and tests in the future, and you will learn to "beat the clock."

exercise Take a minute or two to look over your outline of the selection "Migration and Homing." Then test your understanding of the article by selecting the correct answers to complete the following statements.

1. After becoming mature, salmon swim back to spawn
   a. in the sea.
   b. in the same stream in which they were born.
   c. in any one of hundreds of tributaries.

2. Salmon are able to find their way back because of their good sense of
   a. sight.
   b. taste.
   c. smell.

3. Each year sooty terns fly from Africa to an island near Florida to nest, probably because
   a. there is no food for birds on the nearby African shores.
   b. they are safe there from animals that would eat them.
   c. their wing muscles become developed from the flight.

4. Caged starlings fly in the direction of their migration route on sunny days but make only nondirectional movements when there is no sun. This experiment suggests that the starlings
   a. navigate by an inborn compass.
   b. fly only when it is warm.
   c. use celestial clues for migration.

5. Other experiments indicate that indigo buntings and certain other birds that fly at night navigate by
   a. the position of the stars.
   b. the shape of the land.
   c. their sense of hearing.

6. At present, one of the best hypotheses to explain the homing of birds over areas they do not know is that they use
   a. their keen sense of smell.
   b. the movement of wind currents.
   c. the magnetic field of the earth.

SELECTION three

Recycling: Getting the Most Out of Our Garbage

Before You Read

Timed Reading

The following article from *U.S. News & World Report* discusses another problem that involves the interaction of people and the physical world. Read it quickly; then check your comprehension by taking the quiz at the end. You should be able to complete the reading and the quiz in 10 minutes.

Recycling: Getting the Most Out of Our Garbage

Last fall, the city of Philadelphia put 11 tons of odoriferous garbage on a plane to Leibstadt, Switzerland. Two weeks later the shipment came home. It was shredded, dry, chemically stable, odor-free, and separated into reusable products such as ceramics, plastics, paper fiber, metals, glass for road constructions, and organic material for compost or fuel.

The transatlantic trash flight was undertaken to test out a Swiss-designed recycling system known as ORFA, which turns conventional mixed garbage into a range of raw materials in just 17 mintues.

An ORFA plant is due to come on line in Philadelphia in October, and another one in Somerville, Massachusetts, next year. A similar Swiss system developed by the Bühler-

Miag company is already in the testing stage at Eden Prairie, Minnesota.

Growing European concern over incinerating garbage has spurred a move toward recycling, and the Leibstadt plant is one of several systems designed to bring as much automation as possible into waste recycling.

Increasingly, waste is being seen as a resource that the world can no longer afford to squander. Cynthia Pollock, author of "Worldwatch Paper 76: Mining Urban Wastes: The Potential for Recycling," says society has no choice but to recycle if it is to preserve natural resources that are being depleted at geometrically increasing rates. As she has pointed out, "simply recovering the print run of a Sunday issue of the *New York Times* would leave 75,000 trees standing."

But is recycling a practical solution? Opinions range widely over how much solid waste can be easily recycled. A citizen recycling program in Wilton and several other New Hampshire towns recycles 45 percent of its solid waste. New European mechanical systems can prepare all of the waste stream [waste water] for recycling.

Neil Seldman, who has investigated waste-handling systems in much of the world for the Institute for Local Self-Reliance, says that up to 80 percent of the United States' waste stream could readily be recycled, "and at half the cost of current plans for long-term hauling and incineration if it's done properly."

By "properly," Mr. Seldman means recycling programs must be funded and managed by officials who do more than pay lip service to the concept. Too often, Seldman says, a city will call for recycling a quarter of its waste, but with only 1 or 2 percent of its solid-waste management budget. And cities seeking to recycle are faced with a chicken-or-egg problem. For recycling to pay off, there must be a market for the raw materials generated; but it's difficult to get buyers for the raw material until they can be assured of a steady supply.

The National Recycling Coalition recently called on Congress to pass tax incentives that would encourage development of new applications of waste materials. It also seeks control on freight costs of recycled raw materials, which are now more expensive to transport than virgin raw materials.

Burying waste has long been a freely available and inexpensive option, so recycling has had to prove cost-effective to win public acceptance. Aluminum and tin from the plating on steel cans are among the very few materials profitable enough to recycle. But now, with land fill costs skyrocketing, recycling is becoming a competitive waste-disposal system.

A recent study done for St. Paul, Minnesota, bears this out. It puts the cost of disposing of waste through recycling at $30 a ton, after subtracting revenues from secondary material sales. By comparison, land filling costs $90 a ton now, and will continue to rise; incineration runs $90 to $110 a ton.

Ideally, recycling begins at home, with individuals separating waste into various categories—glass, aluminum, paper—along with curbside pickup programs. Many such programs are now operating in the United States, and this is one aspect, says Seldman, where the United States is ahead of Europe."

To boost citizen participation in its recently introduced curbside recycling program, the city of Rockford, Illinois, gave away $1,000 each week to a resident whose

A recycling center: Waste is now being seen as a valuable resource.

garbage was found, in a random check, to be separated into the appropriate categories.

Following home or office separation, hand picking of garbage from conveyor belts at recycling centers removed easily identifiable and valuable recyclables such as glass containers, plastic beverage bottles, aluminum, and steel cans.

Murray Fox, of Recycling Enterprises, Inc., of North Oxford, Massachusetts, designs systems involving initial hand separation. In one such plant, operated by a non-profit organization in Flint, Michigan, 800 tons a week of garbage is being processed. One of the shifts involves mentally handicapped workers, who have proved outstanding at the job. He describes the improved self-image of these people as one of the "unexpected rewards" to come his way since entering the recycling business more than a decade ago.

At the forefront of American solid-waste technology is the unique Agripost system, which has been tested in the United States and abroad and will soon go into the construction phase in Dade County, Florida (Miami). While not a recycling process in the full meaning of the word, the Agripost system converts solid waste—including steel, glass, rubber, and plastic—into a single, useful product: a finely ground, chemically stable compost, with no leftover needing to be land filled. The end product has been fully approved by the United States Department of Agriculture.

The two Swiss recycling systems, Bühler-Miag and ORFA, also leave little or nothing for the land fill. The processes are designed to handle the waste stream as it comes: everything from yellowing cabbage leaves to the kitchen sink. Simply stated, the waste is shredded in hammermills and cutters before passing through a series of sieves, screens, and classifiers, which separate the waste into its component parts, leaving it in a stable, clean, odor-free condition.

At present the principal salable product from Bühler-Miag's Minnesota plant will be fuel pellets made from recycled organic 150 waste (paper and wood fiber), although the waste could also be diverted to paper manufacture, once there's a market for it, company spokesmen say. For its part, ORFA has contracts to sell recovered paper to manu- 155 facturers in the region. Aluminum and plastic separation will begin soon afterward.

These automated recycling plants, along with the Agripost operation, are designed to process 400 tons of city waste a day, with 160 the capacity for more in the future. A rough calculation shows it would take 1,000 or so of these plants to handle the country's daily garbage production of 400,000 tons a day.

Will America make that commitment 165 someday? At this point, it seems far off.

Peter Tonge

After You Read

Comprehension Quiz

Choose the correct word or phrase to complete each of the following statements about the article.

1. The city of Philadelphia sent 11 tons of garbage by plane to Switzerland in order to
   a. test out a possible system for recycling its garbage.
   b. get rid of dangerous materials.
   c. provide Switzerland with some badly needed chemicals.
   d. show the Swiss that conventional garbage can be turned into a range of products.

2. With the increasing depletion of the natural environment, people are beginning to feel that garbage is not just something to dispose of; instead it is
   a. an organic material.   c. a resource.
   b. a print run.   d. a waste.

3. The "recycling" of waste materials means that they are
   a. completely eliminated.
   b. transported far away.
   c. changed into useful products.
   d. changed into harmless substances

4. When Mr. Seldman says that "cities seeking to recycle are faced with a chicken-or-egg problem," he means that
   a. in some cities there is not enough food for people to eat and so they do not want to try out new recycling systems there.
   b. many people would prefer to buy and sell chickens and eggs rather than working with garbage or recycling.

c. you can't get recycling without a market for recycled goods just as you can't get chickens without eggs or eggs without chickens.

d. to make recycling pay off you must get buyers to produce garbage and sellers to dispose of it just as eggs produce chickens and chickens produce eggs.

5. Before land fill costs became so high, the most inexpensive and freely available option for waste disposal was
   a. recycling.
   b. automation.
   c. incineration.
   d. burying.

6. One aspect of recycling where the United States is ahead of Europe seems to be its
   a. processing of the tin from the plating on steel cans.
   b. curbside pickup programs for glass, aluminum, and paper.
   c. many systems for land fill.
   d. advanced new technologies for incineration.

7. For Murray Fox, one of the "unexpected rewards" of the hand-picking method used at his recycling plant was the
   a. improved self-image of successful handicapped workers.
   b. removal of easily identifiable and valuable recyclables.
   c. operation of a nonprofit organization.
   d. processing of 800 tons of garbage a week at the Michigan plant.

8. One difference between the American Agripost system on the one hand and the Swiss system called ORFA and the one developed by the Bühler-Miag company on the other is that the
   a. American system leaves no leftover for land fill.
   b. Swiss systems handle only one type of waste.
   c. American system converts everything into a compost.
   d. Swiss systems have been tested both in Europe and in the United States.

9. What inference can be made from the article about the level of technology used for waste disposal in America and Europe?
   a. In general, the Americans are ahead of the Europeans.
   b. In general, the Europeans are ahead of the Americans.
   c. The Americans and the Europeans are at about the same level.
   d. Neither has applied modern technology to the problem.

10. Which of the following is the best statement of the main idea of the article?
   a. There is not much of a problem at present with garbage disposal in the United States.
   b. At the present time, the United States is making a large investment in effective new technologies for garbage disposal.
   c. Recycling is a possible solution to the increasingly difficult problem of garbage disposal.
   d. Both the United States and Europe should make a commitment to recycling their garbage as soon as possible.

WHAT DO YOU THINK?

Littering

Wherever you go today, from New York City to Bombay, to the ancient tourist sites of Greece and Egypt, to the beaches of the Mediterranean and Rio, you find litter. Garbage, plastic bags, and bottles are thrown everywhere without regard. In some places in the United States, there is a $500 fine for throwing litter on the ground. Do you think this is a good idea? Why or why not? In other areas, organizations or businesses "adopt a highway." A group, such as a Boy Scout troop, will adopt a portion of the highway and make sure that section stays clean. Do you think this is a good idea? Why or why not? Would it work in your country? Do you have any other ideas as to how the world can clean up its litter?

Hi and Lois, reprinted with special permission of King Features Syndicate, Inc.

CHAPTER **twelve**

Together on a Small Planet

"You look down there, and you can't imagine how many borders and boundaries you cross. . . There you are—hundreds of people killing each other over some imaginary line. . . And you realize that on that small spot, that little blue and white thing is everything that means anything to you. All of history and music and poetry and art and birth and love: tears, joy, games. All of it on that little spot out there you can cover with your thumb."
—*Russel Schweikert, astronaut*

in this chapter

Here you will read selections from four literary genres—essays, poetry, a speech, and a short story—using the skills you practiced in previous chapters. The selections were written by authors from different cultures who share their unique viewpoints and feelings about human existence and values.

Books

In an age of films and TV, with multiscreen cinemas, videotape recorders, and cable systems extending visual communication, many people predict that books will soon become obsolete. In the following short essay, Argentine poet and short-story writer Jorge Luis Borges (1899–1986) gives his opinion on this topic.

Die Weltwoche/Zurich

Books

I believe books will never disappear. It is impossible for it to happen. Of all mankind's diverse tools, undoubtedly the most astonishing are his books. All the others are extensions of the body. The telephone is an extension of his voice; the telescope and microscope extensions of his sight; the sword and the plow are extensions of his arms. In *Caesar and Cleopatra,* when Bernard Shaw refers to the Library of Alexandria, he says it is mankind's memory. I would add it is also mankind's imagination. Humanity's vigils have generated infinite pages of infinite books. Mankind owes all that we are to the written word. Why? What is our past but a succession of dreams? What difference is there between dreaming and remembering? Between remembering dreams and recalling the past? Books are the great memory of the centuries. Consequently their function is irreplaceable. If books were to disappear, history would disappear. So would men.

Jorge Luis Borges

After You Read
Recalling Information

exercise

Select the phrase that best completes the statement about Borges' ideas on books according to the essay.

1. Books are humanity's most astonishing
   a. possibility.
   b. tool.
   c. dream.

2. A book is an extension of the human
   a. body.
   b. voice.
   c. imagination.

3. If books were to disappear, human history would also disappear because people would
   a. feel too sad to live.
   b. no longer remember the past.
   c. keep on dreaming of the future.

Discussion

activity

In small groups, discuss the following questions.

1. In your opinion, what is the main idea of this essay? Do you agree with it or not? Why?

2. Which would you prefer: to read a particular book or to see a film based on it? Why?

3. What is one of the best books you have read? In what language was it written? By whom? To what kind of person would you recommend it?

SELECTION **two**

Three Days to See

Imagine that you are both blind and deaf. You see nothing. You hear no sound. How could you connect to reality? What would your life be like?

Helen Keller (1880–1968), an American born in Alabama, lost her sight and hearing from illness at the age of 19 months, yet she became a world-renowned writer and lecturer who graduated cum laude from Harvard University and received the

Presidential Medal of Freedom in 1963. She tells the chronicle of her journey out of darkness in her most popular book, *The Story of My Life* (1902). She was helped by the famous inventor Alexander Graham Bell and a wonderful teacher named Anne Sullivan. This teacher patiently used the sense of touch to make contact with her young student, who at first behaved like a wild animal, and later to subdue, stimulate, and support the awakening of the brilliant intelligence that speaks to us in the following essay. This amazing story was later made into the film *The Miracle Worker*. The writings of Helen Keller serve as an inspiration not only for people with disabilities but for all people the world over.

Three Days to See

All of us have read thrilling stories in which the hero has only a limited and specified time to live. Sometimes it was as long as a year; sometimes as short as twenty-four hours. But always we were interested in discovering just how the doomed man chose to spend his last days or his last

5   hours. I speak, of course, of free men who have a choice, not condemned criminals whose sphere of activities is strictly limited.

Such stories set us thinking, wondering what we should do under similar circumstances. What events, what experiences, what associations, should we crowd into those last hours as mortal beings? What happiness

10   should we find in reviewing the past, what regrets?

Sometimes I have thought it would be an excellent rule to live each day as if we should die tomorrow. Such an attitude would emphasize sharply the values of life. We should live each day with a gentleness, a vigor, a keenness of appreciation which are often lost when time stretches before

15   us in the constant panorama of more days and months and years to come. There are those, of course, who would adopt the epicurean motto of "Eat, drink, and be merry," but most people would be chastened by the certainty of impending death.

In stories, the doomed hero is usually saved at the last minute by some stroke of fortune, but almost always his sense of values is changed. He becomes more appreciative of the meaning of life and its permanent spiritual values. It has often been noted that those who live, or have lived, in the shadow of death bring a mellow sweetness to everything they do.

Most of us, however, take life for granted. We know that one day we must die, but usually we picture that day as far in the future. When we are in buoyant health, death is all but unimaginable. We seldom think of it. The days stretch out in an endless vista. So we go about our petty tasks, hardly aware of our listless attitude toward life.

The same lethargy, I am afraid, characterizes the use of all our faculties and senses. Only the deaf appreciate hearing, only the blind realize the manifold blessings that lie in sight. Particularly does this observation apply to those who have lost sight and hearing in adult life. But those who have never suffered impairment of sight or hearing seldom make the fullest use of these blessed faculties. Their eyes and ears take in all sights and sounds hazily, without concentration and with little appreciation. It is the same old story of not being grateful for what we have until we lose it, of not being conscious of health until we are ill.

I have often thought it would be a blessing if each human being were stricken blind and deaf for a few days at some time during his early adult life. Darkness would make him more appreciative of sight; silence would teach him the joys of sound.

Now and then I have tested my seeing friends to discover what they see. Recently I was visited by a very good friend who had just returned from a long walk in the woods, and I asked her what she had observed. "Nothing in particular," she replied. I might have been incredulous had I not been accustomed to such responses, for long ago I became convinced that the seeing see little.

How was it possible, I asked myself, to walk for an hour through the woods and see nothing worthy of note? I who cannot see find hundreds of things to interest me through mere touch. I feel the delicate symmetry of a leaf. I pass my hands lovingly about the smooth skin of a silver birch, or the rough shaggy bark of a pine. In spring I touch the branches of trees hopefully in search of a bud, the first sign of awakening Nature after her winter's sleep. I feel the delightful, velvety texture of a flower, and discover its remarkable convolutions, and something of the miracle of Nature is revealed to me. Occasionally, if I am fortunate, I place my hand gently on a small tree and feel the happy quiver of a bird in full song. I am delighted to have the cool waters of a brook rush through my open fingers.

60 To me a lush carpet of pine needles or spongy grass is more welcome than the most luxurious Persian rug. To me the pageant of seasons is a thrilling and unending drama, the action of which streams through my finger tips.

At times my heart cries out with longing to see all these things. If I can get so much pleasure from mere touch, how much more beauty must be
65 revealed by sight. Yet those who have eyes apparently see little. The panorama of color and action which fills the world is taken for granted. It is human, perhaps, to appreciate little that which we have and to long for that which we have not, but it is a great pity that in the world of light the gift of sight is used only as a mere convenience rather than as a means of
70 adding fullness to life.

Helen Keller

After You Read
Recalling Information

 Fill in the blanks of the following summary of Helen Keller's ideas with key words from the essay.

SUMMARY

Helen Keller at times thought that it would be an excellent rule to live each day as if we should _____ tomorrow. In adventure stories, a doomed
1
hero is usually saved from death at the last minute, but almost always his sense of _____ has been changed. Most people who have never suffered
2
impairment of their eyes or ears take in all sights and sounds with very little _____ . Only the _____ seem to truly appreciate hearing
3   4
and only the _____ really appreciate sight. Once a friend of Helen's
5
returned from a walk in the woods and said that she had observed _____ . Helen, however, always found hundreds of things to
6
_____ her in the woods through touch. By feeling leaves, flowers,
7
and trees, she felt that the miracle of _____ was revealed to her. In
8
her opinion, the panorama of color and action that fills the world is taken for _____ by most people.

Talking It Over

In small groups, discuss the following questions.

1. According to Keller, what advantage did her "disabilities" or "handicaps" give her?

2. How are people with disabilities treated in your culture? What kind of education or assistance do they receive? Is there discrimination against them? Should there be?

3. In your opinion, what can we learn from Keller?

SELECTION **three**

Good Friends . . . Dogs, Sons and Others

Willie Morris is a Southern journalist, author, and editor. He is the winner of several literary awards, and in 1981 he was the writer-in-residence at the University of Mississippi. In the following excerpt from his essay "Good Friends . . . Dogs, Sons and Others," Morris writes about the value of a small group of friends from varied backgrounds.

Good Friends . . . Dogs, Sons and Others

We are all terribly alone in this life, I fear. This is part of our mortality, and there is not really much we can do about it. The awful armor of our isolation is pierced only by those fragile loyalties which we pray will abide— children, or a lover, or friends. All of these ask for tenderness and care.

5 I am not just talking here about male friendships and female ones, but also about friendships of a nonsexual nature between men and women. One of the dividends of the women's movement of this generation, per- haps, has been the enhanced freedom of American women to choose af- fectionate relationships with men whom they trust outside the bedroom.

10 Some of my own closest friends are women; I can count four whom I be- lieve I would go to the brink for. Two are married to men I admire, one is a widow, one is divorced, and they are as important to me as anything in my existence, including my male friends, who are also only a few. I suspect a person can only have a handful of steadfast friends, if that. Be wary of

those who claim to count their friendships by the dozens, unless they are politicians up for reelection.

Parenthetically, I must also go so far as to confess that one of my best friends is a big black dog of acute warmth and intelligence. He and I are huckleberry friends who ride the river together. By my personal measure, another of my finest friends is my twenty-year-old son. We have lived through too many moments as a twosome to be forgetful of them. Among genuine friendships, never discount the possibility of good dogs and good sons.

At the core of friendship, I feel, is fidelity. We all make fools of ourselves now and again, and do things which cause us guilt—or worse, shame—and there are our times of ineluctable grief and sorrow. A trusting friend can call us back to earth and remind us of the universal failures and sufferings. Laughter is no less an ingredient of friendship than loyalty, or charity, or forgiveness. Conversely, in the lexicon of human cruelty, I rank the betrayal of a friend—even a friend from an earlier part of one's life—as dastardly almost as child abuse or manslaughter. I am reminded of the New York editor and writer who recently published a memoir belittling old friends, ferreting out their faults in retrospect as finely as a sculptor chiseling at a bust, all in the spirit of his own aggrandizement. Gratuitous betrayal often exacts its own special price.

I am reminded too of a worthier example, one that remains with me as vividly as the moment I first heard of it as a boy, so that it has become a kind of symbol for me. In his rookie season with the Brooklyn Dodgers, Jackie Robinson, the first black man to play Major League baseball, faced venom wherever he traveled—fastballs at his head, spikings on the bases, brutal epithets from the opposing dugouts and from the crowds. During one game on a hot day in St. Louis, the taunts and racial slurs seemed to reach a crescendo. In the midst of all this, the Dodger who was Jackie Robinson's particular friend, a Southern white named Peewee Reese, called time out. He walked from his position at shortstop toward Robinson at second base, put his arm around Robinson's shoulder and stood there with him for a long time. The gesture spoke more eloquently than the words: This man is my friend.

Even across the divide of death, friendship remains, an echo forever in the heart. The writer James Jones has been gone for more than three years, yet so alive was he for me that I have never quite admitted he is dead. He and his family lived down the road from me on eastern Long Island, and he struggled against death in his last months to finish his fictional trilogy of World War II. He was a connoisseur of cigars, a believer in the written word, and an enemy of meanness and pretense. He was courageous without ever talking much about courage; he appreciated mirth and he understood sorrow. I'm not sure why we were closer than brothers, for he was older than I and more inured of the siftings and winnowings of this world. Yet we were. Two years ago, as I began a book which means much to me—struggling with the very first sentences with a radio somewhere in the background—the song that came on was the theme to the movie of Jim's big novel, *From Here to Eternity.* "Keep the faith," he might have said.

When I see an honored friend again after years of separation, it is like reassuming the words of an old conversation which had been halted momentarily by time. Surely, as one gets older, friendship becomes more precious to us, for it affirms the contours of our existence. It is a reservoir of shared experience, of having lived through many things in our brief and mutual moment on earth. To paraphrase another writer from Mississippi, it is a prop, a pillar, to help us not merely endure, but prevail.

Willie Morris

After You Read

Recalling Information

exercise

Write true or false in front of the statements about Morris's essay. Correct the false ones to make them true.

According to Morris . . .

1. _____ one good result of the women's movement is that now American women can have real, nonsexual friendships with men.

2. _____ a person should have dozens of steadfast friends.

3. _____ two of his best friends are his twenty-year-old son and a big black dog.

4. _____ laughter is an important part of a friendship.

5. _____ the New York editor who wrote an article about the faults of his old friends did nothing wrong.

6. _____ sometimes a personal gesture of friendship speaks louder than words.

7. _____ death is the only real end of friendship.

8. _____ friendship becomes more precious as a person gets older.

Talking It Over

activity

In small groups, discuss the following questions.

1. In your opinion, what is the main idea of this essay?

2. What can you infer about the author's character from what he has written?

3. What do you feel are the important qualities of a friend?

4. Do you think a person should have many friends or just a few? Why?

5. Do you think that friendships in North America are different from those in your culture?

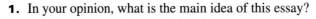

Any object, feeling, or thought can be the subject of a poem, but poets everywhere tend to speak mostly about the traditional themes of love, friendship, life, death, and the meaning of human existence. The following poems are by poets from different cultures and historical eras: Yevgeny Yevtushenko, Russian, twentieth century; Ono no Komachi, Japanese, ninth century (Heian period); Paavo Haavikko, Finnish, twentieth century; Maya Angelou, American, twentieth century; Omar Khayyam, Persian, twelfth century. Most poetry is written to convey feelings more than ideas. Poets generally employ unusual language in an original way to force us to see ordinary aspects of human experience in a new light. Read each poem several times, preferably aloud, to discover what feeling the poet is trying to convey.

People

No people are uninteresting.
Their fate is like the chronicle of planets.

Nothing in them is not particular
and planet is dissimilar from planet.

5 And if a man lived in obscurity
making his friends in that obscurity
obscurity is not uninteresting.

To each his world is private
and in that world one excellent minute.

10 And in that world one tragic minute.
These are private.

In any man who dies there dies with him
his first snow and kiss and fight.
It goes with him.

15 There are left books and bridges
and painted canvas and machinery.

Whose fate is to survive.
But what has gone is also not nothing.

By the rule of the game something has gone.
20 Not people die but worlds die in them.

Whom we knew as faulty, the earth's creatures.
Of whom, essentially, what did we know?

Brother of a brother? Friend of friends?
Lover of lover?

25   We who knew our fathers
In everything, in nothing.

They perish. They cannot be brought back.
The secret worlds are not regenerated.

And every time again and again
30   I make my lament against destruction.

Yevgeny Yevtushenko

Poem

That which fades away
Without revealing its altered color
Is in the world of love
The single flower which blossoms
5   In the fickle heart of man

Ono no Komachi

Poem

You marry the moon
and the sea and the moon and the woman:
    earless all.

You'll listen to their voices, you'll talk to them
5   and they say
    It's a game.

Paavo Haavikko

Caged Bird

A free bird leaps
on the back of the wind
and floats downstream
till the current ends
5 and dips his wing
in the orange sun rays
and dares to claim the sky.

But a bird that stalks
down his narrow cage
10 can seldom see through
his bars of rage
his wings are clipped and
his feet are tied
so he opens his throat to sing.

15 The caged bird sings
with a fearful trill
of things unknown
but longed for still
and his tune is heard
20 on the distant hill
for the caged bird
sings of freedom.

Maya Angelou, poet, writer, and actress

The free bird thinks of another breeze
and the trade winds soft through the sighing trees
25 and the fat worms waiting on a dawn-bright lawn
and he names the sky his own.

But a caged bird stands on the grave of dreams
his shadow shouts in a nightmare scream
his wings are clipped and his feet are tied
30 so he opens his throat to sing.

The caged bird sings
with a fearful trill
of things unknown
but longed for still

35 | and his tune is heard
on the distant hill
for the caged bird
sings of freedom.

Maya Angelou

The Rubaiyat of Omar Khayyam* (Selections)

VIII

Come, fill the Cup, and in the fire of Spring
Your winter garment of Repentance fling.
5 | The Bird of Time has but a little way
To flutter—and the Bird is on the wing.

XII

A Book of Verses underneath the Bough,
A Jug of Wine, a Loaf of Bread and thou†
10 | Beside me singing in the Wilderness—
Oh, Wilderness were Paradise enow!‡

XIII

Some for the Glories of This World and some
Sigh for the Prophet's Paradise§ to come,
15 | Ah, take the Cash, and let the Credit go
Nor heed¶ the rumble of the distant Drum!

*Translated into English verse by Edward Fitzgerald, fifth edition
†You
‡Enough
§Heaven
¶And don't listen to

After You Read
Recalling Information

 Circle the letter of the best response, according to the poems you just read.

"PEOPLE"

1. To Yevtushenko the people who are interesting are
   a. those who live in obscurity.
   b. those who study the planets.
   c. all people.

2. After a person's death, some of the things that are left are
   a. painted canvas and machinery.
   b. his first snow and kiss and fight.
   c. a private world.

3. When a person dies, what dies?
   a. a book
   b. a world
   c. nothing

POEM (ONO NO KOMACHI)

4. Love is compared to
   a. the sea.
   b. a flower.
   c. rain.

5. Love is seen as something
   a. momentary.
   b. permanent.
   c. unchanging.

POEM (PAAVO HAAVIKKO)

6. The moon, women, and the sea are shown as things that cannot
   a. feel.
   b. see.
   c. hear.

7. Love is shown as
   a. serious.
   b. playful.
   c. meaningless.

"CAGED BIRD"

8. The main theme of the poem is
   a. the beauty of birds.
   b. the fear of the unknown.
   c. the importance of freedom.

9. The poem is written with
  a. rhyme.
  b. rhythm.
  c. both rhyme and rhythm.

"THE RUBAIYAT OF OMAR KHAYYAM"

10. The poet tells us that the most important thing in life is
  a. to gain Paradise after death.
  b. to enjoy the present moment.
  c. to earn a lot of money.

Talking It Over

In small groups, discuss the following questions.

1. Which of the poems did you like best for its sound?

2. Which of the poems did you like best for its meaning?

3. Why do you think that people compose poems? Why do people enjoy reading or listening to poems?

4. Think of a short poem or part of a poem that you like from your culture. Write down a simple translation or description of it here to share with your group.

_____

_____

_____

_____

SELECTION **five**

Inaugural Address

John Fitzgerald Kennedy was the thirty-fifth president of the United States. He was the first Roman Catholic to be elected to the office and the youngest president in United States history. A popular and eloquent speaker, Kennedy, in his inaugural address in January 1961, urged his fellow citizens to become committed to a new vision of peace, freedom, and prosperity with these words: "Ask not what your country can do for you—ask what you can do for your country." Unfortunately, Kennedy didn't have much time to see his dreams for a new society become reality; he was assassinated in Dallas, Texas, on November 22, 1963. The following is an excerpt from his famous inaugural address.

Inaugural Address

● ● ● *L*et both sides,* for the first time, formulate serious and precise proposals for the inspection and control of arms—and bring the absolute power to destroy other nations under absolute control of all nations.

Let both sides seek to invoke the wonders of science instead of its terrors. Together let us explore the stars, conquer the deserts, and encourage the arts and commerce.

Let both sides unite to heed in all corners of the earth the command of Isaiah—to "undo the heavy burdens . . . [and] let the oppressed go free."

And if a beachhead of cooperation may push back the angels of suspicion, let both sides join in creating a new endeavor: not a balance of power, but a new world of law, where the strong are just and the weak secure and the peace preserved.

All this will not be finished in the first 100 days. Nor will it be finished in the first 1,000 days, nor in the life of this administration, nor even perhaps in our own lifetime on this planet. But let us begin.

In your hands, my fellow citizens, more than mine, will rest the final success or failure of our course. Since this country was founded, each generation of Americans has been summoned to give testimony to its national loyalty. The graves of young Americans who answered the call to service surround the globe.

Now the trumpet summons us again—not as a call to bear arms, though arms we need—not as a call to battle, though embattled we are—but as a call to bear the burden of a long twilight struggle year in and year out, "rejoicing in hope, patient in tribulation"—a struggle against the common enemies of man: tyranny, poverty, disease, and war itself.

Can we forge against these enemies a grand and global alliance, north and south, east and west, that can assure a more fruitful life for all mankind? Will you join in that historic effort?

In the long history of the world, only a few generations have been granted the role of defending freedom in its hour of maximum danger. I do not shrink from this responsibility—I welcome it. I do not believe that any of us would exchange places with any other people or any other generation. The energy, the faith, the devotion which we bring to this endeavor will light our country and all who serve it—and the glow from that fire can truly light the world.

---

*Kennedy was referring to the tension that existed then between the Communist nations and the non-Communist nations.

President John Fitzgerald Kennedy gives his inaugural address in January, 1961

And so, my fellow Americans: Ask not what your country can do for you—ask what you can do for your country.

My fellow citizens of the world: Ask not what America will do for you but what together we can do for the freedom of man.

40   Finally, whether you are citizens of America or citizens of the world, ask of us here the same high standards of strength and sacrifice which we ask of you. With a good conscience our only sure reward, with history the final judge of our deeds, let us go forth to lead the land we love, asking His blessing and His help, but knowing that here on earth God's work must

45   truly be our own.

John F. Kennedy

After You Read

Recalling Information

 *exercise*

Write true in front of those statements that express ideas from Kennedy's speech and false in front of those that do not. Correct the false statements to make them true.

1. _____ Both sides should try to identify and discuss the problems that divide them.

2. _____ Each side should try to gain complete control for itself of the inspection and control of arms.

3. _____ The two sides together should unite in their efforts to explore space and improve commerce and the arts.

4. _____ These goals should be accomplished in the first 1,000 days of Kennedy's administration as president.

5. _____ The common enemies of human beings are poverty, disease, communism, and socialism.

6. _____ Most people realize that the present moment is one of great challenge and are glad to be alive at this time.

7. _____ Americans should ask how their country can help them.

8. _____ People from other countries should ask how America can help them.

Talking It Over

In small groups, discuss the following questions.

1. Which of the goals mentioned in Kennedy's speech have been accomplished?

2. Do you think all the goals he mentioned are possible to achieve? Why or why not? Which one do you consider the most important for today's world?

3. Why do you think that Kennedy's ideas were very popular with the young people of his time?

4. In 1961, Kennedy created the U.S. Peace Corps, an organization that sends Americans to countries in the developing world to work for two-year periods. In your opinion, is this a good idea or not? Explain.

SELECTION **six**

Susana and the Shepherd

Margaret Craven was born in Helena, Montana, and received her college degree from Stanford University. She is a former journalist and has written many short stories about life in the western United States and in Canada as well as the novel *I Heard the Owl Call My Name.* This short story discusses the loneliness and dreams of a young Basque shepherd in his early days in America.

Susana and the Shepherd

*A*ll the passengers on the big transcontinental plane were interested in the young Basque who occupied the rear seat. He was a good-looking lad with his dark eyes and his proud, inscrutable face, tagged on the jacket with a check badge like a piece of luggage because he couldn't speak an
5 English word.

"He's a sheepherder from the Spanish Pyrenees," the stewardess replied to an inquiry. "The California Range Association is flying over many of them. Usually three or four come together. He's the first to come alone."

Several of the passengers tried to be friendly, but the young Basque only stared at them, too bewildered and confused to smile, and finally a sure blonde, who had traveled in Spain, said she'd draw him out. She'd toss a little Spanish at him. She'd just go over and sit on the arm of his chair and give him the good old American *bienvenida.*

So she did it, and the young Basque fixed upon her a pair of scornful, suspicious eyes and ignored her.

"You know what I think?" said the defeated blonde to the stewardess. "I think his mother warned him to have nothing to do with American women. They'd eat him alive." And she was wrong; it was his grandmother who had warned him.

"Oh, he's a strange one," the stewardess told the navigator. "They're all silent, but this one wouldn't even talk if he knew how. I hope somebody meets him in San Francisco. I have strict orders not to turn him loose unless he's met."

The navigator was wiser. "He's from some small village, probably," he said. "Never seen a big city. Never been in a plane. If he's afraid, it's the kind of fear only the brave know. Otherwise he wouldn't be crossing an ocean and a continent to herd sheep for a stranger in a land he doesn't know. Let him alone. He's a kid with a dream."

And after that, across the plains and the mountains, the boy sat undisturbed, holding his dream, and his was the old dream many Basque boys have held in their hearts. The land was not big or rich enough to support all. By custom, a family's land was left to the eldest son. The younger sons, therefore, must emigrate; their only hope of keeping the land they loved was to leave it—and come back rich.

It was possible. From his own village in the Valle de Arce in the province of Navarra, several had done it. Felipe Lacabe had done it. He had herded sheep for six years in a place called Nevada. In all that time he had learned no more than fifty English words, and been to town twice, and spent not one coin on drink, smokes, and girls. He had come back with twelve thousand dollars—a fabulous fortune—and he had bought himself a band of fine sheep and married the prettiest girl in Uriz.

Many had come back, and more had not. Whenever American tourists came to the remote villages of the Pyrenees some Basque father, prodded by his wife, said slowly, "If you have been to California, is it possible you know our son, Bonifacio?" or Fermin. Or Esteban. But they never did.

He, Juan Varra, was going to be one of the lucky ones. He had made up his mind. The American consul at Bilbao before whom he had appeared for his sheepherder's examination had praised him. The doctor who had given him his physical had spoken of his strength. And while he had waited the long months for the completion of his papers, the priest had strengthened him.

No Basque had ever been remembered for his words, the priest had said. Only for deeds and for courage. And if the ignorant thought he had a mist in his head like the mists of the mountains he loved, what of it? The thing to do was to be strong.

Yet when it was almost time to land, the boy found it hard to be strong. He reminded himself that an unknown *americano* had paid seven hundred and eleven dollars and ten cents for his passage, sight unseen, and why? Because he knew—as who does not?—that for two thousand years the Basques have been famous for their skill with sheep.

He thought hard on *abuelita,* his grandmother. How confidently she had smiled at him as she had prepared his favorite omelet for his last supper at home. With no teeth, she looked like a little old baby, and he vowed now that with his first wages he would send her enough money to buy a set of shiny white store teeth, so she could walk through the village, head high and smiling.

Also he thought of his little brother, who had begged to come along, who must emigrate, too, when he was older. He must set him an example. He must not fail.

Then the plane landed. The passengers began to file out slowly. He followed them. Surely El Cid, the bravest knight in all Christendom, never went forth to battle more staunchly than Juan Varra left that plane, the little stewardess at his heels, praying fervently somebody would meet him and ready to grab his jacket tails if no one did.

He was the first to pass the gate, and as he stepped through he saw the most beautiful sight possible to any Basque far from home. He saw another Basque. He saw a browned face, no longer young, which was smiling and showing some splendid gold teeth. And the voice was speaking his own dialect and it said, "Welcome, Juan Varra, and are the girls still as pretty in Navarra?" And this was Ancelito, thirty years from home and as much of a Basque as ever.

Ancelito collected his luggage and led him to the pickup truck. When they had left the confusion of the city, and were driving through the great wide green Sacramento Valley, Ancelito dropped pleasantries and began to speak so slowly and seriously in Spanish that the boy knew he must remember every word.

Now in early May the alfilaria was already dry. The corkscrew spirals on the wild grass that can work their way into the sheep's hides had already formed. It was vital, therefore, that the sheep be moved at once from the low range. Separated into bands, sheared, and branded, they had been driven to a central campsite, the trailer houses of the herders accompanying them. At the campsite, freight cars waited. The rich *americano* who owned the sheep had rented a whole train, and this very moment he was supervising the loading of the sheep bands into the cars. Tonight the train would carry the sheep across the great mountains into Nevada, where the long summer drive would begin at dawn.

Usually, said Ancelito, a youngster from the homeland was kept on the valley ranch for several weeks to accustom him to the strange American ways. But now they were desperate for herders. Last year they had lost two older men from heart attacks. The camp tender had found them at eight thousand feet, stiff in their blankets. It would be necessary for Juan Varra to go with them to Nevada and to start out at dawn with a band of two thousand sheep. Every other day a camp tender would bring him supplies and tell him where to find water. He would have a burro, of course, and a dog which Ancelito, himself, had trained.

"There is nothing to fear," Ancelito told him gravely. "The dog will know what you do not."

The boy said with dignity, "I have no fear."

Ancelito questioned him carefully, and in response the boy told him, shyly and briefly, a little of his dream. After four hours' driving, they came at last to the campsite.

In the trailer house Juan Varra ate a quick meal while Ancelito checked the clothes and the bedding he'd need. Then it was time to go, and they walked together through the dark to the train.

"You will go in the caboose," said Ancelito. "You will sleep better and tomorrow you will need that sleep. I will go by truck with the others, and I will see you at daybreak."

Once, at night in his bunk, the boy woke and felt the train moving under him and the cold air on his cheek, and he could hear the hard pull of the engine, and knew they were crossing the mountains. When he woke again, it was to the smell of coffee and the touch of a trainman's hand on his shoulder. He put on his shoes and his jacket and drank two cups of coffee. When he left the caboose, he stepped out into the clear dawn and such a sight as he had never seen.

Already the sheep were being spilled out onto the sage, each band at a time, its loaded burro, herder, and dog waiting to drive it away.

Because he was new, his band was the last. Then it, too, was spilled into the sage, and his burro and dog and a sheep tender drove the band away from the tracks as Ancelito motioned him to wait.

The train moved on, the boy waiting by the truck while Ancelito talked earnestly to the *americano* who owned the sheep, and though they spoke English and the boy could not understand a word, he knew the *americano* was worried.

"Andy, I'm scared to death to send him out. Can he do it?"

"Yes. He's used to hardship. He is not an American boy. He does not put his manhood in a car that can go ninety miles an hour. It is in himself."

"I know. He'll have the inbred willingness to endure."

"He has something else. He has a dream."

"All right. Let him go."

Then Ancelito gave the boy his directions and told him where he would find water. The owner shook his hand.

Juan ran into the sage and took the crook from the tender and he gave the old signal to the dog with a lift of his hand and he was off and on his own. He did not permit himself to look back for some moments. When he did so, it was as if the truck, the men, and the other bands of sheep had never existed, so quickly had the land taken them. And it was unlike any land he had ever seen, and vaster than any he had ever imagined.

The sage and the green buckbrush stretched as endlessly as eternity, broken only by a few small yellow sunflowers and a very occasional pine. No friendly villages. No small white houses with cheerful red-tiled roofs. Nothing but mountains which did not stand up proudly as mountains should, but lay rolling beneath his old high shoes.

He could scarcely bear to look at the sheep, so great was his disappointment. How ugly they were with their strange snub-nosed faces. The factory-made crook was awkward to his hand, and so long that he was sure he would never be able to trip a ewe neatly by the hind leg. Even the motley-colored Australian shepherd was unlike any dog he had known.

But the burro was the same. It trudged along with the sheep, carrying his supplies, topped by his big square bedroll. And the sheep baaed like sheep. The lambs frolicked like the lambs at home. And the dog let the sheep scatter only so far, rounding in the strays, circling watchfully.

He counted the black sheep—the markers—carefully. There were twenty-one. He counted the bellwethers. At the nooning-up he would unpack the burro, check his supplies and repack in his own precise way. He would make a fire and set a pot of beans to simmer, and cook himself a meal of ham and eggs. And this night when the coyotes yapped and the dog answered them, prowling the bed grounds, thoughts of home would creep to his little tent and he would begin the long battle against loneliness. And he swore now, by all the lady saints and the gentlemen saints in the entire heaven, that he would fight it each night until he won.

It took him six weeks. He had no calendar and no watch, and he needed neither. Each day followed the familiar pattern. He was up before daylight, building his fire beneath the heavy U-shaped iron, brewing his coffee. When the burro was packed, the daily trek began, the sheep scattering over a mile, the boy following, his beat-up .30.30 in a sling on his back, the dog circling, alert to every sound of his voice, every movement of his hands.

Each nooning-up Juan cooked his meal while the sheep lay in the sage, chewing their cud. And every other day the sheep tender came bumping through the buckbrush in his four-wheel-drive truck, bringing fresh meat and food, even water if necessary, and an eight-pound round loaf of white Basque bread which he had baked in a long pit. The sheep tender was a Basque also, but he had been too long alone. He had lost his dream. He could not talk easily to anyone, and when he spoke, it was always of some café called Estrellita or Española in some valley town where he could fill himself up on red wine, poured from a goatskin, and eat prodigiously.

Sometimes on the rainy nights when the coyotes cried like women, the boy was so homesick for his land and his people that it was an agony within him, and he rose shaken and white. He dreamed one night of his *abuelita,* smiling and showing her toothless gums, and when he awoke, his cheeks were wet, and though never for an instant did he admit it was from anything but rain leaking in the tent, after that he felt better.

Gradually the sheep did not seem quite so snub-nosed and ugly. They became the familiar sheep. He knew them, and a few too well—especially the cantankerous ewe with the twin lambs which he called "*La Bruja,*" the witch. He grew fond of his burro, and he loved the dog as deeply as a man can love a friend.

Then the six weeks were over, and with his band he took the old trail toward the higher mountains, the little burro leading the way because it knew it well. They reached the river, followed and forded it into the great national forest, traveling twenty miles in three days into the juniper range.

They were in the juniper forest a week, working their way up to the ponderosa and the sugar pine, and here the boy's loneliness left him. Often he saw deer browsing at dawn and dusk; a doe keeping herself carefully between him and her fawn. Once, in the early evening when the sheep had settled for the night, he came on a mother bear, scolding, slapping, and cuffing her two cubs to hurry them out of his way. Even the birds were a delight, the mountain bluebirds and jays, and sapsuckers and the black and yellow orioles. Here he was no longer a boy far from home. He was a Basque herder at his best, responsible and resourceful, like a soldier at some lonely outpost.

The tender's truck could not follow them now. The *americano* who owned the sheep had established two cabins at seventy-five hundred feet from which several tenders took supplies to the various sheep bands by pack mule. And when Juan saw Ancelito riding through the trees leading a mule he laughed aloud, startled by the sound of his own voice.

The mule was a walking grocery, its pack bags heavy with flour sacks, each fat with supplies.

Then for the first time Juan Varra was afraid. He was so afraid he wanted to bolt like *La Bruja*, the witch ewe. On the mule bringing up the rear was a girl.

Ancelito dismounted. . . . Had it gone well? . . . Yes. . . . Had he been lonely? . . . No—perhaps a very little at first. And as he spoke not once did the boy glance at the girl.

It was only Susana, said Ancelito; and she was his daughter, come to the cabins for a few days, as he had promised her. She was quite harmless. As women go, she was no trouble. She would get the noon meal while they unpacked the supplies.

And she did. While the boy and Ancelito unpacked the supplies and discussed the best sites for the bed grounds and the danger of bears, Juan could hear the girl moving at the fire.

When the meal was ready and they sat down for slabs of jack cheese, ham and eggs, fresh bread and coffee, he was forced to look at her. Her feet were as big as a boy's. Her legs were encased in thick blue cotton pants like a boy's. Her top half was submerged in a shirt like a boy's. Her hair was drawn tight to the back of her head, and hung in a thick brush, suitable only for a horse's tail. Furthermore, she did not look up at him from under her lashes and touch him with the briefest of cool, sweet glances to tell him she saw every single thing about him and found it good. She looked straight at him, and boldly, as one boy takes the measure of another.

He did not direct to her one word. When the meal was over and Ancelito and his daughter were mounted and leaving, he cast an "*adios*" into the air, which she could take to include her if she wished.

"Is he alive?" Susana asked her father, when the mules had started. "Is he stupid?"

"No. He is silent. He is Basque. I am Basque."

"When you came to this country, you were not like that."

"I was exactly like that. He is afraid of you. But do not worry. I have told him you are harmless."

"Father, you didn't."

"But certainly. It would do you no good to make eyes at this one. He has a dream. He will save his money. He will go back to his village a *millonario* and will marry the most beautiful girl in all Navarra. Now, if you were as wise as your mother—"

"Papacito," said Susana slowly, "are the girls so pretty in Navarra?"

And Ancelito smiled at her and said, "Beyond description."

The voices carried back to the boy in the high clear air, and though they were in English, he did not miss the scorn in the girl's voice. That night among the supplies he found that Ancelito had left him a beginner's Spanish-English reader.

Love may need no words, but resentment can use several. The next day Juan Varra opened the first crack in the dark tomb in which he was determined to bury himself for six years. He began to learn to read English.

Two days later, when the grocery mule came through the trees, the boy put on his most proud and silent Basque face, lest the girl think he was glad to see her. But it was not Ancelito and Susana who followed the mule. It was the dull camp tender who had lost his dreams.

Juan did not admit his disappointment. He had no time to think of girls. The bears were troublesome. One old killer bear followed the sheep band, killing a ewe each night, and the boy tracked him and shot him. In all, he killed four bears.

In July the rams were brought in, and in August all the sheep band were driven to a mountain valley where the ewes were culled, the lambs separated into the fats and the feeders. On the way back to the high range with his reassembled band, Juan passed his first campers, and they were friendly. A little boy chased the lambs and couldn't catch them. The father gave him cigarettes, and the wife smiled at him and made him a present of a kitten.

After that, the cat followed along with the sheep, and though Juan told himself he kept her only to keep the chipmunks from his food, he carried her under his jacket in the thunderstorms, and let her sleep at the foot of his bedroll.

Then, in October, the long drive was done. The sheep were carried by two- and three-decker trucks from the mountains to the low delta to browse on the corn stubble; the burro was left behind, the cook wagon carried supplies. Just before Christmas the bands were driven to the home ranch to wait for the lambing, and it was here, in a neat white house, that Ancelito, the foreman, lived with Susana. The boy did not ask for her.

"Am I rich yet?" he asked Ancelito anxiously.

"In this country you are poor as a thin mouse," said Ancelito. "But at home already you can buy the finest house in the village."

It was Ancelito who helped him send money to his *abuelita* for the store teeth and presents for the family. It was Ancelito who brought from town the clothes he needed. After that, he spent nothing, and each month the *americano* who owned the sheep deposited his wages in a savings account in his name. When, at Christmas, the other herders left the trailer houses and drove to town for a fine binge, he did not go. And when he was working with the sheep near the white house and saw something soft and obviously feminine fluttering on the clothesline in the rear, he looked the other way, so tight was the dream still within him.

Right after Christmas the drop band was collected in a big open field and lambing began. Four hundred lambs were born each night, the boy working out in the cold, helping the young ewes that were having touble with their firstborn, turning the lambs. One morning the *americano* was helping put each ewe and her new lamb into a portable *chiquero,* or pen, so she would claim her lamb, and he watched the boy work.

"He is wonderful," he said. "He will save twenty-five percent more lambs. . . . Andy, we must keep this one."

"I have thought of it," said Ancelito.

The last night of the lambing, through no fault of his own, the boy lost two little lambs, and this, to a Basque herder, is not cause for sadness, but for heartbreak. Ancelito took him to the white house for food and comfort, and there in the warm kitchen waited Susana.

Gone were the boy's shoes, the pants, and the horse's tail. She was as shy as a forest creature and as sweet as any young girl in Navarra on her saint's day. She was the daughter of a Basque and she, too, could be silent. She placed the coffee pot before them without a word, and plates of ham and eggs. Then she left them, turning at the door.

"I am so sorry, Juan," and for an instant her glance touched his cheek and was gone.

He did not see her again, because this was the busy time. Lamb tails to be docked. New sheep bands to be formed. The ewes to be sheared and branded, and the winter was gone, and May here again, and the sheep drive to the campsite to go by train to Nevada. And the first year was over, and the cycle began again.

Now repetition had replaced newness, making the second year even lonelier than the first. In the buckbrush, loneliness became an entity, pressing constantly upon him. The boy talked aloud sometimes to the cat and the burro. The dog, of course, was his abiding friend.

Rarely the camp tender brought him letters from home. Those from his *abuelita* and his little brother were the same. They loved him; they missed him. But the letter from his eldest brother, who was head of the family, held a new tone. How fortunate Juan was to be in that land where everyone was rich and all was easy. How hard it was to be the one who was left behind. Oh, he must not stay away too long. If he worked harder and was given a raise—if he saved all beyond the barest necessities, perhaps five years would be enough or even four.

In the juniper forest one June day he heard a strange little whimpering, crying sound, and came on a lone fawn. He longed to make a pet of it, to keep it with him, as the herders did sometimes. But he could not bear to take it from its mother, to teach it to be unafraid of man, to notch its ear so

that when some hunter shot it he would know that once it had had too
good a friend in man. It reminded him of the girl.

Then again he had driven the sheep band into the ponderosa and
sugar pines of the high ranges, and he was home in the mountains.

When the grocery mule came through the trees, Ancelito was with it,
but not Susana. This time the boy asked for her.

"And how is your daughter?" he asked formally, and Ancelito said she
was well. She was going to school this summer. She was educating her
head.

"It is that she does not wish a husband?" the boy asked slowly, and Ancelito said that, like all girls, she hoped to find one. But in this country it
was the custom for many girls to help their husband get started. Suppose
Susana should marry a man who wished to own a sheep band of his own.
What a fine thing if she could help him. Did Juan know that the sheepman
chosen as the year's best in all California was the son of a Basque whose
father had come first as a herder? No doubt his wife had helped him, as
his mother had helped his father. It was one of the strange American
ways.

Several times this year the forest ranger came by at nooning-up and
shared his meal. And once a party of mountaineers coming out from a
climb passed by and hailed him. He had picked up enough English to say
a few words now, but he was alone so much that the sound of a voice always startled him and filled him with uneasiness, because it broke the
quiet monotony in which he lived.

Then at last it was fall and he and sheep were back on the delta, working their way toward the home ranch.

"How rich am I now?" he asked Ancelito, who took out his pencil for a
bit of figuring and replied gravely, "In this country you have a modest savings, but in Navarra you are a man of some means. All your relatives are
trying to borrow money."

When the sheep band neared the home ranch, the boy watched ea-
gerly for Susana to come home for the holidays from the school she attended, forty miles distant. And one afternoon just before Christmas,
while he was working in the big field where the drop band was to be collected for the lambing, he saw her arrive, and the sight filled him with hor-
ror.

There was a loud and sudden roar, and into the ranch road from the
highway bounced a small, open, ancient and rattletrap car, Susana at the
wheel, her legs in jeans, her hair streaming behind her in a horse-tail.

"She goes back and forth to school this way," said Ancelito calmly.

345

350

355

360

365

370

375

380

"Scares the sheep. It is amazing what an *americana* will do to educate her head and get ready to help her husband."

It was cold during this year's lambing, and again Juan worked each night in the big open field with the ewes, and late one night twin lambs lost their mother, arriving in this world so weak that in the morning he and Ancelito carried them to the house and bedded them in the warmth of the kitchen stove.

When the boy had finished working with the lambs and stood up, ready to return to the field, he saw that Susana was watching him quietly, sweet and feminine as she had been when she had prepared breakfast the year before.

"You had a good year, Juan?" she asked in Spanish.

"Sí."

"You were lonely?"

"A Basque is never lonely."

"See, *papacito,* he is afraid of me."

"I am afraid of no one."

"He is afraid of me. He is like the others. He learns nothing. He gives nothing. All he sees in this country is money. All he wants is to grab. He is stupid, *papacito.* He is more stupid than the sheep."

The boy followed Ancelito back to the field.

"She likes you," said Ancelito complacently. "If she did not like you, she would not be so *furiosa.*

One day from the fields Juan saw the little rattletrap car take off down the road, and he knew Susana had gone back to school. He put her resolutely from his mind, and the months slipped by until the sheep bands were driven to the campsite and the second year was done.

The third year was as like the second as the second had been like the first. The loneliness and the constant movement of the sheep. The noonings-up and the bedding-down, and the watchful eye that never forgot to count the bellwethers and the black sheep. The coyotes yapping in the night, and the bears coming in the night, and the cat, the dog, and the burro. Only the details differed, and the girl's scornful words, and the thought of the girl was constantly in his mind.

In October, two days before the sheep bands were to leave the mountains, an early blizzard caught them; the snow falling so fast and heavily that they could not be driven out in time. The boy built a fire of green wood, so much smoke would rise to guide the camp tender, and Ancelito saw it and came with horses and men to trample and pack the snow so the sheep could move.

"Am I rich now?" Juan asked, sitting beside Ancelito in the truck on their way down to the delta.

"You are not quite a *millonario*," said Ancelito. "You have a little more than five thousand dollars. In your village it would be a very large sum," and he spoke sadly.

"My work has not been good?" asked the boy. "The *americano* is not satisfied?"

"He is much pleased. This morning when the sheep were safe from the blizzard, I called Susana to tell him. She says there are many letters for you. When a Basque family takes thus to the pen, the news must be bad."

They rode in silence, not to the corn stubble this time, but to the white house, and when they went into the kitchen, Susana handed his letters to the boy, her eyes big and worried.

They left him to read them alone, and when they returned to the kitchen, he was sitting quietly, the letters spread on the table before him, his face stricken. He did not look up.

"My *abuelita* is dead," he said, and when Ancelito tried to comfort him, he made no response, and when Susana set hot coffee before him, he did not thank her. He was silent as only a Basque can be silent.

"Shall I tell you what is wrong?" asked Ancelito. "Shall I tell you how I know?"

The boy did not answer.

"When I came to this country," said Ancelito, "I spent ten years alone with the sheep. I had a dream also. I thought only of my people and the day I would return to them. When I did so, I could not stand it. I had forgotten such poverty. Things were bad in my village. Everyone was poor and I was rich, and between us was a wall of jealousy I could not tear down or climb over."

The boy did not look up.

"Have you not seen the wall in these letters? Is not your elder brother already resentful? Does he not complain bitterly of your good fortune?"

The boy was silent.

"I bought my parents the finest house in the village! I paid sixty American dollars for it. I gave them money to care for them, and I came back here where I shall never be rich. It is a friendly country. This is what matters."

"*Papacito,* it is useless!" cried Susana. "He is so stupid! Can you believe it? He does not know we love him of truth. He does not know you feel to him as a man to his own son. Let him save and go back. Let him be rich and miserable. Let him marry the most beautiful girl in all of Navarra.

What do I care?" And she sat down at the table and began to cry as only a
465 Basque girl can cry—loud and furiously.

Then the boy looked up. "Is it possible to bring my little brother to this
country?" he asked slowly.

"It would take time, but it is possible. He could live with us. He could go
to school. Susana could teach him to speak English."

470 "Is it possible Susana could teach me also? Could she teach me to tell
her in English that in the mountains when I am alone with the sheep I do
not think of any girl in Navarra? I think of her."

"This she would do gladly."

"Then if I have lost my dream, I can replace it with another. And if I do
475 not return, it is nothing. I am a Basque," said the boy proudly, "and a
Basque cannot lose his homeland, because he takes it with him always."

Margaret Craven

After You Read
Recalling Information

exercise **1**   Choose the phrase that best answers each question about the story.

1. What was the attitude of the other passengers on the plane toward Juan
Varra?
   a. They were afraid of him because he seemed so proud and silent.
   b. They were friendly and interested in him and wanted to draw him out.
   c. They disliked him and looked down on him for being poor and
   ignorant.

2. Why did so many Basque boys leave their homeland?
   a. They longed for travel and adventure.
   b. They wanted to keep the land they loved.
   c. They needed money for drinks, smokes, and girls.

3. According to tradition, what were Basques especially known for?
   a. Their excellence in speaking
   b. Their courage and actions
   c. Their physical strength

4. The two people Juan missed and thought about the most were his *abuelita*
and
   a. the village priest.
   b. El Cid.
   c. his little brother.

5. Who was Ancelito?
   a. A Basque who had left home long ago
   b. A rich *americano* who owned sheep
   c. A camp tender who brought supplies

6. Why did Juan have to start work right away?
   a. Two of the herders had died recently.
   b. It was the custom to start boys immediately.
   c. The law did not permit rest periods.

7. At first, what did Juan think of the sheep that were given to him?
   a. They were the most beautiful he had ever seen.
   b. They were just like the sheep back in Spain.
   c. They were ugly and different from those he knew.

8. Who was Juan's best friend during his time in the mountains?
   a. *La Bruja*
   b. the dog
   c. his burro

9. When was Juan really afraid for the first time?
   a. When he lost some sheep
   b. When he tracked the killer bear
   c. When he saw the girl

10. Why did Juan begin to learn English?
    a. He had fallen in love with Susana.
    b. He felt resentful toward Susana.
    c. He wanted to talk with Susana's father.

11. What was the important gift that Juan received from one of the campers?
    a. a dictionary
    b. a gun
    c. a cat

12. What was the new tone that Juan noticed in the letters from his oldest brother?
    a. admiration
    b. envy
    c. friendship

13. According to Ancelito, why had Susana gone away to school?
    a. To learn a profession and become famous
    b. To educate herself to help her future husband
    c. To see more of the world and learn about customs

14. What made Ancelito think that Susana liked Juan?
    a. She got very angry with him.
    b. She asked about him often.
    c. She dropped her eyes when she said his name.

15. What was the bad news that Juan received by letter?
    a. His relatives wanted to borrow money.
    b. Susana was going to get married.
    c. His grandmother had died.

16. At the end, what did Juan discover about his dream?
    a. It was silly and worthless.
    b. He could put another in its place.
    c. He would never lose it.

Oinkari Dance Troupe
performing at Boise
Basque Festival,
Boise, Idaho.

Expressing an Opinion

Write down your opinion of the story's ending, answering the following question:
Did Juan Varra make the right decision or not? Why? After ten minutes, read your
answers aloud.

Talking It Over

In small groups, discuss the following questions.

1. What big problem does the main character, Juan Varra, have at first when
   he arrives in California? How does he overcome it? How long does it take
   him?

2. How does Juan change during the story? What people and experiences
   cause this change?

3. In your opinion, which of the characters in the story are realistic? Explain.

4. Have you ever known anyone who left his or her native country to work or
   study for a long period of time? Did that person return or not? Why? Do
   you think it would be possible for most people to live happily in a foreign
   country for the rest of their lives? Why or why not?

WHAT DO YOU THINK?

Although products of the technological age—TV, videos, computer games—have taken many people away from reading books, the book industry is still thriving. What kinds of books do you prefer? Which types do you think are most popular nowadays? Do you think that books will always last in the form that they are in now? What other forms will books take in the future?

Happy Reading!